THE OUTER SOLAR SYSTEM

JUPITER, SATURN, URANUS, NEPTUNE, AND THE DWARF PLANETS

AN EXPLORER'S GUIDE TO THE UNIVERSE

THE OUTER SOLAR SYSTEM

JUPITER, SATURN, URANUS, NEPTUNE, AND THE DWARF PLANETS

EDITED BY ERIK GREGERSEN, ASSOCIATE EDITOR, ASTRONOMY AND SPACE EXPLORATION

Britannica
Educational Publishing

IN ASSOCIATION WITH

ROSEN
EDUCATIONAL SERVICES

Published in 2010 by Britannica Educational Publishing
(a trademark of Encyclopædia Britannica, Inc.)
in association with Rosen Educational Services, LLC
29 East 21st Street, New York, NY 10010.

Distributed exclusively by Rosen Educational Services.
For a listing of additional Britannica Educational Publishing titles, call toll free (800) 237-9932.

First Edition

Britannica Educational Publishing
Michael I. Levy: Executive Editor
Marilyn L. Barton: Senior Coordinator, Production Control
Steven Bosco: Director, Editorial Technologies
Lisa S. Braucher: Senior Producer and Data Editor
Yvette Charboneau: Senior Copy Editor
Kathy Nakamura: Manager, Media Acquisition
Erik Gregersen: Associate Editor, Astronomy and Space Exploration

Rosen Educational Services
Jeanne Nagle: Senior Editor
Nelson Sá: Art Director
Nicole Russo: Designer
Introduction by Greg Roza

Library of Congress Cataloging-in-Publication Data

Outer solar system: Jupiter, Saturn, Uranus, Neptune, and the dwarf planets / edited by Erik Gregersen.—1st ed.
    p. cm.—(An explorer's guide to the universe)
"In association with Britannica Educational Publishing, Rosen Educational Services."
Includes index.
ISBN 978-1-61530-014-3 (library binding)
1. Solar system—Popular system. 2. Sattelites—Popular system. 3. Kuiper Belt—Popular system. I. Gregersen, Erik.
QB501.2.O98 2010
523.2—dc22

2009036104

On the cover: A highly visible ring system differentiates Saturn from the other planets of the outer solar system–Jupiter, Neptune, Uranus–and the dwarf planet Pluto. Cover photo: © www.istockphoto.com/sololos

CONTENTS

20

52

55

83

93

100

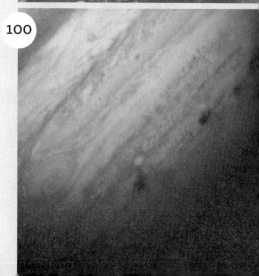

105

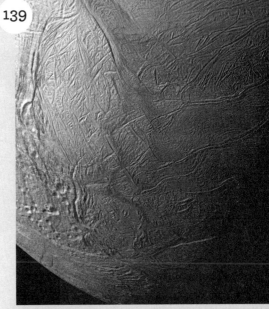

139

141

171

175

188

202

210

225

INTRODUCTION

After hundreds of years of observation, theorizing, exploration, and data collection, the universe is still a mysterious place. Numerous cosmic questions remain unanswered despite the scientific and technological advances made since the telescope was invented in the 1600s. But we are learning more about the cosmos all the time through intense examination of the solar system in which we live.

Still, learning about the outer solar system has proved to be difficult, to say the least. What is known about the farthest reaches of our solar system is discussed, at great length and in fine detail, in this book.

Scientists have launched many spacecraft into orbit. Manned spacecraft have traveled as far as the moon. Unmanned probes have approached most of the planets and even landed on Mars. These probes tell scientists more about the solar system than we could ever learn with telescopes alone. In 1977, the Voyager 1 probe was sent into space for the purpose of exploring Jupiter and Saturn. Other probes were sent in the years that followed. It took decades for these probes to reach the most distant planets and send back data about them. Presently, Voyager 1 is the farthest man-made object from Earth; it is approaching the edge of the known solar system, and scientists hope it will gain new information about the mystifying region known as the Kuiper Belt.

The Voyager and other missions represent the limit of our physical reach within the cosmos. For now, we depend on the data they have collected to gain a better understanding of the outer solar system.

Beyond the orbit of Mars—which represents the planetary boundary between the inner and outer solar system—is a ring of asteroids orbiting the Sun. The asteroid belt contains rocky objects left over from the formation of the solar system. The asteroids range in size from hundreds of kilometers in diameter to dust-sized particles. The largest asteroid in the asteroid belt, Ceres, is considered a dwarf planet. It was the first asteroid ever discovered. By 2009, more than 450,000 asteroids had been discovered.

While most asteroids orbit the sun in the main belt between Mars and Jupiter, some stray closer to Earth. These are called near-Earth asteroids (NEAs). Most NEAs are still far from Earth, but some actually cross Earth's orbit, making them potentially deadly to life on Earth.

Smaller-sized asteroids are often called meteoroids. This term is also often reserved for asteroids that collide with

As they tumble into Earth's orbit, stony or metallic chunks of space matter known as meteors burst into friction-induced flame, creating a fiery show in the night sky. NASA/Getty Images

other objects, or those that have the potential to do so. If a meteoroid comes close enough to Earth, it might enter our atmosphere. The swiftly moving meteoroid becomes so hot that it glows, creating a visible phenomenon we call a meteor or shooting star. A meteor that reaches the ground before burning up is called a meteorite. Large meteorites can create deep impressions in the ground called impact craters, like those we can see on the moon's surface.

The first of the outer planets is the fifth planet from the Sun—Jupiter. It is the most massive planet in the solar system and is larger than all the other planets combined. This "gas giant" has a diameter of about 143,000 km (88,900 miles). Jupiter's mean orbital distance is 778 million km (483 million miles), and it takes about 12 years to make one rotation around the sun.

We can see Jupiter's atmosphere from Earth with a telescope. It is well known for its bands of colour. Close-up views of Jupiter have shown quickly moving clouds and giant, cyclonelike storms. The Great Red Spot—a cyclone larger than Earth and Mars together—is perhaps Jupiter's most notable feature. The clouds around Jupiter contain numerous substances, particularly pure hydrogen and helium, methane, ammonia, and water.

Jupiter doesn't have a solid surface. Since scientists cannot see past its atmosphere, they have come up with theories about what lies below it. Jupiter has a significant magnetic field and constantly radiates radio waves. The planet also creates more energy than it receives from the Sun—another fact that continues to intrigue scientists.

To date, more than 60 moons have been discovered in orbit around Jupiter, and there are likely more. The largest moon in the solar system—Ganymede—is larger than Mercury! Several of these worlds are as interesting to scientists as the planet they circle. Jupiter also has a ring of ice and dust similar to but much smaller than those around Saturn.

You probably recognize Saturn as the ringed planet. It is the second-largest planet in the solar system with a diameter of 120,536 km (74,898 miles). At a mean orbital distance of 1,427,000,000 km (887 million miles), it takes Saturn nearly 30 years to make one trip around the Sun.

Saturn's atmosphere is similar to Jupiter's, but it is much less active. Like Jupiter, Saturn does not have a solid surface. It is surrounded by a dense, complex layer of clouds that appear as light-brown bands circling the planet. Storms are sometimes visible as well. Saturn has the most hydrogen-rich atmosphere of all the planets with 91 percent hydrogen and 6 percent helium. Common compounds include ammonia and methane, among smaller traces of others. Scientists think Saturn's interior is made up mainly of liquid hydrogen. The core is probably a liquid, metallic substance. Saturn's magnetic field is probably due to motions in its metallic core.

Saturn's rings have been a subject of study since Galileo first discovered them in 1610. NASA's Cassini spacecraft gave the world its first up-close views of the planet and its ring system. HO/NASA/AFP/Getty Images

The entire ring system is nearly one million km (600,000 miles) wide, but only about 100 metres (330 feet) thick. The total mass of the rings is about the same as the mass of Saturn's moon Mimas. Titan, Saturn's largest moon, is the second largest moon in the solar system, second to Jupiter's Ganymede. Saturn's moons and rings are closely related. In fact, Saturn's two smallest moons are within the ring structure itself. Each of the particles that make up the rings—which range from dust-sized to house-sized—could be considered satellites orbiting the planet. This may make it impossible to ever know how many moons Saturn truly has.

Uranus is the seventh planet from the Sun and the least massive of the outer planets. Its mean distance from the Sun is nearly 2.9 billion km (1.8 billion miles). At this distance, it takes the planet more than 84 years to orbit the Sun. It has an equatorial diameter of 51,118 km (31,764 miles).

The atmosphere of Uranus is made primarily of hydrogen and helium, but also contains oxygen, nitrogen, sulfur, and carbon. The most common compounds include methane, ammonia, and water. The visible surface of Uranus is blue with no "spots" like those seen on Jupiter and Saturn. This shows that of all the outer planets, Uranus has the lowest amount of storms. Images taken by Voyager 2, however, revealed faint cloud bands on the blue planet.

Scientists believe that, beneath its gaseous outer layer, Uranus is a fluid planet. It radiates the least amount of internal heat of the outer planets. Unlike the other planets, Uranus's axis is nearly parallel with its orbital path, which means that it spins on its side. This may have resulted long ago when a moon-sized body collided with Uranus. The planet's north pole faces the Sun for about 42 years, and then the south pole faces the Sun for an equal period. Like Jupiter, Uranus has thin rings of dust and ice, and currently has 27 known moons.

At approximately 4,498,250,000 km (2,795,083,000 miles), Neptune is the farthest planet from the Sun, and the only one that cannot be seen with the unaided eye. It takes Neptune more than 163 years to orbit the sun. Neptune is the third-most massive planet, but the smallest of the outer planets with an equatorial diameter of 49,528 km (30,775 miles). That is about four times the size of Earth.

Like the other outer planets, Neptune's atmosphere is made up mainly of hydrogen and helium. The planet's blue colour is due to the presence of methane in its atmosphere, which absorbs red light and reflects blue light. Dark, stormy spots and white clouds are sometimes visible on Neptune's surface.

Since Neptune's density is greater than the other outer planets, scientists believe it has a greater percentage of melted ices and molten, rocky materials than the other gas giants. Although Neptune receives less than half the amount of sunlight as Uranus, the temperatures of both planets are very similar. This is because Neptune emits more than twice the energy it receives from the Sun. Scientists are not sure what causes this. Neptune's inner heat creates powerful storms on its surface and the fastest winds in the solar system.

Neptune has at least 13 moons, the largest of which—Triton—is similar in size to Earth's Moon. The rest are much smaller. The four nearest moons are within a system of six rings encircling the

Scientists suspect that the large, dark spots visible on Neptune's surface (middle right) *are fierce storms raging through the planet's atmosphere. High winds have been recorded near Neptune's Great Dark Spot.* NASA Marshall Space Flight Center

planet. Many of the particles that make up Neptune's rings are dust-sized.

Discovered in 1930, Pluto was once known as the ninth and smallest planet of the solar system. However, in 2006 its status was lowered to dwarf planet. With a diameter of 2,344 km (1,456 miles), it is only about two-thirds the size of Earth's Moon. It is interesting to note, however, that Pluto has three of its own moons—Charon, Nix, and Hydra. The latter two are very small, but Charon is similar in size to Pluto, and many scientists consider them "twin planets."

Pluto's mean orbital distance from the sun is 5.9 billion km (3.7 billion miles). Its orbit is more elongated than any of the planets. In fact, it is actually closer to the Sun than Neptune for part of its trip around the Sun. Pluto is so far away from the Sun that it takes sunlight more than 5 hours to reach it, and it receives about 1/1,600 of the amount of sunlight that reaches Earth. This makes Pluto a very cold place. Although the dwarf planet has a thin atmosphere, most gases—especially methane and carbon dioxide—freeze at such low temperatures. These substances and other ices form a reflective layer on Pluto's surface. Like many of the icy moons of Jupiter and Saturn, Pluto probably has a rocky core surrounded by a layer of ice.

Pluto resides in the solar system's most distant orbital region called the Kuiper Belt. Kuiper Belt objects (KBOs) are made of ice and rock left over from the formation of the solar system. Other dwarf planets, most of which were recently discovered, also orbit the Sun within this region beyond Neptune. Pluto isn't even the largest KBO. Eris is an icy dwarf planet with a diameter of 2,500 km (1,550 miles), making it slightly larger than Pluto. It orbits the Sun once every 560 years and has one known moon. Other notable KBO dwarf moons include Makemake with a diameter of about 1,500 km (900 miles), and Haumea, an egg-shaped object with two tiny moons.

Of all the bodies that orbit the Sun, comets are those that travel to the farthest reaches of the solar system. Comets have very eccentric orbits, which means that they are oval-shaped. This brings them very close to the Sun at times; other times they are very far away. Comets are sorted into two categories based on how long their periods, or orbits, last. Short-period comets have orbits of less than 200 years. Long-period comets have orbits longer than 200 years.

You may picture a comet as a fiery ball with a long tail. However, the only permanent characteristic of a comet is a rocky, icy center called the nucleus. A nucleus can remain unchanged in the deepest parts of the solar system for thousands of years. As the comet approaches the Sun it grows warmer. The evaporating gases and dust form an "atmosphere" around the comet called the coma. Still closer to the Sun, solar radiation blows dust away from the coma, producing a tail. Solar wind blows ionized gas away from the coma in a slightly different direction. All comets disappear eventually, and in relatively short time on a cosmic scale. Some are thrown out of the solar system due to the gravitational pulls of the larger planets. Others decay in solar heat.

You might wonder if comets would someday disappear from the solar system altogether. Scientists have discovered that comets are "born" in the farthest reaches of the solar system, in a region called the Oort cloud. The Oort cloud is a large area of gas and dust left over from the formation of the solar system. Much like the planets themselves, the Ort cloud orbits the Sun. Although scientists are still trying to understand the origins and features of this mysterious region, most believe it is the source of our solar system's comets.

The solar system exists in an area scientists call the heliosphere. Beyond the heliosphere is a transition region called the heliosheath. This is where the Sun's solar wind is slowed by forces outside the solar system. Voyagers 1 and 2 have reached this area. Beyond the heliosheath is the heliopause, which marks the outer boundary of the solar system between 17 and 26 billion km (10 and 16 billion miles) from the Sun. What will we learn about this distant boundary when the Voyager probes reach it? We can only wait and see.

CHAPTER 1

ASTEROIDS

Beyond our planet, Earth, and the other terrestrial planets—scorched Mercury, enshrouded Venus, and frigid Mars—lie the rocky bodies of the asteroid belt. Any natural solar system object other than the Sun, a planet, a dwarf planet, or a moon is called a small body; these include asteroids, meteoroids, and comets. Beyond those remnants of the early solar system lie the planets of the outer solar system. These planets, in order of their distance outward from the Sun, are Jupiter, Saturn, Uranus, and Neptune. Many astronomers consider the asteroid belt a demarcation point between the inner solar system (consisting mainly of the terrestrial planets) and the outer solar system.

Most of the rocky asteroids move around the Sun in elliptical orbits in the same direction of the Sun's rotation. Such motion is termed prograde. Looking down on the solar system from a vantage point above Earth's North Pole, an observer would find that prograde orbits are counterclockwise. Orbits in a clockwise direction are called retrograde.

Between the orbits of Mars and Jupiter are a host of rocky small bodies, about 1,000 km (600 miles) or less in diameter, called asteroids that orbit in the nearly flat ring called the asteroid belt. It is because of their small size and large numbers relative to the major planets that asteroids are also called minor planets. The two designations have been used interchangeably, though the term *asteroid* is more widely

By comparison with those of the inner solar system, the planets of the outer solar system are veritable giants. Shown to scale, outward from the Sun, are Mercury, Venus, Earth, Mars, Jupiter, Saturn, Uranus, and Neptune. Also shown is the dwarf planet, Pluto. NASA/Lunar and Planetary Laboratory

recognized by the general public. Among scientists, those who study individual objects with dynamically interesting orbits or groups of objects with similar orbital characteristics generally use the term *minor planet*, whereas those who study the physical properties of such objects usually refer to them as *asteroids*.

MAJOR MILESTONES IN ASTEROID RESEARCH

The first asteroid was discovered on Jan. 1, 1801, by the astronomer Giuseppe Piazzi at Palermo, Italy. At first Piazzi thought that he had discovered a comet. However, after the orbital elements of the object had been computed, it became clear that the object moved in a planetlike orbit between the orbits of Mars and Jupiter.

Owing to illness, Piazzi was able to observe the object only until February 11. As no one else was aware of its existence, it was not reobserved before it moved into the daytime sky. The short arc of observations did not allow computation of an orbit of sufficient accuracy to predict where the object would reappear when it moved back into the night sky, and so it was "lost."

There matters might have stood were it not for astronomers searching for a "missing" planet between Mars and Jupiter during an astronomical conference in 1796. (Unfortunately, Piazzi was not a party to this attempt to locate the missing planet.) In 1801, German mathematician Carl Friedrich Gauss developed a method for computing the orbit of an asteroid from only a few observations.

Using Gauss's predictions, the German Hungarian astronomer Franz von Zach rediscovered Piazzi's "lost" object on Jan. 1, 1802. Piazzi named this object Ceres after the ancient Roman grain goddess and patron goddess of Sicily, thereby initiating a tradition that continues to the present day—asteroids are named by their discoverers.

The discovery of three more faint objects (at least when compared with Mars and Jupiter) in similar orbits over the next six years—Pallas, Juno, and Vesta—complicated this elegant solution to the missing-planet problem and gave rise to the surprisingly long-lived though no longer accepted idea that the asteroids were remnants of a planet that had exploded. Following this flurry of activity, the search for the planet appears to have been abandoned until 1830, when Karl L. Hencke renewed it. In 1845 he discovered a fifth asteroid, which he named Astraea.

There were 88 known asteroids by 1866, when the next major discovery was made: Daniel Kirkwood, an American astronomer, noted that there were gaps (now known as Kirkwood gaps) in the distribution of asteroid distances from the Sun. The introduction of photography to the search for new asteroids in 1891, by which time 322 asteroids had been identified, accelerated the discovery rate. The asteroid designated (323) Brucia, detected in 1891, was the first to be discovered by means of photography. By the end of the 19th century, 464 had been found; this grew to more than 100,000 by the end of the 20th century

BODE'S LAW

Bode's law, also called the Titius-Bode law, is an empirical rule giving the approximate distances of planets from the Sun. It was first announced in 1766 by the German astronomer Johann Daniel Titius but was popularized only from 1772 by his countryman Johann Elert Bode. Once suspected to have some significance regarding the formation of the solar system, Bode's law is now generally regarded as a numerological curiosity with no known justification.

One way to state Bode's law begins with the sequence 0, 3, 6, 12, 24, . . . in which each number after 3 is twice the previous one. To each number is added 4, and each result is divided by 10. Of the first seven answers—0.4, 0.7, 1.0, 1.6, 2.8, 5.2, 10.0—six of them (2.8 being the exception) closely approximate the distances from the Sun, expressed in AU), of the six planets known when Titius devised the rule: Mercury, Venus, Earth, Mars, Jupiter, and Saturn. At about 2.8 AU from the Sun, between Mars and Jupiter, the asteroids were later discovered, beginning with Ceres in 1801. The rule also was found to hold for the seventh planet, Uranus, which lies at about 19 AU, but it failed to predict accurately the distance of the eighth planet, Neptune (30 AU), and that of Pluto (31.5 AU), which was regarded as the ninth planet when it was discovered in 1930.

and to more than four times that number by 2009. This explosive growth was a spin-off of a survey designed to find 90 percent of asteroids with diameters greater than 1 km (0.6 miles) that can cross Earth's orbit and thus have the potential to collide with the planet..

LATER ADVANCES
IN ASTEROID STUDIES

During much of the 19th century, most discoveries concerning asteroids were based on studies of their orbits. The vast majority of knowledge about the physical characteristics of asteroids— for example, their size, shape, rotation period, composition, mass, and density—was learned beginning in the 20th century, in particular since the 1970s. As a result of such studies, these objects went from being merely "minor" planets to becoming small worlds in their own right.

In 1918 the Japanese astronomer Hirayama Kiyotsugu recognized clustering in three of the orbital elements (semimajor axis, eccentricity, and inclination) of various asteroids. He speculated that objects sharing these elements had been formed by explosions of larger parent asteroids, and he called such groups of asteroids "families."

In the mid-20th century, calculations of the lifetimes of asteroids whose orbits passed close to those of the major planets showed that most such asteroids were destined either to collide with a planet or to be ejected from the solar system on

timescales of a few hundred thousand to a few million years. Since the age of the solar system is approximately 4.6 billion years, this meant that the asteroids seen today in such orbits must have entered them recently and implied that there was a source for these asteroids. At first this source was thought to be comets that had been captured by the planets and that had lost their volatile material through repeated passages inside the orbit of Mars. It is now known that most such objects come from regions in the main asteroid belt near Kirkwood gaps and other orbital resonances.

GEOGRAPHY
OF THE ASTEROID BELT

Geography in its most literal sense is a description of the features on the surface of Earth or another planet. Three coordinates—latitude, longitude, and altitude—suffice for locating all such features. Similarly, the location of any object in the solar system can be specified by three parameters—heliocentric ecliptic longitude, heliocentric ecliptic latitude, and heliocentric distance. Such positions, however, are valid for only an instant of time since all objects in the solar system are continuously in motion. Thus, a better descriptor of the "location" of a solar system object is the path, called the orbit, that it follows around the Sun or, in the case of a planetary satellite (moon), the path around its parent planet.

All asteroids orbit the Sun in elliptical orbits and move in the same direction as the major planets. Some elliptical orbits are very nearly circles, while others are highly elongated (eccentric). An orbit is completely described by six geometric parameters called its elements. Orbital elements, and hence the shape and orientation of the orbit, also vary with time because each object is gravitationally acting on, and being acted upon by, all other bodies in the solar system. In most cases, these gravitational effects can be accounted for so that accurate predictions of past and future locations can be made and a mean orbit can be defined. These mean orbits can then be used to describe the geography of the asteroid belt.

NAMES AND
ORBITS OF ASTEROIDS

Because of their widespread occurrence, asteroids are assigned numbers as well as names. The numbers are assigned consecutively after accurate orbital elements have been determined. Ceres is officially known as (1) Ceres, Pallas as (2) Pallas, and so forth. Of the more than 450,000 asteroids discovered by 2009, about 47 percent were numbered. Asteroid discoverers have the right to choose names for their discoveries as soon as they are numbered. The names selected are submitted to the International Astronomical Union (IAU) for approval.

Prior to the mid-20th century, asteroids were sometimes assigned numbers before accurate orbital elements had been determined, and so some numbered asteroids could not later be located. These objects were referred to as "lost" asteroids. The final lost numbered asteroid, (719) Albert, was recovered in 2000 after a lapse of 89 years. Many newly discovered asteroids still become "lost" because of an insufficiently long span of observations, but no new asteroids are assigned numbers until their orbits are reliably known.

The Minor Planet Center at the Harvard-Smithsonian Center for Astrophysics in Cambridge, Mass., maintains computer files for all measurements of asteroid positions. As of 2009, there were more than 60 million such positions in its database.

DISTRIBUTION
AND KIRKWOOD GAPS

The great majority of the known asteroids move in orbits between those of Mars and Jupiter. Most of these orbits, in turn, have semimajor axes, or mean distances from the Sun, between 2.06 and 3.28 AU, a region called the main belt. The mean distances are not uniformly distributed but exhibit population depletions, or "gaps." These so-called Kirkwood gaps are due to mean-motion resonances with Jupiter's orbital period. An asteroid with a mean distance from the Sun of 2.50 AU, for example, makes three circuits around the Sun in the time it takes Jupiter, which has a mean distance of 5.20 AU, to make one circuit. The asteroid is thus said to be

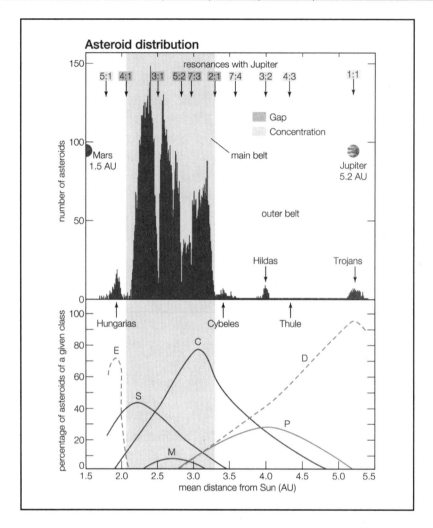

Asteroid distribution between Mars and Jupiter. (Top) Numbers of asteroids from a total of more than 69,500 with known orbits are plotted against their mean distances from the Sun. Major depletions, or gaps, of asteroids occur near the mean-motion resonances with Jupiter between 4:1 and 2:1, whereas asteroid concentrations are found near other resonances. The distribution does not indicate true relative numbers, because nearer and brighter asteroids are favoured for discovery. In reality, for any given size range, three to four times as many asteroids lie between the 3:1 and 2:1 resonances as between the 4:1 and 3:1 resonances. (Bottom) Relative percentages of six major asteroid classes are plotted against their mean distances. At a given mean distance, the percentages of the classes present total 100 percent. As the graph reveals, the distribution of the asteroid classes is highly structured, with the different classes forming overlapping rings around the Sun. Encyclopædia Britannica, Inc.

in a three-to-one (written 3:1) resonance orbit with Jupiter. Consequently, once every three orbits, Jupiter and an asteroid in such an orbit would be in the same relative positions, and the asteroid would experience a gravitational force in a fixed direction. Repeated applications of this force would eventually change the mean distance of this asteroid—and others in similar orbits—thus creating a gap at 2.50 AU. Major gaps occur at distances from the Sun that correspond to resonances with Jupiter of 4:1, 3:1, 5:2, 7:3, and 2:1, with the respective mean distances being 2.06, 2.50, 2.82, 2.96, and 3.28. The major gap at the 4:1 resonance defines the nearest extent of the main belt; the gap at the 2:1 resonance, the farthest extent.

Some mean-motion resonances, rather than dispersing asteroids, are observed to collect them. Outside the limits of the main belt, asteroids cluster near resonances of 5:1 (at 1.78 AU, called the Hungaria group), 7:4 (at 3.58 AU, the Cybele group), 3:2 (at 3.97 AU, the Hilda group), 4:3 (at 4.29 AU, the lone asteroid (279) Thule), and 1:1 (at 5.20 AU, the Trojan groups). The presence of other resonances, called secular resonances, complicates the situation, particularly at the sunward edge of the belt. Secular resonances, in which two orbits interact through the motions of their ascending nodes, perihelia, or both, operate over timescales of millions of years to change the eccentricity and inclination of asteroids. Combinations of mean-motion and secular resonances can either result in long-term stabilization of asteroid orbits at certain mean-motion resonances, as is evidenced by the Hungaria, Cybele, Hilda, and Trojan asteroid groups, or cause the orbits to evolve away from the resonances, as is evidenced by the Kirkwood gaps.

Near-Earth Asteroids

Asteroids that can come close to Earth are called near-Earth asteroids (NEAs), although only some NEAs actually cross Earth's orbit. NEAs are divided into several classes. Asteroids belonging to the class most distant from Earth—those asteroids that can cross the orbit of Mars but that have perihelion distances greater than 1.3 AU—are dubbed Mars crossers. This class is further subdivided into two: shallow Mars crossers (perihelion distances no less than 1.58 AU but less than 1.67 AU) and deep Mars crossers (perihelion distances greater than 1.3 AU but less than 1.58 AU).

The next most distant class of NEAs is the Amors. Members of this group have perihelion distances that are greater than 1.017 AU, which is Earth's aphelion distance, but no greater than 1.3 AU. Amor asteroids therefore do not at present cross Earth's orbit. Because of strong gravitational perturbations produced by their close approaches to Earth, however, the orbital elements of all Earth-approaching asteroids except the shallow Mars crossers change appreciably on timescales as short as years or decades. For this reason, about half the known Amors, including (1221) Amor, the namesake of the group, are part-time Earth crossers. Only asteroids that cross the orbits of planets—i.e., Earth-approaching asteroids and idiosyncratic objects such as (944) Hidalgo and Chiron—suffer significant changes in their orbital elements on timescales shorter than many millions of years.

There are two classes of NEAs that deeply cross Earth's orbit on an almost continuous basis. The first of these to be discovered were the Apollo asteroids, named for (1862) Apollo, which was discovered in 1932 but was lost shortly thereafter and not rediscovered until 1978. The mean distances of Apollo asteroids from the Sun are greater than or equal to 1 AU, and their perihelion distances are less than or equal to Earth's aphelion distance of 1.017 AU; thus, they cross Earth's orbit when near the closest points to the Sun in their own orbits. The other class of Earth-crossing asteroids is named Atens for (2062) Aten, which was discovered in 1976. The Aten asteroids have mean distances from the Sun that are less than 1 AU and aphelion distances that are greater than or equal to 0.983 AU, the perihelion distance of Earth; they cross Earth's orbit when near the farthest points from the Sun of their orbits.

The class of NEAs that was the last to be recognized is composed of asteroids with orbits entirely inside that of Earth. Known as Atira asteroids after (163693) Atira, they have mean distances from the Sun that are less than 1 AU and aphelion distances less than 0.983 AU; they do not cross Earth's orbit.

As of 2009, the known Atira, Aten, Apollo, and Amor asteroids of all sizes numbered 9, 510, 3,081, and 2,577, respectively, although these numbers are steadily increasing as the asteroid survey programs progress. Most of these were discovered since 1970, when dedicated searches for these types of asteroids were begun. Astronomers have estimated that there are roughly 50 Atens, 600 Apollos, and 250 Amors that have diameters larger than about 1 km (0.6 miles).

Because they can approach quite close to Earth, some of the best information available on asteroids has come from Earth-based radar studies of NEAs. In 1968 the Apollo asteroid (1566) Icarus became the first NEA to be observed with radar. Some four decades later, over 200 NEAs had been so observed. Because of continuing improvements to the radar systems themselves and to the computers used to process the data, the information provided by this technique increased dramatically beginning in the final decade of the 20th century. For example, the first images of an asteroid, (4769) Castalia, were made using radar data obtained in 1989, more than two years before the first spacecraft flyby of an asteroid—(951) Gaspra by the Galileo spacecraft in 1991. The observations of Castalia provided the first evidence in the solar system for a double-lobed object, interpreted to be two roughly equal-sized bodies in contact. Radar observations of (4179) Toutatis in 1992 revealed it to be several kilometres long with a peanut-shell shape;

similar to Castalia, Toutatis appears predominantly to be two components in contact, one about twice as large as the other. The highest-resolution images show craters having diameters between 100 and 600 metres (roughly 300 and 2,000 feet). Radar images of (1620) Geographos obtained in 1994 were numerous enough and of sufficient quality for an animation to be made showing it rotating.

The orbital characteristics of NEAs mean that some of these objects make close approaches to Earth and occasionally collide with it. In January 1991, for example, an Apollo asteroid (or, as an alternative description, a large meteoroid) with an estimated diameter of 10 metres (33 feet) passed by Earth within less than half the distance to the Moon. Such passages are not especially unusual. On Oct. 6, 2008, the asteroid 2008 TC3, which had a size of about 5 metres (16 feet), was discovered and crashed in the Nubian desert of the Sudan the next day. The collision of a sufficiently large NEA with Earth is generally recognized to pose a great potential danger to human beings and possibly to all life on the planet.

Because of the small sizes of NEAs and the short time they spend close enough to Earth to be seen, it is unusual for such close passages to be observed. An example of a NEA for which the lead time for observation is large is (99942) Apophis. This Aten asteroid, which has a diameter of about 300 m (984 feet), is predicted to pass within 32,000 km (19,884 miles) of Earth—i.e., closer than

communications satellites in geostationary orbits—on April 13, 2029. During that passage, the probability of the asteroid hitting Earth is thought to be near zero. In 2006, however, it had been estimated that Apophis would have about 1 chance in 50,000 of colliding with Earth during the following close approach, on April 13, 2036.

MAIN-BELT ASTEROID FAMILIES

Within the main belt are groups of asteroids that cluster with respect to certain mean orbital elements (semimajor axis, eccentricity, and inclination). Such groups are called families and are named for the lowest numbered asteroid in the family. Asteroid families are formed when an asteroid is disrupted in a catastrophic collision, the members of the family thus being pieces of the original asteroid. Theoretical studies indicate that catastrophic collisions between asteroids are common enough to account for the number of families observed. About 40 percent of the larger asteroids belong to such families, but as high a proportion as 90 percent of small asteroids (i.e., those about 1 km [0.6 miles] in diameter) may be family members because each catastrophic collision produces many more small fragments than large ones.

The three largest families are named Eos, Koronis, and Themis. Each family has been determined to be compositionally homogeneous—that is, all the members of a family appear to have

Fist-sized meteorite fragment that fell in western Australia in 1960 and is thought to have been ejected from the surface of the asteroid Vesta in a collision. The meteorite has the same unique spectral signature of the mineral pyroxene, which is common in lavas, as that obtained from Vesta. Its shiny black fusion crust was produced by frictional heating as it fell through Earth's atmosphere. R. Kempton/New England Meteoritical Services

collisions similar to those that produced the asteroid families. For example, the asteroid Vesta, whose surface appears to be basaltic rock, is widely believed to be the parent body of the meteorites known as basaltic achondrite HEDs, a grouping of the related howardite, eucrite, and diogenite meteorite types.

HUNGARIAS AND OUTER-BELT ASTEROIDS

Only one known concentration of asteroids, the Hungaria group, occupies the region between Mars and the inner edge of the main belt. The orbits of all the Hungarias lie outside the orbit of Mars, whose aphelion distance is 1.67 AU. Hungaria asteroids have nearly circular (low-eccentricity) orbits but large orbital inclinations to Earth's orbit and the general plane of the solar system.

Four known asteroid groups fall beyond the main belt but within or near the orbit of Jupiter, with mean distances from the Sun between about 3.28 and 5.3 AU. Collectively called outer-belt asteroids, they have orbital periods that range from more than one-half that of Jupiter to approximately Jupiter's period. Three of the outer-belt groups, the Cybeles, the Hildas, and Thule, are named after

the same basic chemical makeup. If the asteroids belonging to each family are considered to be fragments of a single parent body, then their parent bodies must have had diameters of 200, 90, and 300 km (124, 56, and 186 miles), respectively. The smaller families present in the main belt have not been as well studied because their numbered members are fewer and smaller (and hence fainter when viewed telescopically). It is theorized that some of the Earth-crossing asteroids and the great majority of meteorites reaching Earth's surface are fragments produced in

the lowest-numbered asteroid in each group. Members of the fourth group are called Trojan asteroids (see below). As of 2009, about 930 Cybeles, 1,270 Hildas, 1 Thule, and 2,962 Trojans were known.

TROJAN ASTEROIDS

In 1772 the French mathematician and astronomer Joseph-Louis Lagrange predicted the existence and location of two groups of small bodies located near a pair of gravitationally stable points along Jupiter's orbit. These are positions (now called Lagrangian points and designated L4 and L5) where a small body can be held, by gravitational forces, at one vertex of an equilateral triangle whose other vertices are occupied by the massive bodies of Jupiter and the Sun. These positions, which lead and trail Jupiter by 60° in the plane of its orbit, are two of the five theoretical Lagrangian points in the solution to the circular, restricted three-body problem of celestial mechanics. The other three stable points are located along a line passing through the Sun and Jupiter. The presence of other planets, however—principally Saturn—perturbs the Sun-Jupiter-Trojan asteroid system enough to destabilize these points, and no asteroids have been found near them. In fact, because of this destabilization, most of Jupiter's Trojan asteroids move in orbits inclined as much as 40° from Jupiter's orbit and displaced as much as 70° from the leading and trailing positions of the true Lagrangian points.

In 1906 the first of the predicted objects, (588) Achilles, was discovered near the Lagrangian point preceding Jupiter in its orbit. Within a year two more were found: (617) Patroclus, located near the trailing Lagrangian point, and (624) Hektor, near the leading Lagrangian point. It was later decided to continue naming such asteroids after participants in the Trojan War as recounted in Homer's epic work the *Iliad* and, furthermore, to name those near the leading point after Greek warriors and those near the trailing point after Trojan warriors. With the exception of the two "misplaced" names already bestowed (Hektor, the lone Trojan in the Greek camp, and Patroclus, the lone Greek in the Trojan camp), this tradition has been maintained.

Of the 2,962 of Jupiter's Trojan asteroids discovered, 56 percent are located near the leading Lagrangian point and the remainder near the trailing one. Astronomers estimate that 1,800–2,800 of the total existing population of Jupiter's Trojans have diameters greater than 15 km (9 miles).

Since the discovery of Jupiter's orbital companions, the term Trojan has been applied to any small object occupying the equilateral Lagrangian points of other pairs of relatively massive bodies. Astronomers have searched for Trojan objects of Earth, Mars, Saturn, and Neptune, as well as of the Earth-Moon system. It was long considered doubtful whether truly stable orbits could exist near these Lagrangian points because of gravitational perturbations by the major planets.

However, in 1990 an asteroid later named (5261) Eureka was discovered librating (oscillating) about the trailing Lagrangian point of Mars, and since then two others have been found; one additional potential Martian Trojan awaits confirmation of its orbit. Six Trojans of Neptune, all associated with the leading Lagrangian point, were discovered beginning in 2001. Although Trojans of Saturn have yet to be found, objects librating about Lagrangian points of the systems formed by Saturn and its moon Tethys and Saturn and its moon Dione are known.

ASTEROIDS IN
UNUSUAL ORBITS

Although most asteroids travel in fairly circular orbits, there are notable exceptions.

In addition to the near-Earth asteroids, discussed above, some objects are known to travel in orbits that extend far inside or outside the main belt. One of the most extreme is (3200) Phaethon, the first asteroid to be discovered by a spacecraft (the Infrared Astronomical Satellite in 1983). Phaethon approaches to within 0.14 AU of the Sun, well within the perihelion distance of 0.31 AU for Mercury, the innermost planet. By contrast, Phaethon's aphelion distance of 2.4 AU is in the main asteroid belt. This object is the parent body of the Geminid meteor stream, the concentration of meteoroids responsible for the annual Geminid meteor shower seen on Earth each December.

Because the parent bodies of all other meteor streams identified to date are comets, Phaethon is considered by some to be

THE DIFFERENCE BETWEEN ASTEROIDS AND COMETS

Asteroids traditionally have been distinguished from comets by characteristics based on physical differences, location in the solar system, and orbital properties. An object is classified as a comet when it displays "cometary activity"—i.e., a coma, or tail, or any evidence of gas or dust coming from it. In addition, any object on a nonreturning orbit (a parabolic or hyperbolic orbit, rather than an elliptical one) is generally considered to be a comet.

Although these distinctions apply most of the time, they are not always sufficient to classify an individual object as an asteroid or a comet. For example, an object found to be receding from the Sun on a nonreturning orbit and displaying no cometary activity could be a comet, or it could be a planet-crossing asteroid being ejected from the solar system after a close encounter with a planet, most likely Jupiter. Unless such an object reveals itself by displaying cometary activity, there is usually no way to determine its origin and thus to classify it unequivocally. The object may have formed as an icy body, as comets do, but lost its volatile materials during a series of passes into the inner solar system. Its burned-out remnant of rocky material would presently have more physical characteristics in common with asteroids than with other comets.

a defunct comet—one that has lost its volatile materials and no longer displays the classic cometary features of a nebulous coma and a tail. Another asteroid, (944) Hidalgo, is also thought by some to be a defunct comet because of its unusual orbit. This object, discovered in 1920, travels sunward as near as 2.02 AU, which is at the inner edge of the main asteroid belt, and as far as 9.68 AU, which is just beyond the orbit of Saturn, at 9.54 AU.

MEASURING ASTEROIDS

The first measurements of the sizes of individual asteroids were made in the last years of the 19th century. A filar micrometer, an instrument normally used in conjunction with a telescope for visual measurement of the separations of double stars, was employed to estimate the diameters of the first four known asteroids. The results established that Ceres was the largest asteroid, having a diameter estimated to be nearly 800 km (497 miles). These values had remained the best available until new techniques for finding albedos (reflectivities) and diameters, based on infrared radiometry and polarization measurements, were introduced beginning about 1970. The first four asteroids came to be known as the "big four," and, because all other asteroids were much fainter, they all were believed to be considerably smaller as well.

The first asteroid to have its mass determined was Vesta—in 1966 from measurements of its perturbation of the orbit of asteroid (197) Arete. The first

mineralogical determination of the surface composition of an asteroid was made in 1969 when spectral reflectance measurements identified the mineral pyroxene in the surface material of Vesta.

SIZE AND ALBEDO

About 30 asteroids are larger than 200 km (124 miles). The largest, Ceres, has a diameter of about 940 km (584 miles). It is followed by Pallas at 530 km (329 miles), Vesta at 520 km (323 miles), and (10) Hygiea at 410 km (255 miles). Three asteroids are between 300 and 400 km (186 and 249 miles) in diameter, and about 23 between 200 and 300 km (124 and 186 miles). It has been estimated that 250 asteroids are larger than 100 km (62 miles) in diameter and perhaps a million are larger than 1 km (0.6 miles). The smallest known asteroids are members of the near-Earth group, some of which approach Earth to within a few hundredths of 1 AU. The smallest routinely observed Earth-approaching asteroids measure about 100 metres (328 feet) across.

The most widely used technique for determining the sizes of asteroids (and other small bodies in the solar system) is that of thermal radiometry. This technique exploits the fact that the infrared radiation (heat) emitted by an asteroid must balance the solar radiation it absorbs. By using a so-called thermal model to balance the measured intensity of infrared radiation with that of radiation at visual wavelengths, investigators are able to derive the diameter of the asteroid. Other remote-sensing techniques—for example, polarimetry, radar, and adaptive optics (techniques for minimizing the distorting effects of Earth's atmosphere)—also are used, but they are limited to brighter, larger, or closer asteroids.

The only techniques that measure the diameter directly (i.e., without having to model the actual observations) are those of stellar occultation and direct imaging using either advanced instruments on Earth (e.g., large telescopes equipped with adaptive optics or orbiting observatories such as the Hubble Space Telescope) or passing spacecraft. In the method of stellar occultation, investigators measure the length of time that a star disappears from view owing to the passage of an asteroid between the star and Earth. Then, using the known distance and the rate of motion of the asteroid, they are able to determine the latter's diameter as projected onto the plane of the sky.

The necessary techniques for imaging asteroids directly were perfected during the last years of the 20th century. They (and radar) can be used to observe an asteroid over a complete rotation cycle and so measure the three-dimensional shape. These results have made it possible to calibrate the indirect techniques, thermal radiometry in particular, such that diameter measurements made with thermal radiometry on asteroids larger than about 20 km (12 miles) are thought to be uncertain by less than 10 percent; for smaller asteroids the uncertainty is about 30 percent.

The occultation technique is limited to the rare passages of asteroids in front of stars, and, because the technique measures only one cross section, it is best applied to fairly spherical asteroids. On the other hand, direct imaging (at least to date) has been limited to the nearer, brighter, or larger asteroids. Consequently, the majority of asteroid sizes have been and will probably continue to be obtained with indirect techniques. Direct imaging has allowed the accurate determination of the diameters of about two dozen asteroids, including Ceres, Pallas, Juno, and Vesta, compared with 2,300 measured with indirect techniques, principally thermal radiometry.

A property that is closely related to size (and that also provides compositional information) is albedo. Albedo is the ratio between the amount of light actually reflected and that which would be reflected by a uniformly scattering disk of the same size, both observed at opposition. Snow has an albedo of approximately 1 and coal an albedo of about 0.05.

An asteroid's apparent brightness depends on both its albedo and diameter as well as on its distance. For example, if Ceres and Vesta could both be observed at the same distance, Vesta would be the brighter of the two by about 15 percent, even though Vesta's diameter is only a little more than half that of Ceres. Vesta would appear brighter because its albedo is about 0.40, compared with 0.10 for Ceres.

Asteroid albedos range from about 0.02 to more than 0.5 and may be divided into four groups: low (0.02–0.07), intermediate (0.08–0.12), moderate (0.13–0.28), and high (greater than 0.28). After corrections are added for the fact that the brighter and nearer asteroids are favoured for discovery, about 78 percent of known asteroids larger than about 25 km (15 miles) in diameter are found to be low-albedo objects. Most of these are located in the outer half of the main asteroid belt and among the outer-belt populations. More than 95 percent of outer-belt asteroids belong to this group. Roughly 18 percent of known asteroids belong to the moderate-albedo group, the vast majority of which are found in the inner half of the main belt. The intermediate- and high-albedo asteroid groups make up the remaining 4 percent of the population. For the most part, they occupy the same part of the main belt as the moderate-albedo objects.

The albedo distribution for asteroids with diameters less than 25 km (15 miles) is poorly known because only a small fraction of this population has been characterized. However, if these objects are mostly fragments from a few asteroid families, then their albedo distribution may differ significantly from that of their larger siblings.

CLASSIFICATION OF ASTEROIDS

In the mid-1970s astronomers, using information gathered from studies of colour, spectral reflectance, and albedo, recognized that asteroids could be grouped into three broad taxonomic classes, designated C, S, and M. At that time they estimated that about 75 percent belonged to class C, 15 percent to class S, and 5 percent to class M. The remaining 5 percent were unclassifiable owing to either poor data or genuinely unusual properties. Furthermore, they noted that the S class dominated the population at the inner edge of the asteroid belt, whereas the C class was dominant in the middle and outer regions of the belt.

Within a decade this taxonomic system was expanded, and it was recognized that the asteroid belt comprised overlapping rings of differing taxonomic classes, with classes designated S, C, P, and D dominating the populations at distances from the Sun of about 2, 3, 4, and 5 AU, respectively. As more data became available from further observations, additional minor classes were recognized.

ROTATION AND SHAPE

The rotation periods and shapes of asteroids are determined primarily by monitoring their changing brightness on timescales of minutes to days. Short-period fluctuations in brightness caused by the rotation of an irregularly shaped asteroid or a spherical spotted asteroid (i.e., one with albedo differences) produce a light curve—a graph of brightness versus time—that repeats at regular intervals corresponding to an asteroid's rotation period. The range of brightness variation is closely related to an asteroid's shape or spottedness but is more difficult to interpret.

In the early years of the 21st century, rotation periods were known for more than 2,300 asteroids. They range from 42.7 seconds to 50 days, but more than 70 percent lie between 4 and 24 hours. In some cases, periods longer than a few days may actually be due to precession (a smooth slow circling of the rotation axis) caused by an unseen satellite of the asteroid. Periods on the order of minutes are observed only for very small objects (those with diameters less than about 150 metres [492 feet]). The largest asteroids (those with diameters greater than about 200 km [1214 miles]) have a mean rotation period close to 8 hours; the value increases to 13 hours for asteroids with diameters of about 100 km (62 miles) and then decreases to about 6 hours for those with diameters of about 10 km (6 miles).

The largest asteroids may have preserved the rotation rates they had when they were formed, but the smaller ones almost certainly have had their modified by subsequent collisions and, in the case of the very smallest, perhaps also by radiation effects. The difference in rotation periods between 200-km-class (124 mile) and 100-km-class (62 mile) asteroids is believed to stem from the fact that large asteroids retain all of the collision debris from minor collisions, whereas smaller asteroids retain more of the debris ejected in the direction opposite to that of their spins, causing a loss of angular momentum and thus a reduction in speed of rotation.

Major collisions can completely disrupt smaller asteroids. The debris from such collisions makes still smaller asteroids, which can have virtually any shape or spin rate. Thus, the fact that no rotation periods shorter than about 2 hours have been observed for asteroids greater than about 150 metres (492 feet) in diameter implies that their material strengths are not high enough to withstand the centripetal forces that such rapid spins produce.

It is impossible to distinguish mathematically between the rotation of a spotted sphere and an irregular shape of uniform reflectivity on the basis of observed brightness changes alone. Nevertheless, the fact that opposite sides of most asteroids appear to differ no more than a few percent in albedo suggests that their brightness variations are due mainly to changes in the projection of their illuminated portions as seen from Earth. Hence, in the absence of evidence to the contrary, astronomers generally accept that variations in reflectivity contribute little to the observed amplitude, or range in brightness variation, of an asteroid's rotational light curve. Vesta is a notable exception to this generalization because the difference in reflectivity between its opposite hemispheres is known to be sufficient to account for much of its modest light-curve amplitude.

Observed light-curve amplitudes for asteroids range from zero to a factor of 6.5, the latter being the case for the Apollo asteroid Geographos. A rotating asteroid shows a light-curve amplitude of zero (no change in amplitude) when its shape is a uniform sphere or when it is viewed along one of its rotational poles. Before Geographos was studied by radar, its 6.5 to 1 variation in brightness was ascribed to either of two possibilities: the asteroid is a cigar-shaped object that is being viewed along a line perpendicular to its rotational axis (which for normally rotating asteroids is the shortest axis), or it is a pair of objects nearly in contact that orbit each other around their centre of mass. The radar images ruled out the binary model, revealing that Geographos is a single, highly elongated object.

The mean rotational light-curve amplitude for asteroids is a factor of about 1.3. This data, together with the assumptions discussed above, allow astronomers to estimate asteroid shapes, which occur in a wide range. Some asteroids, such as Ceres, Pallas, and Vesta, are nearly spherical, whereas others, such as (15) Eunomia, (107) Camilla, and (511) Davida, are quite elongated. Still others, as, for example, (1580) Betulia, Hektor, and Castalia (the last of which appears in radar observations to be two bodies in contact), apparently have bizarre shapes.

MASS AND DENSITY

Most asteroid masses are low, although present-day observations show that the asteroids measurably perturb the orbits of the major planets. Except for Mars, however, these perturbations are too small to allow the masses of the asteroids in question to be determined. Radio-ranging measurements that were transmitted from the surface of Mars between 1976 and 1980 by the two Viking landers and time-delay radar observations using the Mars Pathfinder lander made it possible to determine distances to Mars with an accuracy of about 10 metres (32 feet). The three largest asteroids—Ceres, Vesta, and Pallas—were found to cause departures of Mars from its predicted orbit in excess of 50 metres (164 feet) over times of 10 years or less. The measured departures, in turn, were used to estimate the masses of the three asteroids. Masses for a number of other asteroids have been determined by noting their effect on the orbits of other asteroids that they approach closely and regularly, on the orbits of the asteroids' satellites, or on spacecraft orbiting or flying by the asteroids. For those asteroids whose diameters are determined and whose shapes are either spherical or ellipsoidal, their volumes are easily calculated. Knowledge of the mass and volume allows the density to be calculated. For asteroids with satellites, the density can be determined directly from the satellite's orbit without knowledge of the mass.

The mass of the largest asteroid, Ceres, is 9.1×10^{20} kg (2×10^{21} pounds), or less than 0.0002 the mass of Earth. The masses of the second and third largest asteroids, Pallas and Vesta, are each only about one-fourth the mass of Ceres. The mass of the entire asteroid belt is roughly three times that of Ceres. Most of the mass in the asteroid belt is concentrated in the larger asteroids, with about 90 percent of the total in asteroids having diameters greater than 100 km (62 miles). The 10th largest asteroid has only about ⅟₆₀ the mass of Ceres. Of the total mass of the asteroids, 90 percent is located in the main belt, 9 percent is in the outer belt (including Jupiter's Trojan asteroids), and the remainder is distributed among the Hungarias and planet-crossing asteroid populations.

The densities of Ceres, Pallas, and Vesta are 2.2, 2.9, and 3.5 grams per cubic cm (1.3, 1.7, and 2 ounces per cubic inch), respectively. These compare with 5.4, 5.2, and 5.5 g/cm³ (3.1, 3, and 3.2 oz/in³) for Mercury, Venus, and Earth, respectively; 3.9 g/cm³ (2.3 oz/in³) for Mars; and 3.3 g/cm³ (1.9 oz/in³) for the Moon. The density of Ceres is similar to that of a class of meteorites known as carbonaceous chondrites, which contain a larger fraction of volatile material than do ordinary terrestrial rocks and hence have a somewhat lower density. The density of Pallas and Vesta are similar to those of Mars and the Moon. Insofar as Ceres, Pallas, and Vesta are typical of asteroids in general, it can be concluded that main-belt asteroids are rocky bodies.

COMPOSITION

The combination of albedos and spectral reflectance measurements—specifically, measures of the amount of reflected sunlight at wavelengths between about 0.3 and 1.1 micrometres (0.00001 and 0.00004 inch)—is used to classify asteroids into various taxonomic groups, as mentioned above. If sufficient spectral resolution is

available, especially extending to wavelengths of about 2.5 μm (0.0001 inch), these measurements also can be used to infer the composition of the surface reflecting the light. This can be done by comparing the asteroid data with data obtained in the laboratory using meteorites or terrestrial rocks or minerals.

By the end of the 1980s, spectral reflectance measurements at wavelengths between 0.3 and 1.1 μm (0.00001 and 0.0004 inch) were available for about 1,000 asteroids, while albedos were determined for roughly 2,000. Both types of data were available for about 400 asteroids. The table summarizes the taxonomic classes into which the asteroids are divided on the basis of such data. Starting in the 1990s, the use of detectors with improved resolution and sensitivity for spectral reflectance measurements resulted in revised taxonomies. These versions are similar to the one presented in the table, the major difference being that the higher-resolution data has allowed many of the classes, especially the S class, to be further subdivided.

Asteroids of the B, C, F, and G classes have low albedos and spectral reflectances similar to those of carbonaceous chondritic meteorites and their constituent assemblages produced by hydrothermal alteration and/or metamorphism of carbonaceous precursor materials. Some C-class asteroids are known to have hydrated minerals on their surfaces, whereas Ceres, a G-class asteroid, probably has water present as a layer of permafrost. K- and S-class asteroids have moderate albedos and spectral reflectances similar to the stony iron meteorites, and they are known to contain significant amounts of silicates and metals, including the minerals olivine and pyroxene on their surfaces. M-class asteroids are moderate-albedo objects, may have significant amounts of nickel-iron metal in their surface material, and exhibit spectral reflectances similar to

ASTEROID TAXONOMIC CLASSES		
CLASS	MEAN ALBEDO	SPECTRAL REFLECTIVITY (AT WAVELENGTHS OF 0.3–1.1 MICROMETRES [µM])
C	0.05	neutral, slight absorption at wavelengths of 0.4 µm or shorter
D	0.04	very red at wavelengths of 0.7 µm or longer
F	0.05	flat
P	0.04	featureless, sloping up into red*
G	0.09	similar to C class but with a deeper absorption at wavelengths of 0.4 µm or shorter
K	0.12	similar to S class but with lower slopes
T	0.08	moderately sloped with weak ultraviolet and infrared absorption bands
B	0.14	similar to C class but with shallower slope toward longer wavelengths
M	0.14	featureless, sloping up into red*
Q	0.21	strong absorption features shortward and longward of 0.7 µm
S	0.18	very red at wavelengths of less than 0.7 µm, typically with an absorption band between 0.9 and 1.0 µm
A	0.42	extremely red at wavelengths shorter than 0.7 µm and a deep absorption longward of 0.7 µm
E	0.44	featureless, sloping up into red*
R	0.35	similar to A class but with slightly weaker absorption bands
V	0.34	very red at wavelengths of less than 0.7 µm and a deep absorption band centred near 0.95 µm
other	any	any object not falling into one of the above classes

*Classes E, M, and P are spectrally indistinguishable at these wavelengths and require an independent albedo measurement for unambiguous classification.

the nickel-iron meteorites. Paradoxically, however, some M-class asteroids have spectral features due to the presence of hydrated minerals. D-class asteroids have low albedos and show reflectance spectra similar to the spectrum exhibited by a relatively new type of carbonaceous chondrite, represented by the Tagish Lake meteorite, which fell in January 2000.

P- and T-class asteroids have low albedos and no known meteorite or naturally occurring mineralogical counterparts, but they may contain a large fraction of carbon polymers or organic-rich silicates or both in their surface material. R-class asteroids are very rare. Their surface material has been identified as being most consistent with a pyroxene- and olivine-rich composition analogous to the pyroxene-olivine achondrite meteorites. The E-class asteroids have the highest albedos and have spectral reflectances that match those of the enstatite achondrite meteorites. V-class asteroids have reflectance properties closely matching those of one particular type of basaltic achondritic meteorite, the eucrites. The match is so good that some believe that the eucrites exhibited in museums are chips from the surface of a V-class asteroid that were knocked off during a major collision. The V class had been thought confined to the large asteroid Vesta and a few very small Earth-approaching asteroids until 2000, when asteroid (1459) Magnya—located at 3.15 AU from the Sun, compared with 2.36

AU for Vesta—was discovered also to have a basaltic surface.

Among the larger asteroids (those with diameters greater than about 25 km [15 miles]), the C-class asteroids are the most common, accounting for about 65 percent by number. This is followed, in decreasing order, by the S class, at 15 percent; the D class, at 8 percent; and the P and M classes, at 4 percent each. The remaining classes constitute less than 4 percent of the population by number. In fact, there are no A-, E-, or Q-class asteroids in this size range, only one member of the R and V classes, and between two and five members of each of the B, F, G, K, and T classes.

The distribution of the taxonomic classes throughout the asteroid belt is highly structured. Some believe this variation with distance from the Sun means that the asteroids formed at or near their present locations and that a detailed comparison of the chemical composition of the asteroids in each region will provide constraints on models for the conditions that may have existed within the contracting solar nebula at the time the asteroids were formed.

SPACECRAFT EXPLORATION

The first mission to rendezvous with an asteroid was the Near Earth Asteroid Rendezvous (NEAR) spacecraft (later renamed NEAR Shoemaker), launched in 1996. The spacecraft entered orbit around (433) Eros, an S-class Amor asteroid, on

Feb. 14, 2000, where it spent a year collecting images and other data before touching down on Eros's surface. Prior to this, spacecraft on the way to their primary targets, or as part of their overall mission, made close flybys of several asteroids. Although the time spent close enough to these asteroids to resolve them was a fraction of the asteroids' rotation periods, it was sufficient to image the portion of the surface illuminated at the time of the flyby and, in some cases, to obtain mass estimates.

The first asteroid studied during a close flyby was (951) Gaspra, which was observed in October 1991 by the Galileo spacecraft en route to Jupiter. Galileo's images, taken from a distance of about 5,000 km (3,107 miles), established that Gaspra, an S-class asteroid, is an irregular body with dimensions of 19 × 12 × 11 km (12 × 7 × 6.8 miles). Pocked with numerous small craters, Gaspra has an irregular shape and groovelike linear markings that suggest it was once part of a larger body that experienced one or more shattering collisions.

Nearly two years later, in August 1993, Galileo flew by (243) Ida, another S-class asteroid. Ida was found to be somewhat crescent-shaped when viewed from the poles, with overall dimensions of about 56 × 15 km (35 × 9 miles), and to have a mean density of about 2.6 g/cm³ (1.5 oz/in³). After Galileo had passed Ida,

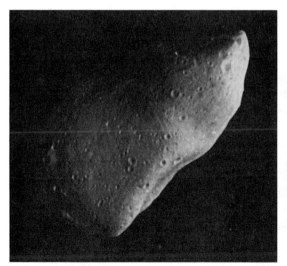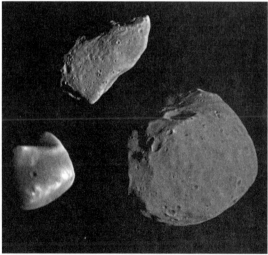

On the left is a close-up image of the asteroid Gaspra, captured by America's Galileo spacecraft. Placed near two moons of Mars (l to r: Deimos, Phobos), courtesy of the NASA photo montage at right, it becomes apparent that Gaspra is roughly the same size. (Left) NASA/JPL/Caltech; (Right) NASA/JPL

Asteroid Ida and its satellite, Dactyl, photographed by the Galileo spacecraft on August 28, 1993, from a distance of about 10,870 km (6,750 miles). Ida is about 56 km (35 miles) long and shows the irregular shape and impact craters characteristic of many asteroids. The Galileo image revealed that Ida is accompanied by a tiny companion about 1.5 km (1 mile) wide, the first proof that some asteroids have natural satellites. Photo NASA/JPL/Caltech

examination of the images it took revealed a tiny object in orbit about the asteroid. Indirect evidence from as early as the 1970s had suggested the existence of natural satellites of asteroids, but Galileo provided the first confirmed instance of one. The moon was given the name Dactyl, from the Dactyli, a group of beings in Greek mythology who lived on Mount Ida in Crete.

In 1999 astronomers using an Earth-based telescope equipped with adaptive optics discovered that the asteroid (45) Eugenia likewise has a moon. Once the orbit of an asteroid's moon has been established, it can be used to derive the density of the parent asteroid without knowing its mass. When this was done for Eugenia, its density turned out to be only 1.2 g/cm³ (0.7 oz/in³). This implies that Eugenia has large voids in its interior, because the materials of which it is composed have densities greater than 2.5.

On its way to Eros, NEAR Shoemaker paid a brief visit to asteroid (253) Mathilde in June 1997. With a mean diameter of 56 km (35 miles), Mathilde is a main-belt asteroid and was the first C-class asteroid to be imaged. The object has a density similar to Eugenia's and likewise is thought to have a porous interior. In July 1999 the Deep Space 1 spacecraft flew by (9969) Braille at a distance of only 26 km (16 miles) during a mission to test a number of advanced technologies in deep space, and about a half year later, in January 2000, the Saturn-bound Cassini-Huygens spacecraft imaged asteroid (2685) Masursky from a comparatively far distance of 1.6 million km (994,194 miles). The Stardust spacecraft, on its way to collect dust from Comet Wild 2, flew by the main-belt asteroid (5535) Annefrank in November 2002, imaging the irregular object and determining it to be at least 6.6 km (4 miles) long, which is larger than estimated from Earth-based observations. The Hayabusa spacecraft, designed to collect asteroidal material and return it to Earth, rendezvoused with the Apollo asteroid (25143) Itokawa between September and December 2005. It found the asteroid's dimensions to be 535 × 294 × 209 metres (1,755 × 965 × 685 feet) and its density to be 1.9 g/cm^3 (1.1 oz/in^3).

The European Space Agency probe Rosetta on its way to Comet Churyumov-Gerasimenko flew by (2867) Steins on Sept. 5, 2008, at a distance of 800 km (500 miles). Steins was the first E-class asteroid to be visited by a spacecraft and had a chain of seven craters on its surface. Rosetta is scheduled to fly by (21) Lutetia, an M-class asteroid, on June 10, 2010, at a distance of 3,000 km (1,900 miles).

The most ambitious mission to the asteroid belt is that of the U.S. spacecraft Dawn, which was launched on Sept. 27, 2007. Dawn will arrive at Vesta in September 2011 and will orbit Vesta until June 2012, when it will leave for Ceres. It will arrive at Ceres in February 2015.

ORIGIN AND EVOLUTION OF THE ASTEROIDS

Available evidence indicates that the asteroids are the remnants of a "stillborn" planet. It is thought that at the time the planets were forming from the low-velocity collisions among asteroid-size planetesimals, one of them, Jupiter, grew at a high rate and to a size larger than the others. In the final stages of its formation, Jupiter gravitationally scattered large planetesimals, some of which may have been as massive as Earth is today. These planetesimals were eventually either captured by Jupiter or another of the giant planets or ejected from the solar system. While they were passing through the inner solar system, however, such large planetesimals strongly perturbed the orbits of the planetesimals in the region of the asteroid belt, raising their mutual velocities to the average 5 km (3 miles) per second they exhibit today. The increased velocities ended the accretionary collisions in this region by transforming them into catastrophic disruptions. Only objects larger than about 500 km (310 miles) in diameter could have survived collisions with objects of comparable size at collision velocities of 5 km (3 miles) per second.

Since that time, the asteroids have been collisionally evolving so that, with the exception of the very largest, most present-day asteroids are either remnants or fragments of past collisions.

As collisions break down larger asteroids into smaller ones, they expose deeper layers of asteroidal material. If asteroids were compositionally homogeneous, this would have no noticeable result. Some of them, however, have become differentiated since their formation. This means that some asteroids, originally formed from so-called primitive material (i.e., material of solar composition with the volatile components removed), were heated, perhaps by short-lived radionuclides or solar magnetic induction, to the point where their interiors melted and geochemical processes occurred. In certain cases, temperatures became high enough for metallic iron to separate out. Being denser than other materials, the iron then sank to the centre, forming an iron core and forcing the less-dense basaltic lavas onto the surface. At least two asteroids with basaltic surfaces, Vesta and Magnya, survive to this day. Other differentiated asteroids, found today among the M-class asteroids, were disrupted by collisions that stripped away their crusts and mantles and exposed their iron cores. Still others may have had only their crusts partially stripped away, which exposed surfaces such as those visible today on the A-, E-, and R-class asteroids. Collisions were responsible for the formation of the

One artist's conception of an asteroid strike, highlighted by a tremendous impact cloud rising from a Caribbean island. Collisions between near-Earth objects and Earth have caught the imagination of people throughout the ages. NASA; illustration by Don Davis

Hirayama families and at least some of the planet-crossing asteroids.

NOTABLE ASTEROIDS

Among the thousands and thousands of asteroids are some that are particularly notable. Some, such as Ceres, are significant in the history of astronomy. Others, such as Vesta, are geologically interesting.

CERES

The dwarf planet Ceres is the largest known asteroid in the asteroid belt and the first asteroid to be discovered. Ceres revolves around the Sun once in 4.61 Earth

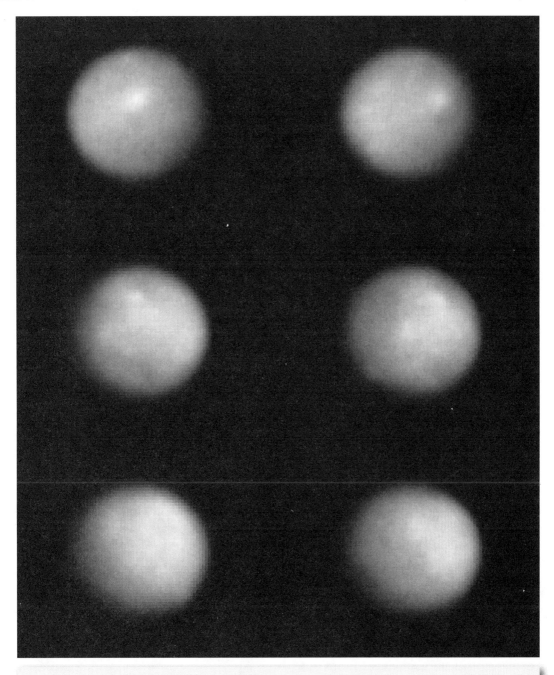

Series of six images showing the rotation of Ceres, taken by the Hubble Space Telescope.
ESA/STScI/NASA

years in a nearly circular, moderately inclined (10.6°) orbit at a mean distance of 2.77 AU (about 414 million km [257 million miles]). Ceres has the shape of a flattened sphere with an equatorial radius of 490 km (304 miles) and a polar radius of 455 km (282 miles), equivalent in volume to a sphere with a diameter of 940 km (94 miles)—i.e., about 27 percent that of Earth's Moon. Although Ceres is the largest asteroid, it is not the brightest. That honour belongs to the second largest asteroid, Vesta, which orbits closer to the Sun than Ceres (Vesta's mean distance is 2.36 AU) and has a surface reflectivity more than three times as high (its albedo is 0.34, compared with 0.10 for Ceres). The mass of Ceres, which accounts for more than one-third the total mass of the main asteroid belt, is about 9.1×10^{20} kg (2×10^{21} pounds), and its density is 2.2 g/cm³ (1.3 oz/in³; about two-thirds that of the Moon). Ceres's shape and density are consistent with a two-layer model of a rocky core surrounded by a thick ice mantle. Ceres rotates once in 9.1 hours, showing no large-scale colour or brightness variations over its surface. Compositionally, the asteroid's surface resembles the carbonaceous chondrite meteorites.

Ceres has been designated a dwarf planet, a new category of solar system objects defined in August 2006 by the IAU.

EROS

Eros was the first asteroid found to travel mainly inside the orbit of Mars and the first to be orbited and landed on by a spacecraft. Eros was discovered in 1898 by the German astronomer Gustav Witt at the Urania Observatory in Berlin. It is named for the god of love in Greek mythology.

A near-Earth asteroid, Eros can pass within 22 million km (14 million miles) of Earth. During a close approach in the 1930s (before the development of direct radar ranging), astronomers were able to observe the asteroid's parallax displacement against the background stars to refine their measurement of Earth's mean distance from the Sun, the basis for the astronomical unit. Eros was the first asteroid found (1901) to display variations in brightness due to its rotation. These periodic light fluctuations were later used to determine its rotation period (5.27 hours), its elongated shape, and, with other observations, its size, which is about twice that of New York City's Manhattan Island. Spectral observations established that Eros belongs to the S compositional class, the most common class among asteroids located in the inner part of the main asteroid belt.

In 2000 the Near Earth Asteroid Rendezvous (NEAR) Shoemaker spacecraft (launched 1996) entered orbit around Eros and collected a full year of data on its surface composition, topography, mass, gravity field, internal structure, and other properties before touching down gently on its surface. NEAR Shoemaker obtained precise dimensions (33 × 13 × 13 km [20.5 × 8 × 8

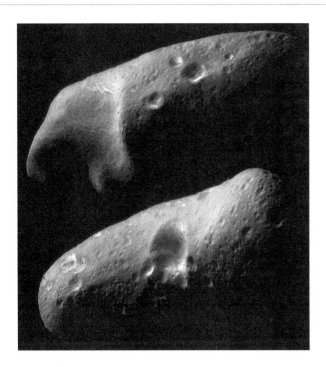

Opposite hemispheres of the asteroid Eros, shown in a pair of mosaics made from images taken by the U.S. Near Earth Asteroid Rendezvous (NEAR) Shoemaker spacecraft on February 23, 2000, from orbit around the asteroid. John Hopkins University/Applied Physics Laboratory/NASA

distinct composition—and so may be a pristine sample of primordial solar system material.

GEOGRAPHOS

Geographos is an asteroid that passes inside Earth's orbit. Geographos was discovered in 1951 by American astronomers Albert Wilson and Rudolf Minkowski at the Palomar Observatory. In 1994 radar observations found that Geographos has dimensions of 5.11 × 1.85 km (3.18 × 1.15 miles) and is thus the most elongated object in the solar system. That same year the U.S. spacecraft Clementine was scheduled to fly by Geographos after leaving lunar orbit, but a computer malfunction canceled that portion of the mission.

HERMES

The binary asteroid Hermes has an eccentric orbit that brings it near Earth. It was discovered in October 1937 by German astronomer Karl Wilhelm Reinmuth when it approached within about 742,000 km (461,000 miles) of Earth; announcement of this near passage occasioned some fear that it might collide with Earth. Hermes was subsequently lost and was not observed again until 2003. Radar observations of Hermes showed that it was actually two asteroids that orbit each other every 14 hours. The

miles]), found evidence of geologic phenomena that could have originated on a much larger parent body from which Eros was derived, and obtained thousands of images revealing numerous ridges, grooves, crater chains, and boulders. A significant discovery was that Eros is an undifferentiated asteroid—i.e., it was never subjected to extensive melting and segregation into layers of

asteroids are 630 and 560 metres (2,070 and 1,840 feet) in diameter.

ICARUS

The asteroid Icarus has a very eccentric orbit with an eccentricity of 0.82 and also approaches quite near to the Sun (within 30 million km [19 million miles]). It was discovered in 1949 by Walter Baade of the Hale Observatories (now Palomar Observatory), California. Its orbit extends from beyond Mars to within that of Mercury; it can approach within 6.4 million km (4 million miles) of Earth. In June 1968 Icarus, the first asteroid to be examined by radar, proved to have a diameter of about 0.8 km (0.5 miles), considerably smaller than previous estimates, and a rotation period of about 2.5 hours.

PALLAS

Pallas is the second largest asteroid in the asteroid belt and the second such object to be discovered, by the German astronomer and physician Wilhelm Olbers on March 28, 1802, following the discovery of Ceres the year before. It is named after Pallas Athena, the Greek goddess of wisdom.

Pallas's orbital inclination of 34.8° is rather large, but its moderate orbital eccentricity (0.23), mean distance from the Sun of 2.77 AU (about 414 million km [257 million miles]), and orbital period of 4.61 years are typical for asteroids located between the orbits of Mars and Jupiter.

Pallas has an ellipsoidal shape with radial dimensions of 285 × 262 × 250 km (177 × 163 × 155 miles), equivalent to a sphere with a diameter of 530 km (329 miles)—i.e., about 15 percent of the diameter of the Moon. Pallas's albedo (reflectivity) is 0.15. Its mass is about 2.2×10^{20} kg (4.8×10^{20} pounds), and its density is about 2.9 g/cm³ (1.7 oz/in³; nearly 90 percent that of the Moon). Pallas turns once on its axis every 7.8 hours. Compositionally, Pallas resembles the carbonaceous chondrite meteorites. Its surface is known to contain hydrated minerals.

VESTA

Vesta is the third largest and the brightest asteroid of the asteroid belt and the fourth such object to be discovered, by the German astronomer and physician Wilhelm Olbers on March 29, 1807. It is named for the ancient Roman goddess of the hearth.

Vesta revolves around the Sun once in 3.63 years in a nearly circular, moderately inclined (7.1°) orbit at a mean distance of 2.36 AU (about 353 million km [219 million miles]). It has an ellipsoidal shape with radial dimensions of 280 × 272 × 227 km (174 × 169 × 141 miles), equivalent to a sphere with a diameter of 520 km (323 miles)—i.e., about 15 percent of the diameter of Earth's Moon. Although Vesta is only about half the size of the largest asteroid, Ceres, it is about four times as reflective (Vesta's albedo, averaged over its rotation, is 0.40, compared

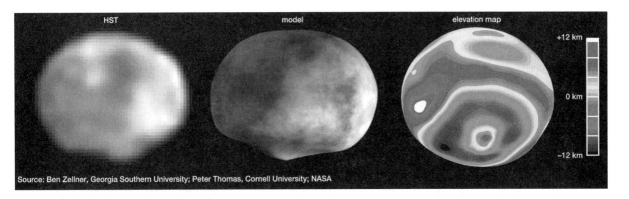

Source: Ben Zellner, Georgia Southern University; Peter Thomas, Cornell University; NASA

The asteroid Vesta, in three renditions based on observations made with the Hubble Space Telescope (HST) in May 1996 during a relatively close approach of the asteroid to Earth. The mottling on the model is artificially added and does not represent true brightness variations on Vesta. Source: Ben Zellner, Georgia Southern University; Peter Thomas, Cornell University; NASA © Encyclopædia Britannica, Inc.

with 0.10 for Ceres), and it orbits closer (Ceres's mean distance is 2.77 AU). Vesta is the only main-belt asteroid visible to the unaided eye. Its mass is about 2.7×10^{20} kg (5.6×10^{20} pounds), and its density is 3.5 g/cm^3 (2 oz/in^3; about the same as that of the Moon). It rotates once in 5.3 hours, showing large-scale colour and brightness variations over its surface.

Compositionally, Vesta resembles the basaltic achondrite meteorites and is widely believed to be the parent body of the meteorites known as basaltic achondrite HEDs (a grouping of the howardite, eucrite, and diogenite types). In other words, most and perhaps all of these meteorites were once part of Vesta.

CHAPTER 2

METEORS AND METEORITES

I f you look long enough at the night sky, eventually you will see a shooting star. This glowing streak in the sky is a meteor, and its cause is a relatively small stony or metallic natural object from space called a meteoroid that enters Earth's atmosphere and heats to incandescence. In modern usage the term *meteoroid*, rather than being restricted to objects entering Earth's atmosphere, is applied to any small object in orbit around the Sun having the same nature as those that result in meteors.

When a meteoroid enters Earth's atmosphere, it is traveling at very high velocity—more than 11 km per second (25,000 miles per hour) at minimum, which is many times faster than a bullet leaving a gun barrel. Frictional heating, produced by the meteoroid's energetic collision with atmospheric atoms and molecules, causes its surface to melt and vaporize and also heats the air around it. The result is the luminous phenomenon recognized as a meteor. The vast majority of meteoroids that collide with Earth burn up in the upper atmosphere. If a meteoroid survives its fiery plunge through the atmosphere and lands on Earth's surface, the object is known as a meteorite.

The term *meteoroid* is usually reserved for chunks of matter that are approximately house-sized—i.e., some tens of metres across—and smaller, to distinguish them from the larger asteroidal bodies. Meteoroids are believed to be mostly fragments of asteroids and comets and are placed, with them, in the category of solar system objects known as small bodies. A few meteoroids also appear to have come from the Moon and Mars. The smallest meteoroids, those less than a few hundred micrometres across (about the size of a period on a printed page), are called interplanetary dust particles or micrometeoroids.

The terms *meteoroid* and *meteor* (and *meteorite* as well) are sometimes confusingly interchanged in common usage. *Meteor* in particular is often applied to a meteoroid hurtling through space, to an incandescent meteoroid (rather than just its luminous streak) in the atmosphere, or to an object that has hit the ground or a man-made object. An example of the last case is found in the name Meteor Crater, a well-known impact structure in Arizona, U.S.

BASIC FEATURES OF METEORS

On any clear night beyond the bright lights of cities, one can see with the naked eye several meteors per hour. Meteors can last for a small fraction of a second up to several seconds. Quite often, as the glowing meteoroid streaks through the sky, it varies in brightness, appears to emit sparks or flares, and sometimes leaves a luminous train that lingers after its flight has ended.

Unusually luminous meteors are termed fireballs or bolides (the latter term is often applied to those meteoroids observed to explode in the sky). When meteor rates increase significantly above normal, the phenomenon is called a meteor shower. Meteors that do not appear to belong to showers are called sporadic.

Meteors are the result of the high-velocity collision of meteoroids with Earth's atmosphere. A typical visible meteor is produced by an object the size of a grain of sand and may start at altitudes of 100 km (60 miles) or higher. Meteoroids smaller than about 500 micrometres (μm; 0.02 inch) across are too faint to be seen with the naked eye but are observable with binoculars and telescopes; they can also be detected by radar. Brighter meteors—ranging in brilliance from that of Venus to greater than that of the full moon—are less common but are not really unusual. These are produced by meteoroids with masses ranging from several grams up to about one ton (centimetre- to metre-sized objects, respectively).

As meteoroids are traveling in interplanetary space near Earth, their velocities relative to Earth's range from a few kilometres per second up to as high as 72 km (44 miles) per second. As they draw closer to the planet, they are accelerated to yet higher velocities by Earth's gravitational field. The minimum velocity with which a meteoroid can enter the atmosphere is equal to Earth's escape velocity of 11.2 km (7 miles) per second. Even at this velocity, the kinetic energy for a meteoroid of a given mass is about 15 times that produced by an equal mass of chemical explosives such as TNT. As the meteoroid is slowed down by friction with atmospheric gas molecules, this kinetic energy is converted into heat.

Even at the very low atmospheric density present at an altitude of 100 km (62 miles), this heat is sufficient to vaporize and ionize the surface material of the meteoroid and also to dissociate and ionize the surrounding atmospheric gas. The excitation of atmospheric and meteoroidal atoms produces a luminous region, which travels with the meteoroid and greatly exceeds its dimensions. About 0.1–1 percent of the original kinetic energy of the meteoroid is transformed into visible light, with most of the remainder going to heat up the air and the meteoroid and pushing aside the air that the meteoroid encounters.

At deeper levels in the atmosphere, a shock wave may develop in the air ahead of the meteoroid. The shock wave interacts with the solid meteoroid and its vapour in a complex way, and it can travel all the way to the ground even when the meteoroid does not. The penetration of a meteoroid in the kilogram range to altitudes of about 40 km (25 miles) can produce sounds on the ground similar to sonic booms or thunder. The sounds can even be intense enough to shake the ground and be recorded by seismometers designed to monitor earthquakes.

This great release of energy quickly destroys most meteoroids, particularly those with relatively high velocities. This destruction is the result both of ablation (the loss of mass from the surface of the meteoroid by vaporization or as molten droplets) and of fragmentation caused by aerodynamic pressure that exceeds the crushing strength of the meteoroid. For these reasons, numerous meteors end their observed flight at altitudes above 80 km (49 miles), and penetration to altitudes as low as 50 km (31 miles) is unusual.

The fragmentation of larger meteoroids due to the stresses of atmospheric entry is often catastrophic. About 10 large explosions (each equivalent to at least 1 kiloton of TNT, but some much larger) occur in the atmosphere every year. Explosions of this size are typically produced by meteoroids that are initially at least 2 metres (6 feet) across. For comparison, the atomic bomb dropped on Hiroshima, Japan, in 1945 had an explosive yield of 15 kilotons of TNT. A particularly spectacular explosion occurred over the Tunguska region of Siberia in Russia on June 30, 1908. The shock wave from that explosion, estimated to be equivalent to 15 megatons of TNT, flattened trees over an area almost 50 km across (about 2,000 square km [500,000 acres]). Witnesses reported that its brightness rivaled that of the Sun.

Despite the fiery end in store for most meteoroids, some lose their kinetic energy before they are completely destroyed. This can occur if the meteoroid is small and has a relatively low entry velocity (less than 25 km [15 miles] per second) or enters the atmosphere at a relatively shallow angle. It also can occur if the meteoroid has a large initial mass (greater than 100 grams [0.2 pound]) and fairly high crushing strength. Very small meteoroids—interplanetary dust particles less than 50–100 μm (0.002–0.004 inch)—are effectively stopped at considerable heights and may take weeks or months to settle out of the atmosphere. Because comet-derived particles tend to enter the atmosphere at high velocities, only those in the above-mentioned size range survive. Meteoroids as large as a few millimetres across that do survive melt either partially or completely and then resolidify.

Somewhat larger meteoroids—those as large as some tens of metres across—that reach the ground as meteorites melt at their surfaces while their interiors remain unheated. Even objects this large are effectively stopped by the atmosphere at altitudes of 5–25 km (3–15 miles), although they generally separate into fragments. Following this atmospheric braking, they begin to cool, their luminosity fades, and they fall to Earth at low velocities—100–200 metres per second (225–450 miles per hour). This "dark flight" may last several minutes, in contrast to the few seconds of visible flight as a meteor. By the time a meteoroid hits the ground, it has lost so much heat that the meteorite can be touched immediately with the bare hand. Often the only obvious sign on a meteorite of its fiery passage through the atmosphere is a dark, glassy crust, called a fusion crust, which is produced by melting of its surface. Sometimes meteorites also end up with aerodynamic shapes and flow structures on their surfaces. These features indicate that the meteoroid remained in the same orientation during atmospheric entry, much like manned spacecraft, rather than having tumbled as most meteoroids seem to do.

METEOR SHOWERS

Showers of meteors, in which the rate of meteor sightings temporarily increases at approximately the same time each year, have been recorded since ancient times. On rare occasions, such showers are very dramatic, with thousands of meteoroids falling per hour. More often, the usual hourly rate of roughly 5 observed meteors increases to about 10–50.

Meteors in showers characteristically are all moving in the same direction in space. As a consequence, plots of observed meteoroid trajectories on a map of the sky converge at a single point, the radiant of the shower, for the same reason that parallel railroad tracks appear to converge at a distance. A shower is usually named for the constellation (or for a star in the constellation) that contains its radiant. The introduction of photography to meteorite studies confirmed the theory developed from naked-eye observations that meteors belonging to a particular shower have not only the same radiant but similar orbits as well. In other words, the meteoroids responsible for meteor showers move in confined streams (called meteor streams) around the Sun. The introduction of radar observation led to the discovery of new meteor showers—and thus of new meteor streams—that were invisible to the eye and to cameras

Intense meteor outburst during the Perseid meteor shower of August 1995. All of the meteors appear to be emerging from a single point in the sky (to the left and outside the image), called the radiant of the shower. S. Molau and P. Jenniskens—NASA Ames Research Center

because they came from radiants in the daytime sky. All told, about 2,000 showers have been identified.

Of great importance, and also fully confirmed by photographic data, is the association of several meteor showers with the orbits of active comets. As a comet travels near the Sun, it is heated and its abundant volatile ices (frozen gases) vaporize, releasing less volatile material in the form of dust and larger grains up to perhaps 1 cm (0.4 inch) across. The shower associated with a given comet thus represents debris shed from that comet along its orbit, which the orbit of Earth intersects annually. When Earth passes through this stream of debris, a meteor shower is produced.

The Leonid meteor shower represents a recently formed meteor stream. Though it occurs every year, this shower tends to increase greatly in visual strength every 33 or 34 years, which is the orbital period of the parent comet, Tempel-Tuttle. Such behaviour results from the fact that these meteoroids are mostly still clustered in a compact swarm moving in the orbit of the comet. Over the next 1,000 years or so, the slightly different orbits of the meteoroids will disperse them more uniformly along the orbit of the comet. Meteor streams for which this has occurred produce showers that are usually weaker but often more consistent in strength from one occurrence to the next. Over a still longer period of about 10,000 years, gravitational perturbations by the planets will disperse the orbits of the meteoroids to the extent that their identities as members of a stream will disappear.

One strange example exists of a major meteor shower clearly associated with an object that at first glance does not resemble a comet. The parent object of the Geminid shower has all the appearances of a small Earth-crossing asteroid. Discovered in 1983, it does not exhibit the usual cometary features of a nebulous head and long tail and so was placed among the asteroids and named Phaethon. Most researchers believe Phaethon is the burned-out remnant of a once-active comet, but its nature may only be established with observations by spacecraft.

METEORITES: SURVIVING ATMOSPHERIC ENTRY

The final impact of meteoroids about a kilogram (2.2 pounds) or less in mass with the ground is usually an anticlimax. The fall can go unnoticed even by those near the impact site, the impact being signaled only by a whistling sound and a thud. Many meteorites are recovered only because at

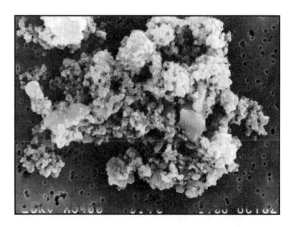

Interplanetary dust particle collected in Earth's atmosphere by a NASA high-altitude research aircraft and imaged in an electron microscope. The particle, measuring about 18 μm (0.0007 inch) in its longest dimension, is of possible cometary origin. Courtesy of D. Brownlee, University of Washington; photograph, M. Wheelock

least one fragment of the meteoroid strikes a house, car, or other object that draws the attention of local people to an unusual event. Recovered meteorites range in mass from a gram up to nearly 60 tons. Most meteorites consist either of stony—chiefly silicate—material (stony meteorites) or of primarily nickel-iron alloy (iron meteorites). In a small percentage of meteorites, nickel-iron alloy and silicate material are intermixed in approximately equal proportions (stony iron meteorites).

In addition to these relatively large meteorites, much smaller objects (less than a few millimetres across) can be recovered on Earth. The smallest, which are in the category of interplanetary dust particles and range from 10 to 100 μm (0.0004 to 0.004 inch) in diameter, are generally collected on filters attached to aircraft flying in the stratosphere at altitudes of at least 20 km (12 miles), where the concentration of terrestrial dust is low. On Earth's surface, somewhat larger micrometeorites have been collected from locations where other sources of dust are few and weathering rates are slow. These include sediments cored from the deep ocean, melt pools in the Greenland ice cap, and Antarctic ice that has been melted and filtered in large amounts. Researchers also have collected

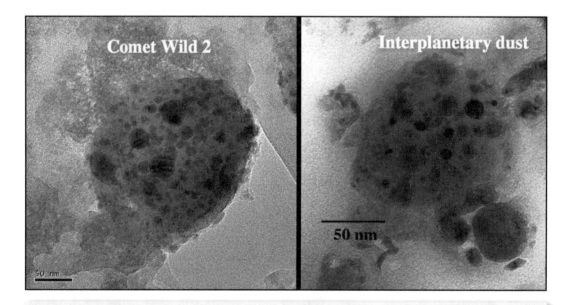

Microscopic components of dust particles collected from the vicinity of Comet Wild 2 (left) and interplanetary space (right) by the Stardust mission and returned to Earth. Both components consist of glass with embedded rounded grains of metal and sulfides. They may be preserved interstellar grains that were incorporated into bodies of the early solar system. NASA

meteoroidal particles outside Earth's atmosphere with special apparatus on orbiting spacecraft, and in 2006 the Stardust mission returned dust that it had trapped in the vicinity of Comet Wild 2.

When meteoroids are sufficiently large—i.e., 100 metres (328 feet) to several kilometres in diameter—they pass through the atmosphere without slowing down appreciably. As a result, they strike Earth's surface at velocities of many kilometres per second. The huge amount of kinetic energy released in such a violent collision is sufficient to produce an impact crater. In many ways, impact craters resemble those produced by nuclear explosions. They are often called meteorite craters, even though almost all of the impacting meteoroids themselves are

Meteors can have an explosive effect on the objects they impact. Though it is an impressive 1,200 metres (4,000 feet) in diameter, the Barringer Crater in Arizona, U.S., exhibits the low end of the scale with regard to the damage meteoroids can inflict. D.J. Roddy/ U.S. Geological Survey

vaporized during the explosion. Arizona's Meteor Crater, one of the best-preserved terrestrial impact craters, is about 1.2 km (0.74 miles) across and 200 metres (656 feet) deep. It was formed about 50,000 years ago by an iron meteoroid that is estimated to have been roughly 50–100 metres (164–328 feet) across, equivalent to a mass of about four million tons. Myriad nickel-iron fragments and sand-grain-sized nickel-iron droplets have been found in and around the crater.

The geologic record of cratering on Earth (and many other bodies in the solar system) attests to the impact of meteoroids much more massive than the one that produced Meteor Crater, including objects with kinetic energies equivalent to as much as one billion megatons of TNT. Fortunately, impacts of this magnitude now occur only once or twice every 100 million years, but they were much more common in the first 500 million years of solar system history. At that time, as planet formation was winding down, the asteroid-size planetesimals that were left over were being swept up by the new planets. The intensity of the bombardment during this period, often referred to as the late heavy bombardment, can be seen in the ancient, heavily cratered terrains of the Moon, Mars, Mercury, and many other bodies.

Some scientists have suggested that very large impacts may have played a major role in determining the origin of life on Earth and the course of biological evolution. The first signs of life are found

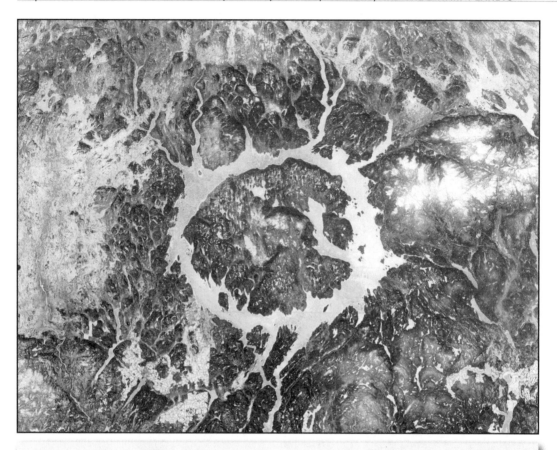

Asteroid strikes may occur irregularly, but their impacts last a long time. The hit that created Manicouagan Crater in Quebec, Can., happened an estimated 210 million years ago. NASA/ Johnson Space Center

in rocks that are only slightly younger than the end of the late heavy bombardment. Until the end of the bombardment, life could have started many times but would have been repeatedly wiped out by large impacts that boiled the oceans and melted the surface rocks. When life did finally establish a foothold, it may have done so in the deep oceans or deep in Earth's crust where it would have been protected from all but the largest impacts. Later, once impact rates had dropped dramatically and life was well-established, rare large impacts may have altered the course of evolution by causing simultaneous extinctions of many species. Perhaps the best-known of these associations is the mass extinction believed by many scientists to have been triggered by a huge impact some 65 million years ago, near the end of the Cretaceous Period. The most-cited victims of this impact were the dinosaurs, whose demise led to the replacement of reptiles by mammals as the dominant land animals and eventually to the rise of the human species. The object responsible for this destruction is estimated to have been about 10 km (6 miles) across, and it produced a crater roughly 150 km (93 miles) in diameter that is thought to be buried under sediments off the Yucatán Peninsula in Mexico.

MEASUREMENT OF METEOROID ORBITS

Even though the likely sources of most meteoroids entering Earth's atmosphere are known, the most direct way to determine the number and types of meteoroids coming from each of these sources is by measuring their orbits. When two or more observers at well-separated locations document the same meteor in the sky and determine its coordinates, the direction in which the meteoroid was moving in space before it encountered Earth—i.e., its radiant—can be estimated reasonably well by triangulation. To determine the meteoroid's orbit, however, also requires ascertaining its speed.

This latter requirement was satisfied in the 1940s with the introduction of wide-field astronomical cameras specially designed for studying meteors. Each camera was equipped with a rotating shutter that interrupted the light to the photographic plate at a known rate. The resulting breaks in the photographed meteor streak permitted calculation of the speed of a meteor along its path. The position of the meteor's trajectory with respect to the stars photographed on the same plate also was measured accurately. Information from such observations made at two or more stations could then be combined to calculate precisely the orbit of the meteoroid before it encountered Earth. About the same time, special radar instruments also were applied to the study of meteors generally fainter than those observed photographically.

A very significant development in meteor science occurred about two decades later. This was the establishment of large-scale networks for photographing very bright meteors, or fireballs. These networks were designed to provide all-sky coverage of meteors over about a million square kilometres (386,102 square miles) of Earth's surface. Three such networks were developed—the Prairie Network in the central United States, the MORP (Meteorite Observation and Recovery Project) network in the Prairie Provinces of Canada, and the European Network with stations in Germany and Czechoslovakia. The most complete set of published data is that of the Prairie Network, which was operated by the Smithsonian Astrophysical Observatory (later merged into the Harvard-Smithsonian Center for Astrophysics) from 1964 to 1974.

Apart from measuring meteoroid orbits, one of the goals of the fireball networks was to determine probable impact areas based on the observed meteor paths and recover any surviving meteorites for laboratory studies. This would enable a comparison of the inferences of theory regarding the density and mechanical strength of meteoroids with "ground truth" provided by the study of the same meteorites in the laboratory. The networks compiled data that became the basis for a new outlook on meteor science and the sources of meteoroids, but the goal of recovering meteorites had only limited success. Only three meteorites were recovered, one by each of the networks. All three meteorites were ordinary chondrites, the most abundant type of stony meteorite.

In spite of this meagre recovery record, the study of the recovered meteorites not only confirmed that they came from the asteroid belt but also led to an improved understanding of what happens to meteoroids when they enter and travel through the atmosphere. This enabled better estimates of the physical properties of meteoroids, allowing researchers to distinguish between meteors resulting from dense, meteorite-like objects and meteors resulting from less substantial objects that, for instance, might come from comets. Prior to this effort, studies of meteors by astronomers and of meteorites by geochemists tended to be pursued as independent scientific fields that had little to contribute to each other.

RESERVOIRS OF METEOROIDS IN SPACE

Most of the mass of the solar system resides in its larger bodies, the Sun and the planets. On the other hand, a smaller fraction of the mass of the solar system is in objects of such small size or in orbits so eccentric (elongated) that their physical survival or orbital stability has been in jeopardy throughout the history of the solar system. Many of these bodies are now found in the asteroid belt, between the orbits of Mars and Jupiter. Small bodies would have been distributed throughout the early solar system, but most were rapidly swept up by the planets during a period that ended about four billion years ago. The flux of material from space that now falls on Earth (in the range of tens of thousands of tons per year) and other planets pales in comparison with this early intense bombardment. Since that time, large impacts have become relatively rare. Nevertheless, when they do occur, the results can be dramatic, as in the case of the impact of Comet Shoemaker-Levy 9 with Jupiter in 1994 or the impact of an asteroid or comet thought to be responsible for the extinction of the dinosaurs and other species at the end of the Cretaceous Period 65 million years ago.

For an object to hit Earth, it must be in an orbit which crosses that of Earth. In the case of the rocky asteroids and their fragments, a limited number of processes can put these bodies into Earth-crossing orbits. Collisions can inject material directly into such orbits, but a more efficient process involves gravitational resonances between asteroidal material and planets, particularly Jupiter. Dust particles can also be moved into an Earth-crossing orbit from the asteroid belt through interactions with solar radiation. In the outermost solar system, icy objects in the Kuiper Belt and Oort cloud, which are believed to be the source reservoirs of comets, are perturbed into orbits that ultimately become Earth-crossing through gravitational interactions with Neptune or even with passing stars and interstellar clouds. When such a frozen body travels inside Jupiter's orbit and approaches the Sun, it gives off gas and sheds small particles, typically taking on the characteristic appearance of a comet. Some of these particles remain in the vicinity of the comet's orbit and may collide with Earth if the orbit is an Earth-crossing one.

The asteroid belt and the outermost solar system, therefore, can be thought of as long-lived though somewhat leaky reservoirs of meteoroidal material. They are long-lived enough to retain a significant quantity of primordial solar system material for 4.567 billion years but leaky enough to permit the escape of the observed quantity of Earth-crossing material. This quantity of Earth-crossing material represents an approximate steady-state balance between the input from the storage regions and the loss by ejection from the solar system, by

collision with Earth, the Moon, and other planets and their satellites, or by impacts between meteoroids.

In addition to cometary and asteroidal sources, a very minor but identifiable fraction of the meteoroidal population comes from the Moon and Mars. From studies of meteorites, scientists believe that pieces of the surfaces of these planets have been ejected into space by large impacts. They also know from the deep-space missions of the Galileo and Ulysses spacecraft that dust particles from outside the solar system are streaming through it as it orbits the centre of the Milky Way Galaxy. These interstellar grains are small and are traveling at high velocities (about 25 km [15 miles] per second) and thus have high kinetic energies, which must be dissipated as heat. Consequently, few are likely to survive atmospheric entry. Even if they do survive, they are rare and hard to discriminate among the much more abundant asteroidal and cometary dust.

DIRECTING
METEOROIDS TO EARTH

There is compelling evidence that nearly all meteoroids that reach the ground and can be studied as meteorites are derived from the asteroid belt. Ideally, scientists would like to know which asteroids are the sources of particular types of meteorites and the mechanisms by which meteorites are transported from the asteroid belt to Earth. The question of which meteorites came from which asteroids may not be comprehensively answered until asteroids are explored by spacecraft. (One exception is the HED meteorites and their relationship to the asteroid Vesta.) Nevertheless, there is considerable information about how they have gotten to Earth.

Only two processes are known that can put meteoroidal fragments into Earth-crossing orbits on the short timescales indicated by their cosmic-ray exposure ages. These processes are direct collisional ejection from the asteroid belt and gravitational acceleration by dynamic resonances with the planets. As mentioned above, collisions at velocities of 5 km (3 miles) per second are relatively common in the asteroid belt. In such a collision, some material is ejected at the velocity needed to put it into an Earth-crossing orbit, but the quantity is small, and most of it is pulverized by the associated shock pressures. High-velocity ejection is the likely explanation for those meteorites determined to have come from Mars or the Moon, but it completely fails to provide the observed quantity of meteorites from the asteroid belt.

Resonance mechanisms are believed to be of much greater importance in sending material toward Earth. These resonances efficiently expel material from the belt, producing the Kirkwood gaps. One of the most prominent of these gaps lies at a distance of about 2.5 AU from the Sun. An asteroidal fragment orbiting the Sun near 2.5 AU completes three revolutions in the time that Jupiter, the most massive planet in the solar system and a strong source of gravitational perturbations, executes one revolution. It is thus said to be in a 3:1 resonance with the planet. The regular nudges resulting from the resonance cause the orbit of the asteroidal fragment to become chaotic, and its perihelion (the point of its orbit nearest the Sun) becomes shifted inside Earth's orbit over a period of about one million years. Numerical simulations on computers support the idea that the 3:1 resonance is one of the principal mechanisms that inject asteroidal material into ultimately Earth-crossing orbits.

If gravitational resonance with Jupiter is an efficient mechanism for removing material from the asteroid belt, one might expect the region close to a strong resonance to be cleared of material over the lifetime of the solar system so that by now nothing would be left to send into Earth-crossing orbits. A number of processes, however, cause asteroids to migrate within the asteroid belt, thereby maintaining a constant supply of material to the resonances.

Meteoroids less than a few hundred micrometres across—i.e., interplanetary dust particles—come to Earth from the asteroid belt via a rather different mechanism than the larger ones. Interaction with solar radiation causes them to spiral into Earth-crossing orbits from the asteroid belt through a process called Poynting-Robertson drag. The time it takes a particle to traverse the distance from the asteroid belt to Earth depends inversely on its radius and where in the asteroid belt it started out. For 10–50 μm (0.0004–0.002 inch) dust particles, traverse time is calculated to be about 100,000 years. (Particles that are much smaller than a micrometre are actually blown out of the solar system by radiation pressure from the Sun.) Estimates of cosmic-ray exposure ages for micrometeoroids collected on Earth are broadly consistent with their traverse times calculated from the Poynting-Robertson drag process. In principle, some dust particles could be much younger than the calculated traverse times, either because they were produced in collisions of larger Earth-crossing objects or because they are not asteroidal in origin but rather have been shed by comets during comparatively recent passages through the inner solar system.

METEORITES

As stated earlier, some meteoroids survive their passage through Earth's atmosphere and land on the surface. In modern usage the term *meteorite* is broadly applied to similar objects that land on the surface of other comparatively large bodies. For instance, meteorite fragments have been found in samples returned from the Moon, and at least one meteorite has been identified on the surface of Mars by the robotic rover Opportunity. The largest meteorite that has been identified on Earth was found in 1920 in Namibia. Named the Hoba

meteorite, it measures 2.7 metres (9 feet) across, is estimated to weigh nearly 60 tons, and is made of an alloy of iron and nickel. The smallest meteorites, called micrometeorites, range in size from a few hundred micrometres (μm) to as small as about 10 μm (0.0004 inch) and come from the population of tiny particles that fill interplanetary space.

The principal driving force behind meteorite studies is the fact that small bodies such as asteroids and comets are most likely to preserve evidence of events that took place in the early solar system. There are at least two reasons to expect that this is the case. First, when the solar system began to form, it was composed of gas and fine-grained dust. The assembly of planet-size bodies from this dust almost certainly involved the coming together of smaller objects to make successively larger ones, beginning with dust balls and ending, in the inner solar system, with the rocky, or terrestrial, planets— Mercury, Venus, Earth, and Mars. In the outer solar system the formation of Jupiter, Saturn, and the other giant planets is thought to have involved more than simple aggregation, but their moons—and comets—probably did form by this basic mechanism. Available evidence indicates that asteroids and comets are leftovers of the intermediate stages of the aggregation mechanism. They are therefore representative of bodies that formed quite early in the history of the solar system.

Second, in the early solar system various processes were in operation that heated up solid bodies. The primary ones were decay of short-lived radioactive isotopes within the bodies and collisions between the bodies as they grew. As a result, the interiors of larger bodies experienced substantial melting, with consequent physical and chemical changes to their constituents. Smaller bodies, on the other hand, generally radiated away this heat quite efficiently, which allowed their interiors to remain relatively cool. Consequently, they should preserve to some degree the dust and other material from which they formed. Indeed, certain meteorites do appear to preserve very ancient material, some of which predates the solar system.

Recovery of Meteorites

Meteorites traditionally are given the name of a geographic feature associated with the location where they are found. Until quite recently, there were no systematic efforts to recover them. This was largely because meteorites fall more or less uniformly over Earth's surface and because there was no obvious way to predict where they would fall or could be found. When a meteorite was seen to fall or when a person chanced upon an unusual-looking rock, the specimen was simply taken to a museum or a private collector.

In the 1930s and '40s, enterprising meteorite collectors began crisscrossing the prairie regions of North America,

asking farmers to bring them unusual rocks that they had found while plowing their fields. Prairie soil is largely derived from fine glacial loess and contains few large rocks. The collectors realized that there was a reasonable chance that any rocks the farmers unearthed would include meteorites.

A better approach to finding meteorites than searching places with few rocks,

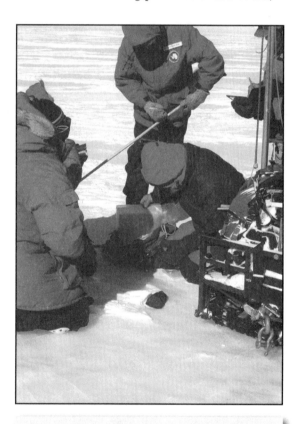

Scientists of the Antarctic Search for Meteorites (ANSMET) team log and collect a meteorite discovered lying on an ice field during the 2001–02 season. Linda Martel—ANSMET/NASA

however, is to search places where they can accumulate over time—i.e., where the surface is quite old and rates of weathering are low. Because meteorites contain minerals, such as iron metal, that are easily weathered, they do not normally last long on Earth's surface. Liquid water is one of the principal agents of weathering. In desert environments, where there is little water, meteorites survive much longer. Indeed, they tend to accumulate on the surface in arid regions if weathering rates are slower than the rates at which meteorites fall to Earth, provided that little windblown sand accumulates to bury them. Areas of the Sahara in North Africa and the Nullarbor Plain region in Australia have proved to be good places to look for meteorites. The most-successful collection efforts, however, have been in Antarctica.

The Antarctic can be viewed as a cold desert. Annual snowfall is quite low over most of the interior, and the intense cold slows weathering rates considerably. Most meteorites that fall on the ice sheet become buried and are stored for 20,000–30,000 years, although some appear to have been in Antarctica for a million years or more. The ice of the Antarctic sheet gradually flows radially from the South Pole northward toward the coast. In places, the ice encounters an obstruction, such as a buried hill, that forces it to flow upward. Strong katabatic winds, which sweep down the gently sloping ice sheets from the centre of the continent, sandblast the upwelling ice with snow and ice particles, eroding it at rates as high as 5–10 cm (2–4 inches) per year and leaving the meteorites stranded on the surface. Areas of upwelling ice, called blue ice for its colour, can be recognized from aerial or satellite photographs, and on foot the dark meteorites are relatively easy to spot against the ice and snow.

The drawback of collecting in Antarctica is the harsh conditions that the collection teams must endure for weeks to months while camping out on the ice. Since the 1970s several countries, notably the United States and Japan, have operated scientific collection programs. Some tens of thousands of meteorites have been brought back from Antarctica by the two countries' programs, increasing the number of meteorites available to researchers manyfold. These include one-third of all known Martian meteorites, one-third of known lunar meteorites, and numerous other rare or unique samples. Because large numbers of Antarctic meteorites are found within small areas, the traditional geographic naming system is not used for them; rather, an identifier is made up of an abbreviated name of some local landmark plus a number that identifies the year of recovery and the specific sample.

TYPES OF METEORITES

Meteorites traditionally have been divided into three broad categories—stony meteorites (or stones), iron meteorites (irons), and stony iron meteorites (stony irons)—based on the proportions of rock-forming minerals and nickel-iron (also called iron-nickel) metal alloy they contain. Stony meteorites make up about 94 percent of all known meteorites, irons about 5 percent, and stony irons about 1 percent. There is considerable diversity within each category, leading to numerous subdivisions (classes, groups, etc.) based on variations in chemistry, mineralogy, and structure.

It is important to realize that meteorite classification is based primarily on observable characteristics. Just because subdivisions belong to the same category, it does not necessarily follow that they all consist of meteorites that have the same or similar parent bodies. Indeed, more often than not, they are unrelated. Conversely, subdivisions from different categories may have a common origin. For instance, if a large asteroid were to melt, its denser metallic components would tend to sink to its centre (its core), while its less-dense rocky material would form a mantle around it, much like what happened to Earth. This separation process is known as geochemical differentiation. When the differentiated asteroid is later broken up by collisions, samples of its rocky mantle, iron core, and core-mantle interface might be represented in the three main categories. Thus, the challenge for researchers is to determine which types of meteorites are related and which are not, as well as to identify the processes that were responsible for the tremendous diversity that is seen among them.

CHONDRITES

The most fundamental distinction between the various stony meteorites is between those that were once molten, the achondrites, and those that were not, the chondrites. Chondrites have been subdivided into three main classes—ordinary, carbonaceous, and enstatite chondrites—and these in turn have been divided into a number of groups.

Chondrites are the most abundant meteorites (about 87 percent of stony meteorites) in collections. They also are arguably the most important. In terms of terrestrial rocks, these meteorites seem akin to sedimentary conglomerates—i.e., fragments of preexisting rock cemented together. They are a mechanical mixture of components that formed in the solar nebula or even earlier. Perhaps more remarkably, the compositions of chondrites are very similar to that of the Sun, except for the absence (in chondrites) of very volatile elements such as hydrogen and helium. The Sun contains more than 99 percent of the mass of the solar system. The composition of the Sun must therefore be very close to the average composition of the solar system when it formed. As a result, the Sun's composition can serve as a reference. Deviations in a meteorite's composition from this reference composition provide clues to the processes that influenced the formation of its parent body and the components in it.

Chondrules

Meteorites are classified as chondrites based on the presence within them of small spherical bodies (typically about 1 mm [0.04 inch] in diameter) called chondrules. From their shapes and the texture of the crystals in them, chondrules appear to have been free-floating molten droplets in the solar nebula. Simulation experiments show that chondrules formed by "flash" heating (to peak temperatures of 1,400–1,800 °C) and then rapid cooling (10–1,000 °C per hour). The sizes, compositions, and proportions of different types of chondrules vary from one chondrite meteorite to the next, which means that chondrule formation must have been a fairly localized process. There is also good evidence for its occurring many times. If chondrule abundance in chondrites is any guide, the chondrule-forming process was one of the most energetic and important in the solar nebula, at least in the region of the asteroid belt. Nevertheless, despite more than a century of study and speculation, scientists have yet to determine definitively what the process was.

Refractory Inclusions

Minor but important constituents of chondrites are refractory inclusions. They are so termed because they are highly enriched in the least-volatile, or refractory, elements. Because calcium and aluminum are two of the most abundant refractory elements in them, they are often called calcium-aluminum-rich inclusions, or CAIs. They range in shape from highly irregular to spherical and in size from tens of micrometres up to a centimetre or more. Like chondrules, they formed at high temperatures but appear to have been heated for more prolonged periods. Many but not all types of inclusions appear to have been formed from a molten state, which probably came about by the heating of preexisting solids. Others seemed to have formed as crystalline solids that condensed directly from a hot gas. Like chondrules, there is no consensus on the mechanism or mechanisms that formed refractory inclusions.

Matrix

The space between the chondrules and refractory inclusions is filled with a fine-grained matrix that cements the larger meteoritic components together. The matrix is richer in volatile elements than are chondrules and inclusions, suggesting that at least some fraction of it formed at a lower temperature. The matrix of many chondrites contains organic matter (up to about 2 percent by weight). The isotopic compositions of the hydrogen and nitrogen atoms in the organic matter are often very unusual. These compositions are best explained if at least some of the organic matter was produced in the interstellar molecular cloud from which the solar system formed.

Other materials that predate the solar system survive in the matrix, albeit at much lower concentrations. Unlike the organic matter, these materials formed not in the interstellar medium but around stars that died millions to hundreds of millions of years before the solar system formed. The evidence that these tiny grains (a few nanometres to 10 micrometres [0.0004 inch] in size) have circumstellar origins lies in their isotopic compositions. These are so different from the compositions of solar system materials that they could only have been produced by nucleosynthesis (formation of elements) in stars. For instance, the average ratio of carbon-12 to carbon-13 observed in solar system objects is about 89 to 1, with a range of about 85–94 to 1. For some material isolated from chondrites, the carbon-12/carbon-13 ratios of individual particles range from about 2 to 1 to about 7,000 to 1. Types of minerals of circumstellar origin that have been isolated from chondrites include diamond, graphite, silicon carbide, silicon nitride, olivine, corundum, spinel, chromite, and hibonite.

Alteration Processes

Few if any chondrites have remained completely unaltered since they formed as part of their larger parent asteroids. Three processes have modified the chondrites to varying degrees: aqueous alteration, thermal metamorphism, and shock.

Soon after the chondritic parent bodies were formed, they were all heated to some degree. In some bodies, temperatures were modest but high enough for liquid water to exist; reaction of the original minerals with water—aqueous alteration—transformed them to complex mixtures of minerals.

Other chondritic parents were heated more intensely, and, if they once contained water, it was driven off. The temperatures achieved were high enough to induce changes in mineralogy and physical structure—thermal metamorphism—but insufficient to cause widespread melting. At an early stage, this heating resulted in an increasing uniformity of mineral composition and recrystallization of the matrix. Organic matter and circumstellar grains in the matrix were also destroyed at this stage. With more intense heating, even the chondrules recrystallized. In the most-metamorphosed chondrites examined, those whose parent bodies experienced temperatures of roughly 1,000 °C (about 1,800 °F or 1,270 K), the chondrules are quite difficult to see.

The third modification process, shock, is caused by collisions of meteoritic parent bodies. Not just chondrites but all major types of meteorites exhibit shock features, which range from minor fracturing to localized melting. The processes of aqueous alteration and thermal metamorphism were probably finished within about 50 million years of the formation of the solar system. On the other hand, collisions of asteroids and their fragments continue to this day.

Classification Systems

The features seen in chondrites reflect processes from two distinct episodes—those that led to the formation of the chondritic parent bodies and those that later altered the material in the parent bodies. As a result, chondrites are classified in two complementary ways. Based on the concentrations of their major elements (iron, magnesium, silicon, calcium, and aluminum) and on their oxidation states, oxygen isotopic compositions, and petrology (e.g., abundance of chondrules and matrix, chondrule size, and mineralogy), chondrites naturally cluster. It is generally believed that the defining characteristics of the classes and groups were determined by conditions prior to and during the formation of the meteorites' parent bodies and that each group comes from a different parent asteroid or set of asteroids.

In addition, within each of the groups, the meteorites differ in the degree to which they were thermally metamorphosed or aqueously altered. These differences are referred to as petrologic types. Types 2 and 1 represent increasing degrees of alteration by water, and types 3 through 6 (some researchers extend the types to 7) reflect increasing degrees of modification by heating. Thus, a meteorite that experienced extensive aqueous alteration would be classified type 1, and one that experienced temperatures just short of melting would be type 6 (or 7). A meteorite that remained completely unmodified by either process since its formation would lie at the boundary of types 2 and 3.

As an example of how the two classification methods are applied, the carbonaceous chondrite known as the Allende meteorite, whose fall was witnessed in 1969, is classified CV3. This indicates that it belongs to the CV group and petrologic type 3.

Meteorites are also classified according to the severity of shock and the terrestrial weathering they have experienced, but these schemes are less commonly used. Still another way to distinguish meteorites is as "falls" or "finds," depending on whether or not they were observed to fall to Earth.

CI Carbonaceous Chondrites

Perhaps the most interesting type of chondrite is the CI group of carbonaceous chondrites. Strictly speaking, it could be questioned why such meteorites are called chondrites at all, inasmuch as they do not contain chondrules. They are aqueously altered so heavily that, if they once contained chondrules, all evidence of them has been erased. When their elemental abundances are compared with those of the Sun, however, it turns out that the two are extremely similar. In fact, of all meteorite types, the CI chondrites most closely resemble the Sun in composition. Consequently, in devising a classification scheme, it makes sense to group them with the chondrites.

Because CI chondrites are chemically so Sun-like—and thus so like the average composition of the forming solar system—some scientists have speculated that they are of cometary rather than of asteroidal origin. Comets are believed to represent the most unaltered material in the solar system. Although there are difficulties with this idea, scientific knowledge about the nature and origin of comets is still limited, which makes it unwise to entirely dismiss this intriguing possibility.

ACHONDRITES

Achondrites, their name meaning "without chondrites," are a relatively small but diverse group of meteorites. They exhibit a range of features that would be expected if their parent bodies experienced widespread melting: igneous features similar to those observed in terrestrial volcanic rocks, segregation of molten metal (possibly into a core) from molten silicate rock (magma), and magmatic segregation of silicate crystals and melt. Most achondrites collected on Earth are derived from asteroids, but one small group is thought to come from Mars and another from the Moon.

The three most numerous asteroidal achondrite groups are the aubrites, the howardite-eucrite-diogenite association, and the ureilites. Aubrites are also known as enstatite achondrites. Like the enstatite class of chondrites, the aubrites derive from parent bodies that formed under highly chemically reducing conditions. As a result, they contain elements in the form of less-common compounds—for example, calcium as the sulfide mineral oldhamite (CaS) rather than in its more usual silicate and carbonate forms.

The howardite, eucrite, and diogenite (HED) meteorites all seem to be related to one another and probably came from the same asteroidal body, tentatively identified as Vesta, the second largest member of the asteroid belt. They have also been linked to the mesosiderites, a group of stony iron meteorites. The HED parent body seems to have had a complex history that included melting, segregation of metal into a core, crystallization, metamorphism, and impact brecciation (the process in which an impact shatters rock).

The eucrites are subdivided into cumulate eucrites and basaltic eucrites. Cumulate eucrites are like terrestrial gabbros in that they seem to have formed at depth in their parent body and crystallized quite slowly. By contrast, basaltic eucrites are similar to terrestrial basalts, apparently having formed at or near the surface of their parent body and cooled relatively fast. The diogenites, composed predominantly of the mineral pyroxene, also seem to have formed at depth. The howardites are impact breccias composed of cemented fragments of diogenite and eucrite materials.

The third main class of asteroid-derived achondrites, the ureilites, are carbon-bearing. They consist of a silicate rock, made primarily of the minerals olivine and pyroxene, that has dark veins running through it. The veins, which constitute as much as 10 percent of the meteorites, are composed of carbon (graphite and some diamond), nickel-iron metal, and sulfides. The silicates clearly crystallized from magma, but there is debate about how they formed. The carbon-rich veins seem to have formed by shock-induced redistribution of graphite that originally crystallized along with the silicates. In addition to the three main achondrite classes, there exist several minor classes and a collection of unique achondrite specimens, all of which reflect the variability of melting processes in the asteroids.

More than 50 meteorites have been identified as having come from Mars, and all are volcanic rocks. All but one of these belong to one of three classes—shergottites, nakhlites, and chassignites—which were established well before a Martian origin was suspected. The three groups are often referred to collectively as SNCs. One piece of evidence for a planetary origin of the SNCs is their young age, between 150 million and 1.3 billion years. To retain enough heat so that volcanic activity could continue until just 1.3 billion years ago, let alone more recently, required a planet-sized parent body. Because there is considerable geochemical evidence

that the rocks did not originate on Earth, the only likely candidates that remain are Venus and Mars, both of which appear to have experienced recent volcanic activity.

The most convincing evidence for a Martian origin comes from an Antarctic meteorite, an SNC named EETA79001. This meteorite contains trapped gases (noble gases, nitrogen, and carbon dioxide) whose relative abundances and isotopic compositions are almost identical to those of the Martian atmosphere as measured by the two Viking landers. Scientists believe that the Martian meteorites are fragments of the planet's near surface that were launched into space by large impacts and that eventually found their way to Earth. In the case of EETA79001, atmospheric gases apparently became trapped in glasses produced during the violent shock event that excavated the rock from Mars. As the only samples of Mars available to scientists on Earth, Martian meteorites provide a unique window into the evolution of this enigmatic planet.

Several Martian meteorites have been aqueously altered to some degree, which is in line with other evidence that liquid water was present at least periodically on Mars at some time in the past. The most unique Martian meteorite is another Antarctic specimen, ALH84001. This rock, an orthopyroxenite, has a crystallization age of about 4.5 billion years, which is roughly the same age as asteroidal meteorites, but several of its properties clearly tie it to the other Martian meteorites. About 3.9 billion years ago, aqueous fluids passed through it, precipitating carbonate-magnetite-sulfide mineral assemblages. Some researchers interpreted these rather unusual assemblages as evidence for life on Mars. They also reported features in the meteorite that they interpreted as fossilized bacteria. These claims created considerable controversy, but they also generated important debate on how life might originate and how it might be recognized even if it is unlike the life known on Earth.

A number of lunar meteorites have been found in Antarctica and hot deserts on Earth. They probably would not have been recognized as having come from the Moon were it not for the lunar samples brought back by the manned Apollo and robotic Luna missions. The meteorites, which likely are fragments blasted off the Moon by large impacts, resemble the various rock types represented in the lunar samples (e.g., mare basalts, highland regolith breccias, and highland impact-melt breccias), but they almost certainly came from areas that were not sampled by the various missions. Therefore, like the Martian meteorites, they are an important source of new information on the formation and evolution of their parent body.

IRON METEORITES

Iron meteorites are pieces of denser metal that segregated from the less-dense silicates when their parent bodies were at least partially melted. They most probably came from the cores of their parent asteroids, although some researchers have suggested that metal, rather than forming a single repository, may have pooled more locally, producing a structure resembling raisin bread, with metal chunks as the "raisins." The latter would have been likely to occur if the asteroid underwent localized shock melting rather than melting of the entire body.

Iron meteorites are principally composed of two nickel-iron minerals, nickel-poor kamacite and nickel-rich taenite. The abundances of these two minerals strongly influence the structure of iron meteorites. At one extreme is the class known as hexahedrites, which are composed almost entirely of kamacite. Being nearly of a single mineral, hexahedrites are essentially structureless except for shock features. At the other extreme is the class known as ataxites, which are made up primarily of taenite. Ataxites are the rarest class and can contain up to about 60 percent nickel by weight. Again, because they are nearly monomineralic, they are almost featureless structurally. Between these two classes are the octahedrites. In these meteorites, kamacite crystals form as interlocking plates in an octahedral arrangement, with taenite filling the interstices. This interlocking arrangement, called the Widmanstätten pattern, is revealed when a cut and polished surface of the meteorite is etched with dilute acid. The pattern is an indication that octahedrites formed at relatively low pressure, as would be expected if they formed in asteroid-sized bodies.

At one time iron meteorites were classified in terms of nickel content and Widmanstätten structure, but this has been largely superseded by a chemical classification based on gallium, germanium, and nickel content. The most-common classes have the rather uninspiring names IAB, IIAB, IIIAB, IVA, and IVB. There are numerous other smaller classes and unique iron meteorites. On the assumption that most iron meteorites formed in the cores of their parent asteroids, variations in the composition and properties of iron meteorites in a given class reflect the changing conditions during solidification of these cores. Gallium and germanium abundances in molten nickel-iron metal are relatively unaffected by the process of crystallization, but they are sensitive to the conditions under which the parent asteroid formed. Thus, iron meteorites with similar gallium and germanium abundances are probably related to one another, either because they came from the same asteroid or because their parent asteroids formed at similar times and places. Nickel abundances, on the other hand, are influenced by crystallization because nickel tends to concentrate in those portions of nickel-iron metal that are still molten. As a result, nickel abundances can be used to determine the sequence of crystallization within iron meteorite classes.

The IAB, IIICD, and IIE iron meteorites exhibit geochemical characteristics that are distinct from those of the other classes of irons. Their origin remains uncertain, but they may have been produced by impact processes.

STONY IRON METEORITES

Stony iron meteorites contain roughly equal amounts of silicate minerals and nickel-iron metal. They fall into two groups: pallasites and mesosiderites. Pallasites are composed of a network of nickel-iron metal in which are set crystals of the silicate mineral olivine. Olivine crystals are typically about 0.5 cm (0.2 in) across. The centres of large areas of metal exhibit the Widmanstätten structure. Pallasites formed at the interface between regions of molten nickel-iron metal and molten silicates. The molten nickel-iron metal regions could have been the outer cores of asteroids or, less likely, nuggets in the asteroids where the metal had collected.

Similarly, the molten silicate regions could have been the deepest layers of the silicate mantle. Mesosiderites are probably related to the three classes of achondrites collectively called HEDs. Like one of the HED classes, howardites, mesosiderites are impact breccias containing fragments belonging to the other two classes, eucrites and diogenites. In addition, however, the mesosiderites contain a large amount of dispersed nickel-iron metal. The origin of the metal is not known for certain, but it may be from the core of the body that collided with and brecciated the mesosiderite parent body.

ASSOCIATION OF METEORITES WITH ASTEROIDS

If meteoritic material comes from specific regions of the asteroid belt, then the asteroids in such regions should have the chemical and mineralogical composition observed in the meteorites. The surface mineralogical composition of asteroids, in principle, can be determined directly by observations from Earth of the fraction of sunlight they reflect (albedo) and the spectrum of the reflected light (reflectance spectrum). A number of processes conspire, however, to make the association of certain asteroids with the various meteorite groups much more difficult than might be expected.

Although no two asteroidal reflectance spectra are exactly alike in detail, most asteroids fall into one of two general groups, the S class and the C class. S class asteroids (e.g., Gaspra and Ida, observed by the Galileo spacecraft, and Eros, visited by the NEAR Shoemaker spacecraft) have moderate albedos and contain mixtures of olivine, pyroxene, and metallic iron. These are the same minerals found in ordinary chondrites, but they also are present in a number of other meteorite types. The C class asteroids (e.g., Mathilde, observed by NEAR Shoemaker) have low albedos, and their more featureless spectra indicate the presence of light-absorbing materials, although at least half have a spectral feature associated with iron-bearing hydrous silicates. It is plausible to consider the C class asteroids as candidate sources for certain groups of carbonaceous chondrite meteorites. Their low albedos and spectral evidence of hydrous silicates, however, make them unlikely sources of ordinary chondrites.

When the S class asteroids are considered in more detail, there are difficulties in identifying them all as sources of ordinary chondrites. Largely because of their apparent range of mineralogies—specifically their ratios of olivine to pyroxene—the S class asteroids have been divided into seven subclasses. In light of this, it is possible that the S class actually represents a number of unrelated groups of asteroids. In addition, some research has linked the S class asteroids to several groups of achondrites. On the other hand, if most S type asteroids are not related to the ordinary chondrites, scientists would be challenged to explain how an uncommon and unidentified class of asteroid is supplying most of the meteorites to Earth.

The asteroids in the S(IV) subclass seem to have mineralogies that best match those of the ordinary chondrites. This is supported by measurements made by NEAR Shoemaker of the elemental composition of the surface of Eros, which is classified as an S(IV) asteroid. With the notable exception of a low sulfur content, the composition of Eros was found to be consistent with that of an ordinary chondrite.

Scientists have come to recognize relatively recently that the surfaces of asteroids and other solid bodies are not necessarily representative of what lies just a short distance beneath those surfaces.

Both Eros's low-sulfur measurement and the fact that, overall, the spectra of S class asteroids do not exactly match those of ordinary chondrites may be due, at least partially, to the effects of a poorly understood set of processes collectively called space weathering. Important component processes of space weathering are thought to be the impacts of meteorites and micrometeorites and the impingement of energetic solar wind particles and solar radiation on surface materials. Over time these processes act to modify the chemical and physical surface properties of airless bodies such as Mercury, the Moon and some other planetary satellites, and asteroids and comets.

Comparisons of younger surfaces around craters with older terrains on Eros by NEAR Shoemaker, and on Gaspra and Ida by Galileo, support the idea that space weathering occurs on asteroids.

Asteroids are thought to be covered by a layer of pulverized rock, called regolith, produced by bombardment with meteorites of all sizes over millions to billions of years. The regolith need only be as thin as a few sheets of paper to completely mask the underlying material from reflectance spectroscopy, although on most asteroids it is probably much thicker. Unfortunately, because it is so loosely bound together, this regolith material does not survive entry into Earth's atmosphere in pieces that are large enough to identify as meteorites and analyze. Consequently, scientists do not have samples of regolith that can be compared with meteorites or asteroids

directly. On the Moon, however, systematic changes are observed in the mineralogy and reflectance properties of the surface material as a result of this collisional grinding and other space weathering processes. Thus, although it seems likely that ordinary chondrites do come from S class asteroids, space weathering may be making it difficult to determine with certainty which S class asteroids are the parent bodies of these meteorites and which are unrelated but have a grossly similar mineralogy.

Space weathering must also affect the spectra of the asteroidal sources of the other meteorite groups. Nevertheless, a number of more-or-less convincing associations between groups of meteorites and types of asteroids have been made. It has been proposed that the CV and CO groups of carbonaceous chondrites come from the K class asteroids. As mentioned above, a number of lines of evidence, including spectral measurements, point to the asteroid Vesta being the source of the howardite-eucrite-diogenite association and the mesosiderites. The most likely source of the iron meteorites is the M class of asteroids, but enstatite chondrites and mesosiderites have also been linked to them. The pallasites may come from A class asteroids.

THE AGES OF METEORITES AND THEIR COMPONENTS

When the planets and asteroids formed, they contained a number of different radionuclides, which are radioactive isotopes that decay at characteristic rates. The time it takes for half of the atoms of a quantity of of a radionuclide to decay, the half-life, is a common way of representing its decay rate. Many radionuclides have half-lives that are similar to or longer than the age of the solar system; for this reason they are often called long-lived radionuclides. As a result of their longevity, they are still present in meteorites and on Earth, and they are commonly used for dating rocks and meteorites.

Scientists typically determine the age of a rock or meteorite using the isochron method. For purposes of illustration, consider the rubidium-strontium decay system. In this system, the radioactive parent rubidium-87 (^{87}Rb) decays to the stable daughter isotope strontium-87 (^{87}Sr). The half-life for ^{87}Rb decay is 48.8 billion years. Strontium has a number of other stable isotopes, including strontium-86 (^{86}Sr), which is often used as a reference. When a rock forms, the minerals within it have identical strontium isotopic compositions (e.g., $^{87}Sr/^{86}Sr$ ratios) but often have different rubidium/strontium ratios (e.g., $^{87}Rb/^{86}Sr$ ratios). In this case, as ^{87}Rb decays, the $^{87}Sr/^{86}Sr$ ratios in the minerals all increase with time but at different rates—the $^{87}Sr/^{86}Sr$ ratios increase more rapidly in minerals with higher initial $^{87}Rb/^{86}Sr$ ratios. If the minerals' $^{87}Sr/^{86}Sr$ ratios as they exist now are plotted on a graph against their $^{87}Rb/^{86}Sr$ ratios, the data points form a straight line, called an isochron. The slope of the line is proportional

to the time since the minerals formed, and the point where the line intercepts the $^{87}Sr/^{86}Sr$ axis (i.e., when $^{87}Rb/^{86}Sr$ is zero) gives the initial ratio when the minerals formed.

In this illustration, the minerals within a single rock are used to date it, and the line on the graph is called an internal isochron. The same principle can be applied if one uses numerous rocks that formed at the same time and place but which had different initial $^{87}Rb/^{86}Sr$ ratios. The result is called a whole-rock isochron. In practice, an isochron is ambiguous in that it dates the time either when the minerals or rocks formed or when they were last heated and the strontium isotopes in them rehomogenized. Consequently, other evidence about a rock or suite of rocks is needed to determine what the isochron is actually dating. If the data points for minerals or rocks do not fall on a line, it indicates that the system has been disturbed and cannot be used for dating. Shock is the most common cause of disturbed systems in meteorites.

In addition to the long-lived radionuclides, a number of short-lived radionuclides were present in the early solar system. Most of these have half-lives of only a few million years or less. They will have decayed away long ago and cannot be used to obtain absolute ages directly. However, their original abundances in some objects can still be determined by the isochron method. By comparing the original abundances of a short-lived radionuclide in different objects, scientists can determine their relative ages. If one or more of these objects also have had their absolute ages determined using long-lived radionuclides, the relative ages can be converted into absolute ones. Trying to establish absolute ages for relative ages that have been determined from various short-lived radionuclides has been the focus of much modern research, but it has proved to be difficult. This is because the short-lived radionuclides typically behave chemically quite differently from one another and from the long-lived isotopes. Nevertheless, given the antiquity of meteorites, scientists have developed a remarkably accurate picture of the timing of events in the early solar system.

The oldest objects in meteorites, with ages of approximately 4,567,000,000 years, are refractory inclusions. With a few exceptions, these are also the objects with the highest abundances of short-lived radionuclides. The absolute ages of chondrules have not been accurately measured. The abundances of the short-lived radionuclide aluminum-26 in chondrules from ordinary and carbonaceous chondrites have been interpreted to indicate that they formed over an extended period from 1 million to at least 3 and perhaps as long as 10 million years after the refractory inclusions. There is some debate, however, over whether these ages, particularly the later ones, really date when chondrules formed or, rather, when their isotopes were reset by later

processes. Metamorphism in the ordinary chondrites ended between 5 and 55 million years after refractory inclusions formed, and in enstatite chondrites between 9 and 34 million years after. This age span probably reflects both the size of the chondrite parent bodies and how deeply within their parent bodies the meteoritic materials were located. Larger bodies cool more slowly, as do more deeply buried regions of a body.

The formation ages of ordinary and enstatite chondrites are uncertain, but, given the age ranges established for the end of metamorphism, they can be no more than 5 and 9 million years after the formation of refractory inclusions, respectively. There is some evidence that enstatite chondrites formed about 2 million years after refractory inclusions. The formation ages of carbonaceous chondrites are also not known, but dating of minerals produced during their alteration by liquid water indicates they must have formed within 3–7 million years, and possibly less than 1 million years, after the formation of refractory inclusions. The crystallization ages of achondrites from their magmas range from about 4,558,000,000 to roughly 4,399,000,000 years. There is some indication that the parent body of the HED meteorites started melting about 4,565,000,000 years ago. Iron and stony iron meteorites crystallized within 10–20 million years of refractory inclusions, while relatively recent evidence suggests that metal-silicate differentiation of their parent asteroids occurred less than 1.5 million years after the formation of refractory inclusions. This again demonstrates the rapidity with which many asteroids melted, differentiated, and solidified.

Cosmic-Ray Exposure Ages of Meteorites

The time it takes for a meteoroid to reach Earth from the asteroid belt is an important constraint when trying to identify the mechanism or mechanisms responsible for delivering meteoroids to Earth. The time cannot be measured directly, but an indication of it can be found from cosmic-ray exposure ages of meteorites. This age measures how long a meteorite existed as a small meteoroid (less than a few metres across) in space or near the surface (within a few metres) within a larger body.

High-energy galactic cosmic rays—primarily protons—have a range of penetration on the order of a few metres in meteoroidal material. Any meteoroid of smaller dimensions will be irradiated throughout by this proton bombardment. The high-energy protons knock protons and neutrons out of the atomic nuclei of various elements present in the meteoroid. As a consequence, a large number of otherwise rare isotopic species, both stable and radioactive, are produced. They include the stable noble gas isotopes helium-3, neon-21, argon-38, and krypton-83 and various short- and moderately long-lived radioactive isotopes, including beryllium-10 (half-life 1.6×10^6 years), aluminium-26 (7.3×10^5 years), chlorine-36 (3×10^5 years), calcium-41 (10^5 years), manganese-53 (3.7×10^6 years), and krypton-81 (2.1×10^5 years). The concentration of the radioactive isotopes can be used to monitor the cosmic-ray bombardment rate, and the accumulation of the stable species (e.g., neon-21) measures the total time since this bombardment began—i.e., the time since the meteoroid was excavated by collisions from an object that was large enough to shield it from cosmic rays.

The vast majority of meteorites have exposure ages that are greater than one million years. For chondritic meteorites, the number of meteorites with a given cosmic-ray exposure age drops off quite quickly as the age increases. Most ordinary chondrites have exposure ages of less than 50 million years, and most carbonaceous chondrites less than 20 million years. Achondrites have ages that cluster between 20 and 30 million years. Iron meteorites have a much broader range of exposure ages, which extend up to about two billion years. There are often peaks in the exposure age distributions of meteorite groups; these probably reflect major impact events that disrupted larger bodies.

The ranges of exposure ages relate both to the dynamic evolution of meteoroid orbits and to the collisional lifetime of the meteoroids. The almost total absence of meteorites with exposure ages of less than a million years suggests that meteoroid orbits cannot become Earth-crossing in much less than a million years. Numerical simulations on computers are consistent with this, but they also predict that orbital lifetimes should fall off much faster than do the cosmic-ray exposure ages. This has prompted the suggestion that meteorites spend a significant fraction of their time as small meteoroids migrating within the asteroid belt until their orbits intersect a resonance—i.e., a region in the belt where they experience strong gravitational perturbations by the planets, particularly Jupiter—that puts the meteoroids in Earth-crossing orbits. The general drop-off in the frequency of meteorites with older exposure ages and the upper limit for most stony meteorites of 50 million years are consistent with estimates that half of any given meteoroid population is eliminated by collisions in 5–10 million years. The longer exposure ages of iron meteorites suggest that their greater strength allows them to survive longer in space.

METEORITES AND THE FORMATION OF THE EARLY SOLAR SYSTEM

As mentioned, scientists study meteorites for insights into the events that took place surrounding the birth and early evolution of the solar system. They know from astronomical observations that all stars form by gravitational collapse of dense regions in interstellar molecular clouds. This is almost certainly how the solar nebula formed, and the presence of preserved circumstellar and interstellar material in meteorites is consistent with this idea. Less clear is what precipitated the gravitational collapse of the region of the molecular cloud that became the solar system.

Gravitational collapse can occur spontaneously—i.e., through random fluctuations of density. Another possibility, however, is suggested by the finding in meteorites (particularly in their refractory inclusions) of short-lived radionuclides that were present at formation (as opposed to the later production of radionuclides by recent cosmic-ray irradiation). The shortest-lived of the radionuclides found to date, calcium-41, has a half-life of only about 100,000 years. This radionuclide must have been made and incorporated into refractory inclusions within just a few half-lives (less than a million years), or its abundance would have been too low to detect. This is remarkably short by astronomical standards. Because the other short-lived radionuclides have longer half-lives, they do not put such stringent time constraints on the interval between their synthesis and formation of refractory inclusions. Nevertheless, the absolute and relative abundances of the short-lived radionuclides can be compared with the values predicted for likely sources of the radionuclides.

One potential source of radionuclides is nucleosynthesis in stars ending their lives in catastrophic explosions called supernovas and in a class of dying stars known as asymptotic giant branch (AGB) stars. Both supernovas and AGB stars produce massive, fast-moving winds (flows of matter) that are rich in short-lived radionuclides. Numerical simulations show that under some conditions, when these winds hit an interstellar molecular cloud that cannot collapse spontaneously, they compress it to the point that it becomes gravitationally unstable and collapses. The simulations also show that some of the wind material with its complement of short-lived radionuclides is mixed into the collapsing cloud. Thus, in this scenario, the radionuclides are fingerprints of the stellar wind responsible for triggering the collapse of the molecular cloud that evolved into the Sun and planets.

An alternative explanation for the short-lived radionuclides in meteorites has not been ruled out—their synthesis in the solar nebula by intense radiation from an early active Sun. This concept has proved somewhat less successful than the stellar-wind idea at explaining the absolute and relative abundances of the short-lived radionuclides. Nevertheless, no model incorporating either of these explanations has been completely successful in this regard.

After collapse was initiated, the first solids known to have formed in the solar nebula were the refractory inclusions, which apparently were made in relatively short-lived heating events about 4,567,000,000 years ago. The gradation of planetary compositions from dry,

rocky, metal-rich Mercury to gas-rich Jupiter and its icy moons suggests that there was a temperature gradient in the inner solar system. Astrophysical models predict such gradients, although the absolute value of the gradient varies with the conditions assumed for a given model. One of many ideas for producing the refractory inclusions is that they formed in convection currents circulating at the edge of the hottest region of the inner nebula.

The ambient environment in the asteroid belt at the time the asteroids were being assembled must have been thermally a rather tranquil one. The fact that presolar material is preserved in meteorites argues against widespread heating of the asteroidal region, as do the presence of water-bearing minerals and the relatively high content of volatile elements in many chondrites. Again, this is consistent with most current astrophysical models. Despite the evidence for an overall low temperature in this region of the solar system, the abundance of chondrules in all chondritic meteorites except the CI chondrites attest to local, transient episodes of very high temperatures.

If chondrules were relatively rare in meteorites, their formation could be regarded as of secondary importance in the early solar system. Chondrules and their fragments, however, make up most of the mass of the most abundant class of meteorites, the ordinary chondrites, and a major portion of other chondrites, which indicates that their formation must have been of central importance. Even if the parent bodies of ordinary chondrites formed only within a restricted region of the asteroid belt adjacent to the major resonance that is thought to put chondritic material into Earth-crossing orbits, this region still represents about 10 percent of the asteroid belt. It also is likely that the parent asteroids of other chondrule-bearing meteorites formed outside this region, even though they may be in that region today.

Ideas abound for how chondrules formed—e.g., electrical discharges, shock waves, collisions between molten asteroids, and outflows associated with the early active Sun—but none has gained general acceptance. The ages of chondrules are crucial to distinguishing between some of these ideas. If they really formed over a period of 1–10 million years after refractory inclusions, this would be problematic for certain models. Fewer problems would arise if it turned out that the measured ages of most chondrules reflect when they were reheated or altered in their parent body.

Asteroidal bodies began to form perhaps as early as one million years after refractory inclusions. Certainly, within 5–10 million years they were being heated, aqueously altered, and melted. Volcanic activity on some asteroidal bodies, presumably the larger ones, continued for as long as about 170 million years. The process responsible for this heating remains to be clearly identified. The short-lived radioactive isotopes aluminum-26 and iron-60 appear to be the most likely heat sources, but heat from electric currents induced by early solar activity and from the release of gravitational potential energy as asteroids formed also may have contributed.

Asteroid-sized bodies presumably were forming not just in the asteroid belt but everywhere in the solar system. Concurrently, they would have begun aggregating into larger bodies in a process that eventually produced the rocky inner planets. This process was remarkably rapid. The Moon probably formed by an impact of a Mars-sized body with the growing Earth. The oldest Moon rocks that have been dated are about 4.44 billion years old, but there is evidence that the Moon actually formed within 30 million years of the refractory inclusions. Similarly, the oldest meteoritic material from Mars is about 4.5 billion years old, but there is evidence that Mars itself formed about 13 million years after the refractory inclusions. Thus, within as little as 30 million years of the appearance of the first solids, the aggregation process that started with tiny particles had produced the rocky inner planets.

In order for asteroids to have formed and developed at all on the timescale of a few million years, theoretical calculations suggest that the density of matter required was more like that in the regions occupied by the giant planets. The quantity of material observed in the asteroid belt today, however, is quite small, perhaps as little as 1/10,000 of that originally present. Some natural process must have removed almost all the material in this region of the solar system after the formation of the asteroidal bodies.

Although the details are not yet fully understood, it seems most likely that the formation of the giant planets, particularly Jupiter, quickly resulted in the evacuation of most of the matter from this region of the solar system.

The foregoing scenario of early solar system evolution is likely to be wrong in some, and perhaps many, of the details. Nevertheless, without the samples of asteroids and primitive solar system materials provided by meteorites, there would be little observational basis at all for formulating models of this kind. For good reason, meteorites have been dubbed "poor man's space probes." Until spacecraft missions bring back a variety of samples from asteroids and comets, the most precise and detailed data for the evolution of the solar system will come from meteorites.

METEORITE CRATERS

When a meteorite impacts with Earth or with other comparatively large solid bodies such as the Moon, other planets and their satellites, or larger asteroids and comets, a depression results that is called a meteorite crater. For this discussion, the term *meteorite crater* is considered to be synonymous with *impact crater*. As such, the colliding objects are not restricted by size to meteorites as they are found on Earth. Rather, they include chunks of solid material of the same nature as comets or asteroids and in a wide range of sizes—from small meteoroids up to comets and asteroids themselves.

Meteorite crater formation is arguably the most important geologic process in the solar system, as meteorite craters cover most solid-surface bodies, Earth being a notable exception. Meteorite craters can be found not only on rocky surfaces like that of the Moon but also on the surfaces of comets and ice-covered moons of the outer planets. Formation of the solar system left countless pieces of debris in the form of asteroids and comets and their fragments. Gravitational interactions with other objects routinely send this debris on a collision course with planets and their moons. The resulting impact from a piece of debris produces a surface depression many times larger than the original object. Although all meteorite craters are grossly similar, their appearance varies substantially with both size and the body on which they occur. If no other geologic processes have occurred on a planet or moon, its entire surface is covered with craters as a result of the impacts sustained over the past 4.6 billion years since the major bodies of the solar system formed. On the other hand, the absence or sparseness of craters on a body's surface, as is the case for Earth's surface, is an indicator of some other geologic process (e.g., erosion or surface melting) occurring during the body's history that is eliminating the craters.

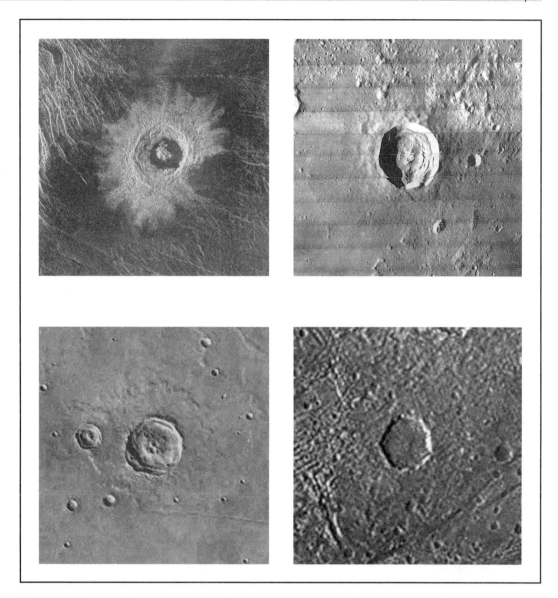

Four impact craters imaged by spacecraft on different solid bodies of the solar system and reproduced at the same scale. They are (clockwise from upper left) Golubkhina crater on Venus, Kepler crater on the Moon, an unnamed crater on Jupiter's moon Ganymede, and an unnamed crater on Mars. (Venus and Moon) Robert Herrick/Lunar and Planetary Institute; (Mars) Calvin Hamilton/Los Alamos National Laboratory; (Ganymede) Paul Schenk/Lunar and Planetary Institute

The Impact-Cratering Process

When an asteroidal or cometary object strikes a planetary surface, it is traveling typically at several tens of kilometres per second—many times the speed of sound. A collision at such extreme speeds is called a hypervelocity impact. Although the resulting depression may bear some resemblance to the hole that results from throwing a pebble into a sandbox, the physical process that occurs is actually much closer to that of an atomic bomb explosion. A large meteorite impact releases an enormous amount of kinetic energy in a small area over a short time. Planetary scientists' knowledge of the crater-formation process is derived from field studies of nuclear and chemical explosions and of rocket missile impacts, from laboratory simulations of impacts using gun-impelled high-velocity projectiles, from computer models of the sequence of crater formation, and from observations of meteorite craters themselves. A generally accepted model of impact cratering postulates the following sequence of events, which for purposes of illustration refers to a planet as the impacted body.

Immediately after a meteorite strikes the surface of the planet, shock waves are imparted both to the surface material and to the meteorite itself. As the shock waves expand into the planet and the meteorite, they dissipate energy and form zones of vaporized, melted, and crushed material outward from a point below the planet's surface that is roughly as deep as the meteorite's diameter. The meteorite is usually vaporized completely by the released energy. Within the planet, the expanding shock wave is closely followed by a second wave, called a rarefaction, or release, wave, generated by the reflection of the original wave from the free surface of the planet. The dissipation of these two waves sets up large pressure gradients within the planet. The pressure gradients generate a subsurface flow that projects material upward and outward from the point of impact. The material being excavated resembles an outward-slanted curtain moving away from the point of impact.

The depression that is produced has the form of an upward-facing parabolic bowl about four times as wide as it is deep. The diameter of the crater relative to that of the meteorite depends on several factors, but it is thought for most craters to be about 10 to 1. Excavated material surrounds the crater, causing its rim to be elevated above the surrounding terrain. The height of the rim accounts for about 5 percent of the total crater depth. The excavated material outside the crater is called the ejecta blanket. The elevation of the ejecta blanket is highest at the rim and falls off rapidly with distance.

When the crater is relatively small, its formation ends when excavation stops. The resulting landform is called a simple crater. The smallest craters require no

Moltke crater, a simple crater on the Moon photographed by Apollo 10 astronauts in 1969. The depression, about 7 km (4.3 miles) in diameter, is parabolic in shape, and the excavated material forms a raised rim and a surrounding ejecta blanket. NASA

more than a few seconds to form completely, whereas craters that are tens of kilometres wide probably form in a few minutes. As meteorite craters become larger, however, the formation process does not cease with excavation. For such craters, the parabolic hole is apparently too large to support itself, and it collapses in a process that generates a variety of features. This collapse process is called the modification stage, and the final depression is known as a complex crater.

The modification stage of complex crater formation is poorly understood because the process is mostly beyond current technological capability to model or simulate and because explosion craters on Earth are too small to produce true complex crater landforms. Although conceptually the modification stage is considered to occur after excavation, it may be that collapse begins before excavation is complete. The current state of knowledge of complex crater formation relies primarily on inferences drawn from field observations of Earth's impact structures and spacecraft imagery of impact craters on other solid bodies in the solar system.

Features associated with complex craters are generally attributed to material moving back toward the point of impact. Smaller complex craters have a flat floor caused by a rebound of material below the crater after excavation. This same rebound causes large complex craters to have a central peak; even-larger craters have a raised circular ring within the crater. Analogues to the central peak and ring are the back splash and outward ripple that are seen briefly when a pebble is dropped into water. Also associated with the modification stage is downward faulting, which forms terraces of large blocks of material along the inner rim of the initial cavity. In the case of very large craters, discrete, inward-facing, widely spaced faults called megaterraces form well outside the initial excavation cavity. Craters with megaterraces are called impact basins.

Variations in Craters Across the Solar System

Although impact craters on all the solid bodies of the solar system are grossly similar, their appearances from body to body can vary dramatically. The most-notable differences are a result of variations among the bodies in surface gravity and crustal properties. A higher surface gravitational acceleration creates a greater pressure difference between the floor of the crater and the surface surrounding the crater. That pressure difference is thought to play a large role in driving the collapse process that forms complex craters, the effect being that the smallest complex craters seen on higher-gravity bodies are smaller than those on lower-gravity bodies. For example, the diameters of the smallest craters with central peaks on the Moon, Mercury, and Venus decrease in inverse proportion to the bodies' surface gravities; Mercury's surface gravity is more than twice that of the Moon, whereas Venus's gravity is more than five times that of the Moon.

The inherent strength of the impacted surface has an effect similar to that of surface gravity in that it is easier for craters to collapse on bodies with weaker near-surface materials. For example, the presence of water in the near-surface materials of Mars, a condition thought to be likely, would help explain why the smallest complex craters there are smaller than on Mercury, which has a similar surface gravity. Layering in a body's near-surface material in which weak material overlies stronger strata is thought to modify the excavation process and contribute to the presence of craters with flat floors that contain a central pit. Such craters are particularly prominent on Ganymede, the largest moon of Jupiter.

Observations of the solid planets show clearly that the presence of an atmosphere changes the appearance of impact craters, but details of how the cratering process is altered are poorly understood. Comparison of craters on planets with and without an atmosphere shows no obvious evidence that an atmosphere does more than minimally affect the excavation of the cavity and any subsequent collapse. It does show, however, that an atmosphere strongly affects emplacement of the ejecta blanket. On an airless body the particles of excavated material follow ballistic trajectories. In the presence of an atmosphere most of this material mixes with the atmosphere and creates a surface-hugging fluid flow away from the crater that is analogous to volcanic pyroclastic flow on Earth. On an airless body an ejecta blanket shows a steady decrease in thickness away from the crater, but on a planet with an atmosphere the fluid flow of excavated material lays down a blanket that is relatively constant in thickness away from the crater and that ends abruptly at the outer edge of the flow. The well-preserved ejecta blankets around Venusian craters show this flow emplacement, and field observations of Earth's impact structures indicate that much of their ejecta were emplaced as flows. On Mars most of the ejecta blankets also appear to have been emplaced as flows, but many of these are probably mudflows caused by abundant water near the Martian surface.

METEORITE CRATERS AS MEASURES OF GEOLOGIC ACTIVITY

A common misconception is that Earth has very few impact craters on its surface because its atmosphere is an effective shield against meteoroids. Earth's atmosphere certainly slows and prevents typical asteroidal fragments up to a few tens of metres across from reaching the surface and forming a true hypervelocity impact crater, but kilometre-scale objects of the kind that created the smallest telescopically visible craters on the Moon are not significantly slowed by Earth's atmosphere. The Moon and Earth certainly experienced similar numbers of these larger impact events, but on Earth subsequent geologic processes (e.g., volcanism and plate tectonic processes) completely eliminated or severely degraded the craters. The dominant role of erosion as a geologic process that destroys craters is unique to Earth among the solid bodies that have been well-studied. Erosional processes may be important in eliminating craters on Titan, Saturn's largest moon, if methane proves to play the role there that water does in Earth's hydrologic cycle. Elsewhere only volcanic and tectonic processes are capable of eliminating large meteorite craters.

An absence or sparseness of craters in a given region of a large solid body indicates that relatively recent geologic activity has resurfaced it or otherwise greatly altered its surface appearance. For example, on the Moon the dark mare regions are much less heavily cratered than the light highland areas because the mare were flooded by basaltic volcanic flows about one billion years after formation of the highland areas. From simple counts of the craters larger than a given size per unit area for different regions of a body, it is possible to determine relative surface ages of different regions in order to gain insight into a body's geologic history. For the Moon absolute ages can be assigned to regions with different numbers of craters per unit area because surface samples from several regions were collected during Apollo lunar landing missions and dated in laboratories on Earth.

For other large bodies, assigning absolute ages to given regions based on the number of craters is based on estimates of asteroidal and cometary impact rates, the size range of those objects, and the size of the crater that forms from a given impacting object. Very little data exist as a basis for these estimates, particularly for impact rates. Absolute ages determined for planetary surfaces other than the Moon consequently have large uncertainties relative to the age of the solar system.

METEORITICS

The scientific discipline concerned with meteors and meteorites is called meteoritics. The awe-inspiring noise and lights accompanying some meteoric falls convinced early humans that meteorites came from the gods; accordingly these objects were widely regarded with awe and veneration. This association of meteorites with the miraculous and religious made 18th-century scientists suspicious of their reality. Members of the French Academy, which was then considered the highest scientific authority, were convinced that the fall of stones from heaven was impossible. Keepers of European museums discarded genuine meteorites as shameful relics of a superstitious past. Against this background, the German physicist Ernst Florens Friedrich Chladni began the science of meteoritics in 1794, when he defended the trustworthiness of accounts of falls. A shower of stones that fell in 1803 at L'Aigle, Fr., finally convinced the scientific world of the reality of meteorites. Interest was intensified by the great meteor shower of Nov. 12, 1833, which was visible in North America. Most natural-history museums now have meteorite collections.

For many years the only method of observing meteors was with the naked eye. The observer would plot the path of a meteor among the stars on a chart and note its apparent magnitude, the time, and other information. A similar plot of the same meteor made about 60 km (40 miles) away permitted rough estimates to be made of its altitude and the true angle of its path. This data can now be obtained more accurately with photographic or radar techniques, but visual observation continues to provide information on the magnitudes of meteors and serves as a check of instrumental methods.

Binoculars and telescopes extend the range of visual observations from the 5th or 6th magnitude, the limit of the unaided eye, to the 12th or 13th. Direct photographs of a meteor's trail (the column of ionized gases formed by the passage of a meteoric body through the upper atmosphere) taken at two points on Earth's surface several kilometres apart yield the most accurate data for tracing the path of a meteor. Specially designed wide-angle, high-speed cameras are employed. A rapidly rotating shutter in front of the open lens makes it possible to photograph the meteor trail in short segments, from which the velocity and deceleration of a meteor can be computed.

Radar is also widely used for meteor detection and observation. Radar pulses (short bursts of radio-frequency energy) emitted from a ground-based transmitter are reflected by a meteor's trail. The distance to the meteor can be determined by measuring the time lapse between the transmitted and reflected radar signals. Its motion toward (or away from) the radar facility can be derived from the rate at which the distance changes, which in turn yields the velocity of the object in the line of sight.

NOTABLE METEORITES

For centuries, meteorites have fallen from the sky, and some of the more notable are discussed here. Some, like the Allende meteorite, revealed much about the early solar system. Others, like the Ensisheim meteorite, came as strange omens from the heavens.

ALLENDE METEORITE

The Allende meteorite fell as a shower of stones after breaking up in the atmosphere at Chihuahua, Mex., near the village of Pueblito de Allende, in February 1969. More than two tons of meteorite fragments were collected. Fortuitously, the Allende meteorite fell shortly before the first rock samples from the Moon were brought to Earth by Apollo astronauts, and its pieces were analyzed by many scientists in preparation for handling lunar rocks.

The Allende meteorite, which is classified as a carbonaceous chondrite, consists of large, irregularly shaped white inclusions and rounded chondrules in a dark matrix. The inclusions are composed of minerals believed to have condensed at high temperatures from a gas having the composition of the Sun, and their time of formation is older than that of any other known solar system material. The inclusions in Allende and other carbonaceous chondrites are thought to be the earliest-formed solids in the solar nebula.

ENSISHEIM METEORITE

One of the earliest instances of a meteorite fall on record is that of the Ensisheim meteorite, which descended from the sky onto a wheat field in Alsace (now part of France) in 1492. Maximilian I, who was proclaimed Holy Roman emperor soon afterward, assembled his council to determine the significance of this event; their verdict was that the meteorite was a favourable omen for success in Maximilian's wars with France and Turkey. Accordingly, Maximilian ordered the Ensisheim stone to be placed with an appropriate inscription in the local parish church. The meteorite was fixed to the wall with iron crampons to prevent it from wandering at night or departing in the same violent manner in which it had arrived. It resides in the town of Ensisheim today, although visitors in the intervening centuries chipped off all but 56 kg (123 pounds) of its original 127-kg (280-pound) mass. The Ensisheim meteorite is classified as an ordinary chondrite.

MURCHISON METEORITE

The Murchison meteorite fell as a shower of stones in Victoria, Austl., in 1969. More than 100 kg (220 pounds) of the meteorite were collected and distributed to museums all over the world.

The Murchison meteorite is classified as a carbonaceous chondrite. It was pervasively altered by water, probably when it was part of its parent asteroid, and it consists mostly of hydrated clay minerals. Because of the availability of samples and its freedom from contamination with terrestrial material, the meteorite has been widely studied for the organic matter that it contains. Amino acids, alcohols, aldehydes, ketones, amines, kerogens, and other organic compounds have been detected and analyzed. The molecular structures of these organic compounds preclude their origin in biological life on Earth. Their unusual hydrogen isotopic compositions suggest that the compounds originally formed in interstellar space, although they have been modified in the early solar nebula and in asteroids.

ORGUEIL METEORITE

The Orgueil meteorite fell on the village of Orgueil, near Toulouse, Fr., in May 1864 and is often used to infer the relative proportions of elements in the solar system (cosmic abundances). Like the Allende and Murchison meteorites, it is classified as a carbonaceous chondrite, a type that comprises the most primitive meteorites—ones having a chemical composition much like that of the Sun and thus of the solid material that formed at the birth of the solar system.

About 20 fragments of the Orgueil meteorite were recovered. Their analysis soon after the fall revealed the presence of hydrogen, carbon, and oxygen and that its substance resembled peat and coal. Subsequent examination showed that hydrocarbons were present. The meteorite was once at the centre of a dispute about extraterrestrial life, prompted by similarities between its organic matter and hydrocarbons of biological origin on Earth. Determination of the optical properties of the organic material, however, indicated that its origin was not associated with biological processes. Later, small objects found in the meteorite were suggested to be the decayed or fossilized remains of organisms. These were later shown to be pollen and starch grains resulting from terrestrial contamination.

CHAPTER 3

JUPITER

Beyond the asteroid belt is Jupiter, the most massive planet of the solar system and the fifth in distance from the Sun. It is one of the brightest objects in the night sky; only the Moon, Venus, and sometimes Mars are more brilliant. Jupiter is designated by the symbol ♃.

When ancient astronomers named the planet Jupiter for the Roman ruler of the gods and heavens (also known as Jove), they had no idea of the planet's true dimensions, but the name is appropriate, for Jupiter is larger than all the other planets combined. It takes nearly 12 Earth years to orbit the Sun, and the planet rotates once about every 10 hours, more than twice as fast as Earth. Its colourful cloud bands can be seen with even a small telescope.

Jupiter has a narrow system of rings and more than 60 known moons, one larger than the planet Mercury and three larger than Earth's Moon. Some astronomers speculate that Jupiter's moon Europa may be hiding an ocean of warm water—and possibly even some kind of life—beneath an icy crust.

Jupiter has an internal heat source; it emits more energy than it receives from the Sun. The pressure in its deep interior is so high that the hydrogen there exists in a fluid metallic state. This giant has the strongest magnetic field of any planet, with a magnetosphere so large that, if it could be seen from Earth, its apparent diameter would exceed that of the

Photograph of Jupiter taken by Voyager 1 on February 1, 1979, at a range of 32.7 million km (20.3 million miles). Prominent are the planet's pastel-shaded cloud bands and Great Red Spot (lower centre). NASA/JPL

result of explorations by three spacecraft missions—Pioneers 10 and 11 in 1973–74, Voyagers 1 and 2 in 1979, and the Galileo orbiter and probe, which arrived at Jupiter in December 1995. The Pioneer spacecraft served as scouts for the Voyagers, showing that the radiation environment of Jupiter was tolerable and mapping out the main characteristics of the planet and its environment. The greater number and increased sophistication of the Voyager instruments provided so much new information that it was still being analyzed when the Galileo mission began. The previous missions had all been flybys, but Galileo released a probe into Jupiter's atmosphere and then went into orbit about the planet for intensive investigations of the entire system over several years. Yet another view of the Jovian system was provided in 2000 by the flyby of the Cassini spacecraft on its way to Saturn and in 2007 by the flyby of the New Horizons spacecraft on its way to Pluto. Observations of the impacts of the fragmented nucleus of Comet Shoemaker-Levy 9 with Jupiter's atmosphere in 1994 also yielded information about its composition and structure.

BASIC ASTRONOMICAL DATA

Jupiter has an equatorial diameter of about 143,000 km (88,900 miles) and

Moon. Jupiter's system is also the source of intense bursts of radio noise, at some frequencies occasionally radiating more energy than the Sun. Despite all its superlatives, however, Jupiter is made almost entirely of only two elements, hydrogen and helium, and its mean density is not much more than the density of water.

Knowledge about the Jovian system grew dramatically after the mid-1970s as a

orbits the Sun at a mean distance of 778 million km (483 million miles). Of special interest are the planet's low mean density of 1.33 g/cm³ (0.77 oz/in³)—in contrast with Earth's 5.52 g/cm³ (3.19 oz/in³)—coupled with its large dimensions and mass and short rotation period. The low density and large mass indicate that Jupiter's composition and structure are quite unlike those of Earth

PLANETARY DATA FOR JUPITER	
mean distance from Sun	778,000,000 km (5.2 AU)
eccentricity of orbit	0.049
inclination of orbit to ecliptic	1.3°
Jovian year (sidereal period of revolution)	11.86 Earth years
visual magnitude at mean opposition	-2.70
mean synodic period*	398.88 Earth days
mean orbital velocity	13.1 km/sec
equatorial radius**	71,492 km
polar radius**	66,854 km
mass	18.99×10^{26} kg
mean density	1.33 g/cm³
gravity**	2,312 cm/sec²
escape velocity	59.5 km/sec
rotation periods	
System I (±10° from equator)	9 hr 50 min 30 sec
System II (higher latitudes)	9 hr 55 min 41 sec
System III (magnetic field)	9 hr 55 min 29 sec
inclination of equator to orbit	3.13°
dimensions of Great Red Spot	20,000 × 12,000 km
magnetic field strength at equator	4.3 gauss
number of known moons	more than 60
planetary ring system	1 main ring; 3 less-dense components

*Time required for the planet to return to the same position in the sky relative to the Sun as seen from Earth.

**Calculated for the altitude at which 1 bar of atmospheric pressure is exerted.

and the other inner planets, a deduction that is supported by detailed investigations of the giant planet's atmosphere and interior.

Three rotation periods, all within a few minutes of each other, have been established. The two periods called System I (9 hours 50 minutes 30 seconds) and System II (9 hours 55 minutes 41 seconds) are mean values and refer to the speed of rotation at the equator and at higher latitudes, respectively, as exhibited by features observed in the planet's visible cloud layers. Jupiter has no solid surface; the transition from the gaseous atmosphere to the fluid interior occurs gradually at great depths. Thus the variation in rotation period at different latitudes does not imply that the planet itself rotates with either of these mean velocities. In fact, the true rotation period of Jupiter is System III (9 hours 55 minutes 29 seconds). This is the period of rotation of Jupiter's magnetic field, first deduced from Earth-based observations at radio wavelengths and confirmed by direct spacecraft measurements. This period, which has been constant for 30 years of observation, applies to the massive interior of the planet, where the magnetic field is generated.

THE ATMOSPHERE

Even a modest telescope can show much detail on Jupiter. The region of the planet's atmosphere that is visible from Earth contains several different types of clouds that are separated both vertically and horizontally. Changes in these cloud systems can occur over periods of a few hours, but an underlying pattern of latitudinal currents has maintained its stability for decades. It has become traditional to describe the appearance of the planet in terms of a standard nomenclature for its alternating dark bands, called belts, and bright bands, called zones. The underlying currents, however, seem to have a greater persistence than this pattern.

The close-up views of Jupiter transmitted to Earth from the Voyager spacecraft revealed a variety of cloud forms, including many elliptical features reminiscent of cyclonic and anticyclonic storm systems on Earth. All these systems are in motion, appearing and disappearing on time scales that vary with their sizes and locations. Also observed to vary are the pastel shades of various colours present in the cloud layers—from the tawny yellow that seems to characterize the main layer, through browns and blue-grays, to the well-known salmon-coloured Great Red Spot, Jupiter's largest, most prominent, and longest-lived feature. Chemical differences in cloud composition, which astronomers presume to be the cause of the variations in colour, evidently accompany the vertical and horizontal segregation of the cloud systems.

Jovian meteorology can be compared with the global circulation of Earth's atmosphere. On Earth huge spiral cloud systems often stretch over many degrees of latitude and are associated with motion around high- and low-pressure regions.

NATURE OF THE GREAT RED SPOT

The true nature of Jupiter's unique Great Red Spot was still unknown at the start of the 21st century, despite extensive observations from the Voyager and Galileo spacecraft. On a planet whose cloud patterns have lifetimes often counted in days, the Great Red Spot has survived as long as detailed observations of Jupiter have been made—at least 300 years. There is some evidence that the spot may be slowly shrinking, but a longer series of observations is needed to confirm this suggestion. Its present dimensions are about 20,000 by 12,000 km (12,400 by 7,500 miles), making it large enough to accommodate both Earth and Mars. These huge dimensions are probably responsible for the feature's longevity and possibly for its distinct colour.

The rotation period of the Great Red Spot around the planet does not match any of Jupiter's three rotation periods. It shows a variability that has not been successfully correlated with other Jovian phenomena. Voyager observations revealed that the material within the spot circulates in a counterclockwise direction once every seven days, corresponding to superhurricane-force winds of 400 km (250 miles) per hour at the periphery. The Voyager images also recorded a large number of interactions between the Great Red Spot and much smaller disturbances moving in the current at the same latitude. The interior of the spot is remarkably tranquil, with no clear evidence for the expected upwelling (or divergence) of material from lower depths.

The Great Red Spot, therefore, appears to be a huge anticyclone, a vortex or eddy whose diameter is presumably accompanied by a great depth that allows the feature to reach well below and well above the main cloud layers. Its extension above the main clouds is manifested by lower temperatures and by less gas absorption above the Great Red Spot than at neighbouring regions on the planet. Its lower extension remains to be observed.

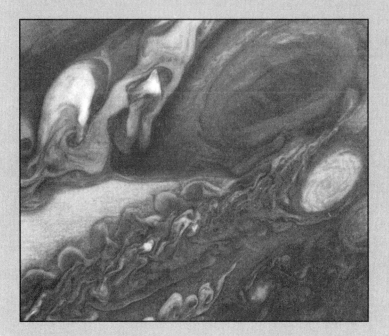

Jupiter's Great Red Spot (top right) and the surrounding region, as seen from Voyager 1 on March 1, 1979. Below the spot is one of the large white ovals associated with the feature. NASA/JPL

These cloud systems are much less zonally confined than the cloud systems on Jupiter and move in latitude as well as longitude. Local weather on Earth is often closely tied to the local environment, which in turn is determined by the varied nature of the planet's surface.

Jupiter has no solid surface—hence, no topographic features—and the planet's large-scale circulation is dominated by latitudinal currents. The lack of a solid surface with physical boundaries and regions with different heat capacities makes the persistence of these currents and their associated cloud patterns all the more remarkable. The Great Red Spot, for example, moves in longitude with respect to all three of the planet's rotation systems, yet it does not move in latitude. The white ovals found at a latitude just south of the Great Red Spot exhibit similar behaviour; white ovals of this size are found nowhere else on the planet. The dark brown clouds, evidently holes in the tawny cloud layer, are found almost exclusively near 18° N latitude. The blue-gray or purple areas, from which the strongest thermal emission is detected, occur only in the equatorial region of the planet.

Cloud Composition

The clouds that are seen through Earth-based telescopes and recorded in pictures of Jupiter are formed at different altitudes in the planet's atmosphere. Except for the top of the Great Red Spot, the white clouds are the highest, with cloud-top temperatures of about 120 kelvins (K; -240 °F, or -150 °C). These white clouds consist of frozen ammonia crystals and are thus analogous to the water-ice cirrus clouds in Earth's atmosphere. The tawny clouds that are widely distributed over the planet occur at lower levels. They appear to form at a temperature of about 200 K (-100 °F, -70 °C), which suggests that they probably consist of condensed ammonium hydrosulfide and that their colour may be caused by other ammonia-sulfur compounds such as ammonium polysulfides. Sulfur compounds are invoked as the likely colouring agents because sulfur is relatively abundant in the cosmos and hydrogen sulfide is notably absent from Jupiter's atmosphere above the clouds.

Jupiter is composed primarily of hydrogen and helium. Under equilibrium conditions—allowing all the elements present to react with one another at an average temperature for the visible part of the Jovian atmosphere—the abundant chemically active elements are all expected to combine with hydrogen. Thus it was surmised that methane, ammonia, water, and hydrogen sulfide would be present. Except for hydrogen sulfide, all these compounds have been found by spectroscopic observations from Earth. The apparent absence of hydrogen sulfide can be understood if it combines with ammonia to produce the postulated ammonium hydrosulfide clouds. Indeed, hydrogen sulfide was detected at lower levels in the atmosphere by the Galileo probe. The absence of detectable hydrogen sulfide above the clouds, however, suggests that the chemistry that forms coloured sulfur compounds (if indeed there are any) must be driven by local lightning discharges rather than by ultraviolet radiation from the Sun. In fact, the causes of the colours on Jupiter remain undetermined, although investigators have developed several viable hypotheses.

Sulfur compounds have also been proposed to explain the dark brown coloration of the ammonia clouds detected at still lower levels, where the measured temperature is 260 K (8 °F, –13 °C). These clouds are seen through what are apparently holes in the otherwise ubiquitous tawny clouds. They appear bright in pictures of Jupiter that are made from its thermal radiation detected at a wavelength of 5 micrometres (0.0002 inch), consistent with their higher temperatures.

The colour of the Great Red Spot has been attributed to the presence of complex organic molecules, red phosphorus, or yet another sulfur compound. Laboratory experiments support these ideas, but there are counterarguments in each case. Dark regions occur near the heads of white plume clouds near the planet's equator, where temperatures as high as 300 K (80 °F, 27 °C) have been measured. Despite their blue-gray appearance, these so-called hot spots have a reddish tint. They appear to be cloud-free regions—hence the ability to "see" into them to great depths and measure high temperatures—that exhibit a blue colour (from Rayleigh scattering of sunlight) overlain with a thin haze of reddish material. That these so-called hot spots occur only near the equator, the elliptical dark brown clouds only near latitude 18° N, and the most prominent red colour on the planet only in the Great Red Spot implies a localization of cloud chemistry that is puzzling in such a dynamically active atmosphere.

At still lower depths in the atmosphere, astronomers expect to find water-ice clouds and water-droplet clouds, both consisting of dilute solutions of ammonium hydroxide. Nevertheless, when the probe from the Galileo spacecraft entered Jupiter's atmosphere on Dec. 7, 1995, it failed to find these water clouds, even though it survived to a pressure level of 22 bars—nearly 22 times sea-level pressure on Earth—where the temperature was more than 400 K (260 °F, 130 °C). In fact, the probe also did not sense the upper cloud layers of ammonia and ammonium hydrosulfide. Unfortunately for studies of Jovian cloud physics, the probe had entered the atmosphere over a hot spot, where clouds were absent, presumably caused by a large-scale meteorological phenomenon related to the downdrafts observed in some storms on Earth.

ATMOSPHERIC CHARACTERISTICS

Prior to the deployment of the Galileo probe, astronomers had relied upon studies of the planet's spectrum to provide

ATMOSPHERIC ABUNDANCES FOR JUPITER			
GAS	PERCENT	ELEMENT MEASURED (RELATIVE TO HYDROGEN)	JUPITER/SUN RATIO
EQUILIBRIUM SPECIES			
hydrogen (H_2)	86.4		
helium (He)	13.56	helium-4	0.81
water (H2O)	> 0.026	oxygen	> 0.82
methane (CH_4)	0.21	carbon	2.9 ± 0.5
ammonia (NH_3)	0.07	nitrogen	3.6 ± 0.5
hydrogen sulfide (H_2S)	0.007	sulfur	2.5 ± 0.2
hydrogen deuteride (HD)	0.004	deuterium	no deuterium on Sun
neon (Ne)	0.002	neon-20	0.10 ± 0.01
argon (Ar)	0.002	argon-36	2.5 ± 0.5
krypton (Kr)	6×10^{-8}	krypton-84	2.7 ± 0.5
xenon (Xe)	6×10^{-9}	xenon-132	2.6 ± 0.5
NONEQUILIBRIUM SPECIES			
phosphine (PH_3)	5×10^{-5}	phosphorus	0.8
germane (GeH_4)	6×10^{-8}	germanium	0.05
arsine (AsH_3)	2×10^{-8}	arsenic	0.5
carbon monoxide (CO)	1×10^{-7}		
carbon dioxide (CO_2)	detected in stratosphere		
ethane (C_2H_6)	$1–4 \times 10^{-4}$ (stratosphere)		
acetylene (C_2H_2)	$3–9 \times 10^{-6}$ (stratosphere)		
ethylene (C_2H_4)	6×10^{-7} (north polar region)		
benzene (C_6H_6)	2×10^{-7} (north polar region)		
propyne (C_3H_4)	2×10^{-7} (north polar region)		

GAS	PERCENT	ELEMENT MEASURED (RELATIVE TO HYDROGEN)	JUPITER/SUN RATIO
DETECTED SPECIES NOT YET QUANTIFIED			
methyl radical (CH_3)	(polar regions)		
propane (C_3H_8)			
diacetylene (C_4H_2)	(polar regions)		

information about the composition, temperature, and pressure of the atmosphere. In the particular version of this technique known as absorption spectroscopy, light or thermal radiation from the planet is spread out in wavelengths (colours, in visible light, as in a rainbow) by the dispersing element in a spectrograph. The resulting spectrum contains discrete intervals, or lines, at which energy has been absorbed by the constituents of the planet's atmosphere. By measuring the exact wavelengths at which this absorption takes place and comparing the results with spectra of gases obtained in the laboratory, astronomers can identify the gases in Jupiter's atmosphere.

The presence of methane and ammonia in Jupiter's atmosphere was deduced in this way in the 1930s, while hydrogen was detected for the first time in 1960. (Although 500 times more abundant than methane, molecular hydrogen has much weaker absorption lines because it interacts only very weakly with electromagnetic waves.) Subsequent studies led to a growing list of new constituents, including the discovery of the arsenic compound arsine in 1990.

If the condition of chemical equilibrium held rigorously in Jupiter's atmosphere, one would not expect to find molecules such as carbon monoxide or phosphine in the abundances measured. Neither would one expect the traces of acetylene, ethane, and other hydrocarbons that have been detected in the stratosphere. Evidently, there are sources of energy other than the molecular kinetic energy corresponding to local temperatures. Solar ultraviolet radiation is responsible for the breakdown of methane, and subsequent reactions of its fragments produce acetylene and ethane. In the convective region of the atmosphere, the Voyager and Galileo spacecraft observed lightning discharges that contribute to these processes. Still deeper, at temperatures around 1,200 K (1,700 °F, 930 °C), carbon monoxide is made by a reaction between methane and water vapour. Vertical mixing must be sufficiently strong to bring this gas up to a region where it can be detected from outside the atmosphere. Some carbon monoxide, carbon dioxide, and water in the atmosphere comes from icy particles bombarding the planet from space.

Galileo's probe carried a mass spectrometer that detected the constituent atoms and molecules in the atmosphere by first charging them and then spreading them out with a magnetic field according to their masses. This technique had the advantage that it could measure noble gases like helium and neon that do not interact with visible and infrared light. As the probe descended through the atmosphere on its parachute, its spectrometer also studied variations in abundance with altitude. This experiment finally detected the previously missing hydrogen sulfide, which was found to be present even lower in the atmosphere than anticipated. Evidently this cloud-forming gas, like ammonia and water vapour, was depleted in the upper part of the hot spot by the aforementioned downdraft. It was not possible to measure oxygen, because this element is bound up in water, and the probe did not descend into the hot spot deeply enough to reach the atmospheric region where this condensable vapour is well-mixed.

The elemental abundances in Jupiter's atmosphere can be compared with the composition of the Sun. If, like the Sun, the planet had formed by simple condensation from the primordial solar nebula that is thought to have given birth to the solar system, their elemental abundances should be the same. A surprising result from the Galileo probe was that all the globally mixed elements that it could measure in the Jovian atmosphere showed the same approximately threefold enrichment

of their values in the Sun, relative to hydrogen. This has important implications for the formation of the planet (see Origin of the Jovian System later in this chapter). Spectroscopy from Earth reveals a large spread in the values of other elements (phosphorus, germanium, and arsenic) not measured by the probe. The abundances of the gases from which these elemental abundances are derived depend on dynamical phenomena in Jupiter's atmosphere—principally chemical reactions and vertical mixing.

Another difference with solar values is indicated by the presence of deuterium on Jupiter. This heavy isotope of hydrogen has disappeared from the Sun as a result of nuclear reactions in the solar interior. Because no such reactions occur on Jupiter, the ratio of deuterium to hydrogen there should be identical to the ratio of those isotopes in the cloud of interstellar gas and dust that collapsed to form the solar system 4.6 billion years ago. Since deuterium was made in the big bang that is postulated to have begun the expansion of the universe, a still more accurate measurement of the deuterium/hydrogen ratio on Jupiter would allow the calibration of expansion models.

TEMPERATURE AND PRESSURE

In addition to measuring atmospheric composition, the Galileo probe carried instruments to measure both the temperature and pressure during its descent into the Jovian atmosphere. Notably, temperatures higher than the freezing point of water (273 K, 32 °F, 0 °C) were measured at pressures just a few times greater than sea-level pressure on Earth (about one bar). This is mainly a consequence of Jupiter's internal energy source, although some warming would occur just through the trapping of infrared radiation by the atmosphere via a process comparable to Earth's greenhouse effect.

The increase in temperature above the tropopause is known as an inversion, because temperature normally decreases with height. The inversion is caused by the absorption of solar energy at these altitudes by gases and aerosol particles. A similar inversion is caused in Earth's atmosphere by the presence of ozone.

OTHER LIKELY
ATMOSPHERIC CONSTITUENTS

Astronomers expect monosilane to be present in the deep atmosphere, along with many other exotic species. Other nonequilibrium species should occur in the higher regions, accessible to future atmospheric probes, as a result of chemical reactions driven by lightning discharges or solar ultraviolet radiation, or at the poles (where, for example, benzene has been detected) by the precipitation of charged particles.

The formation of complex organic molecules in Jupiter's atmosphere is of great interest in the study of the origin of life. The initial chemical processes that gave rise to living organisms on Earth

may have occurred in transient microenvironments that resembled the present chemical composition of Jupiter, although without the enormous amounts of hydrogen and helium. Thus, Jupiter may well represent a vast natural laboratory in which the initial steps toward the origin of life are being pursued again and again. Determining how complex prelife chemical processes can become under such conditions constitutes one of the most fascinating problems confronting any program of space exploration.

COLLISION WITH
A COMET AND AN ASTEROID

On March 25, 1993, a previously unknown comet positioned close to Jupiter was noted by Eugene and Carolyn Shoemaker and David Levy in photographs taken at Palomar Observatory in California. Most unusual was its appearance—it comprised at least a dozen cometary nuclei lined up like glowing pearls on a string. Week after week the nuclei spread farther apart until a total of 21 fragments were visible. An analysis of their common orbit revealed that the original comet, which had been revolving about the Sun, had grazed Jupiter's atmosphere and nearly crashed into it on July 8, 1992. At that time, tidal gravitational forces from the giant planet had broken the nucleus into many pieces, which were captured by Jupiter's gravity and thrown into an elongated two-year orbit around the planet. Astronomers calculated that

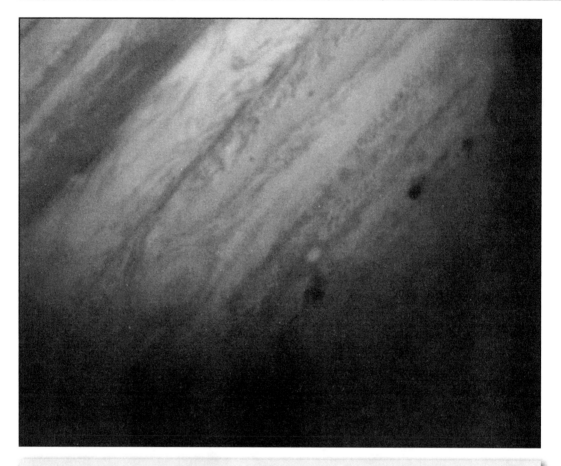

Jupiter's southern hemisphere, showing several dark scars created by collisions of fragments of Comet Shoemaker-Levy 9. The image was made by the Hubble Space Telescope on July 22, 1994, the last day of the impacts. NASA/Hubble Space Telescope Comet Team

the new orbit would bring the pieces back to Jupiter in July 1994.

The train of fragments from Shoemaker-Levy 9 smashed into Jupiter's atmosphere with a velocity of 216,000 km (134,000 miles) per hour beginning July 16, 1994. They all hit the unobservable side beyond the limb of Jupiter as seen from Earth, but the planet's 10-hour rotation quickly brought each impact site into view. Separated in time by an average of seven to eight hours, each fragment plunged deeply into the Jovian atmosphere, leaving conspicuous scars aligned in a zone near latitude 44° S. Astronomers labeled the individual fragments with capital letters in order of arrival. Fragment G, with an estimated diameter of 3–4 km (1.9–2.5 miles), was probably the largest and heaviest. It left a dark multiringed blemish twice as large as Earth's diameter. Its impact delivered energy equivalent to several trillion tons of TNT—hundreds of times the yield of the world's supply of nuclear weapons. Each impact transformed quickly into an immense bubble of hot gas that glowed warmly in infrared images of Jupiter as it expanded for a few days in the atmosphere. The planet-girdling string of dark brown bruises, assumed to be fine organic cometary dust, remained visible for weeks. It faded slowly into a new, narrow belt induced by Jupiter's strong winds.

Spectroscopic studies revealed that the impacts had produced or delivered many chemicals such as water, hydrogen cyanide, and carbon monoxide, substances that exist on Jupiter but in much smaller concentrations. The excess carbon monoxide and hydrogen cyanide remained detectable in the upper atmosphere several years after the event. In addition to its intrinsic interest, the collision of a comet with Jupiter stimulated detailed studies of the effects that cometary impacts would have on Earth.

In 2009 a dark spot similar to those left behind by the fragments of Comet Shoemaker-Levy 9 appeared near the south pole of Jupiter. Since only one spot was seen, it was believed that the impacting body was a single body—either a comet or an asteroid—rather than a chain of fragments.

RADIO EMISSION

In 1955, Jupiter became the first planet found to be a source of radiation at radio wavelengths. The radiation was recorded at a frequency of 22 megahertz (corresponding to a wavelength of 13.6 metres (44.6 feet), or 1.36 decametres) in the form of noise bursts with peak intensities sometimes great enough to make Jupiter the brightest source in the sky at this wavelength, except for the Sun during its most active phase. The bursts of radio noise from three distinct areas constituted the first evidence for a Jovian magnetic field. Subsequent observations at shorter (decimetre) wavelengths revealed that Jupiter is also a source of steady radio emission. It has become customary to refer to these two types of emission in terms of their characteristic wavelengths—decametre radiation and decimetre radiation.

The nonthermal component of the continuous decimetre radiation is interpreted as synchrotron emission—that is, radiation emitted by extremely high-speed electrons moving in the planet's magnetic field within a toroidal, or doughnut-shaped, region surrounding Jupiter—a phenomenon closely analogous to that of Earth's Van Allen belts. The maximum emission occurs at a distance of two planetary radii from the centre of the planet and has been detected from Earth at 178–5,000 megahertz and by the Cassini orbiter at 13,800 megahertz, the operating frequency of the spacecraft's radar instrument. The

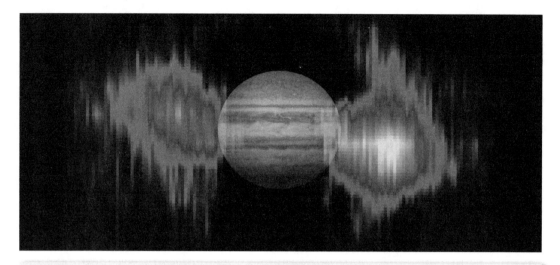

Image of Jupiter's radiation belts measured by the U.S. Cassini orbiter in January 2001 during its flyby of the planet. A superposed telescopic image of Jupiter to scale shows the size and orientation of the belts relative to the planet. NASA/JPL

intensity of the emission and its plane of polarization (the plane in which the oscillations of the radio emission lie preferentially) vary with the same period. Both effects are explained if the axis of the planet's magnetic field is inclined by about 10° to the rotational axis. The period of these variations is the rotation period designated as System III.

The intermittent radio emission at the decametre wavelengths has been studied from Earth in the accessible range of 3.5–39.5 megahertz. Free of Earth's ionosphere, which blocks lower frequencies from reaching the surface, the radio-wave experiment on the Voyager spacecraft was able to detect emissions from Jupiter down to 60 kilohertz, corresponding to a wavelength of

5 km (3 miles). The strength of the radio signal and the frequency of noise storms show a marked time dependence that led to the early detection of three "sources," or emitting regions. The System III rotational period was initially defined through the periodicity of these sources.

The decametre noise storms are greatly affected by the position of Jupiter's moon Io in its orbit. For one source, events are much more likely to occur when Io is 90° from the position in which Earth, Jupiter, and Io are in a straight line (known as superior geocentric conjunction) than otherwise. The noise sources appear to be regions that lie in the line of sight toward the visible disk of the planet, unlike the nonthermal decimetric radiation.

The most promising explanation of the effect of the orbital motion of Io on noise storms relates the emission to a small region of space linked to Io by magnetic field lines (a flux tube) that move with Io. Electrons moving in spirals around the magnetic field lines could produce the observed radiation. Interactions between these electrons and the Jovian ionosphere are expected and indeed were observed by the Voyager and Galileo spacecraft. The "footprint" of Io's flux tube on Jupiter's upper atmosphere can even be observed from Earth as a glowing spot associated with Jupiter's polar auroras.

THE MAGNETIC FIELD AND MAGNETOSPHERE

The nonthermal radio emissions described above are the natural result of trapped charged particles interacting with Jupiter's magnetic field and ionosphere. Interpretation of these observations led to a definition of the basic characteristics of the planet's magnetic field and magnetosphere that was shown to be remarkably accurate by direct exploration of the vicinity of Jupiter by the Pioneer and Voyager spacecraft. The basic magnetic field of the planet is dipolar in nature, generated by a hydromagnetic dynamo that is driven by convection within the electrically conducting outer layers of Jupiter's interior. The magnetic moment is 19,000 times greater than Earth's, leading to a field strength at the equator of 4.3 gauss, compared with 0.3 gauss at Earth's surface. The axis of the magnetic dipole is offset by a tenth of Jupiter's equatorial radius of 71,500 km (44,400 miles) from the planet's rotational axis, to which it is indeed inclined by 10°. The orientation of the Jovian magnetic field is opposite to the present orientation of Earth's field, such that a terrestrial compass taken to Jupiter would point south.

The magnetic field dominates the region around Jupiter in the shape of an extended teardrop. The round side of the teardrop faces the Sun, where the Jovian field repels the solar wind, forming a bow shock at a distance of about 3 million km (1.9 million miles) from the planet. Opposite the Sun, an immense magnetotail stretches out to the orbit of Saturn, a distance of 650 million km (404 million miles), which is almost as far as Jupiter's distance from the Sun. These dimensions make Jupiter's magnetosphere the largest permanent structure in the solar system, dwarfing the Sun's diameter of 1.4 million km (870,000 miles). Within this huge region, the most striking activity is generated by the moon Io, whose influence on the decametric radiation is discussed in the section above. An electric current of approximately five million amperes flows in the magnetic flux tube linking Jupiter and Io. This satellite is also the source of a toroidal cloud of ions, or plasma, that surrounds its orbit.

The energy to power this huge magnetosphere comes ultimately from the planet's rotation, which must accordingly be slowing down at an immeasurably small rate. Charged particles such as electrons that are spiraling along the magnetic field lines are forced to move around the planet with the same speed as the field and, hence, with the rotation period of the planet itself. That is why radio astronomers on Earth were able to deduce the System III rotation period long before any spacecraft measured it directly. This trapping of charged particles by the Jovian magnetic field means that the ions shed by Io in its orbit move with the System III period of nearly 10 hours rather than the 42 ½ hours that Io takes to revolve around Jupiter. Thus, Io's plasma wake precedes the moon in its orbit about Jupiter.

THE AURORAS

Just as charged particles trapped in the Van Allen belts produce auroras on Earth when they crash into the uppermost atmosphere near the magnetic poles, so do they also on Jupiter. Cameras on the Voyager and Galileo spacecraft succeeded in imaging ultraviolet auroral arcs on the nightside of Jupiter. The Hubble Space Telescope also captured images of far-ultraviolet auroras on the planet's dayside. In addition, Earth-based observations have recorded infrared emissions from H_3^+ ions at both poles and imaged the associated polar auroras. Evidently protons (hydrogen ions, H^+) from the magnetosphere spiral into the planet's ionosphere along magnetic field lines, forming the excited H_3^+ ions as they crash into the atmosphere dominated by molecular hydrogen.

The resulting emission produces the auroras, which are observable from Earth at wavelengths where methane in Jupiter's atmosphere has very strong absorption bands and thereby suppresses the background from reflected sunlight. The relation of the ultraviolet and infrared auroras, the detailed interaction of Io's flux tube with Jupiter's ionosphere, and the possibility that ions from Io's torus are impinging on the planet's atmosphere remain active topics of research.

THE INTERIOR

The atmosphere of Jupiter constitutes only a very small fraction of the planet, much as the skin of an apple compares with its contents. Because nothing can be directly observed below this thin outer layer, indirect conclusions are drawn from the evidence in order to determine the composition of the interior of Jupiter.

The observed quantities with which astronomers can work are the atmospheric temperature and pressure, mass, radius, shape, rate of rotation, heat balance, and perturbations of satellite orbits and spacecraft trajectories. From these can be calculated the ellipticity—or deviation from a perfect sphere—of the planet and its departure from an ellipsoidal shape. These latter quantities may also be predicted using theoretical

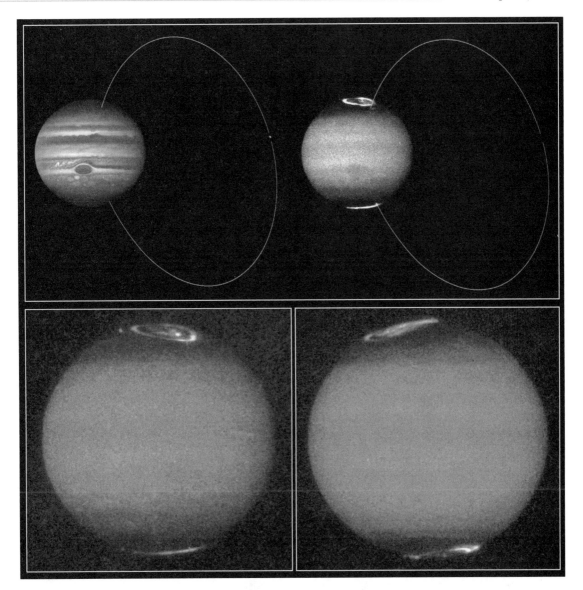

Jupiter's auroral arcs at its north and south poles, as imaged by the Hubble Space Telescope between May 1994 and September 1995. The offset between the planet's rotational and magnetic axes is apparent. In the top images, taken in visible and ultraviolet light (left and right, respectively), the path of the magnetic flux tube, or current of charged particles, that links Jupiter and its moon Io is traced with an added line. In the top left image, Io appears as a faint dot on the trace near the plane of Jupiter's equator. AURA/STScI/NASA/JPL

descriptions, or models, for the internal distribution of material. Such models can then be tested by their agreement with the observations.

The basic difficulty in constructing a model that will adequately describe the internal conditions for Jupiter is the absence of extensive laboratory data on the properties of hydrogen and helium at pressures and temperatures that would exist near the centre of this giant planet. The central temperature is estimated to be close to 25,000 K (44,500 °F, 24,700 °C), to be consistent with an internal source of heat that allows Jupiter to radiate about twice as much energy as it receives from the Sun. The central pressure is in the range of 50–100 million atmospheres (about 50–100 megabars). At such tremendous pressures hydrogen is expected to be in a metallic state.

Despite the problems posed in establishing the properties of matter under these extreme conditions, the precision of the models has improved steadily. Perhaps the most significant early conclusion from these studies was the realization that Jupiter cannot be composed entirely of hydrogen; if it were, it would have to be considerably larger than it is to account for its mass. On the other hand, hydrogen must predominate, constituting at least 70 percent of the planet by mass, regardless of form—gas, liquid, or solid. The Galileo probe measured a proportion for helium of 24 percent by mass in Jupiter's upper atmosphere, compared with the 28 percent predicted if the atmosphere had the same composition as the original solar nebula. Because the planet as a whole should have that original composition, astronomers have concluded that some helium that was dissolved in the fluid hydrogen in the planet's interior has precipitated out of solution and sunk toward the planet's centre, leaving the atmosphere depleted of this gas. Evidently it has taken much of the neon with it. This precipitation is persisting as the planet continues to cool down. Current models agree on a transition from molecular to metallic hydrogen at approximately one-fourth of the distance down toward Jupiter's centre. It should be stressed that this is not a transition between a liquid and a solid but rather between two fluids with different electrical properties. In the metallic state the electrons are no longer bound to their nuclei, thus giving hydrogen the conductivity of a metal. No solid surface exists in any of these models, although most (but not all) models incorporate a dense core with a radius of 0.03–0.1 that of Jupiter (0.33–1.1 the radius of Earth).

The source of internal heat has not been completely resolved. The currently favoured explanation invokes a combination of the gradual release of primordial heat left from the planet's formation and the liberation of thermal energy from the precipitation of droplets of helium in the planet's deep interior, as is also known to occur on Saturn. The lower helium abundance in Jupiter's atmosphere relative to the Sun supports this latter deduction. The first process is simply the cooling phase of the original "collapse" that converted potential energy to thermal energy at the time when the planet accumulated its complement of solar nebula gas (see Origin of the Jovian system).

JUPITER'S MOONS AND RING

The first objects in the solar system discovered by means of a telescope—by Galileo in 1610—were the four brightest moons of Jupiter, now called the Galilean satellites. The fifth known Jovian moon, Amalthea, was discovered by the visual observation of Edward Emerson Barnard in 1892. All the other known satellites were found in photographs or electronic images taken with Earth-based telescopes or by the cameras on the Voyager spacecraft. Jupiter's multi-component ring was detected in Voyager images in 1979. (A table summarizing data for the known Jovian moons can be found in Appendix A, "Moons of Jupiter.")

The orbits of the inner eight moons have low eccentricities and low inclinations; i.e., the orbits are all nearly circular and in the plane of the planet's equator. Such moons are called "regular." The orbits of the dozens of moons found beyond Callisto have much higher inclinations and eccentricities, making them "irregular." The two innermost moons, Metis and Adrastea, are intimately associated with Jupiter's ring system, as sources of the fine particles and as gravitationally controlling "shepherds."

Amalthea and Thebe also contribute to the ring system by producing very tenuous gossamer rings slightly farther from the planet. There may well be additional, undiscovered small moons close to Jupiter. There almost certainly are more distant irregular moons than those so far detected.

THE GALILEAN SATELLITES

Galileo proposed that the four Jovian moons he discovered in 1610 be named the Medicean stars, in honour of his patron, Cosimo II de' Medici, but they soon came to be known as the Galilean satellites in honour of their discoverer. Galileo regarded their existence as a fundamental argument in favour of the Copernican model of the solar system, in which the planets orbit the Sun. Their orbits around Jupiter were in flagrant violation of the Ptolemaic system, in which all celestial objects must move around Earth. In order of increasing distance from the planet, these satellites are called Io, Europa, Ganymede, and Callisto, for figures closely associated with Jupiter in Greek mythology. The names were assigned by the German astronomer Simon Marius, Galileo's contemporary and rival, who likely discovered the satellites independently. There proved to be a particular aptness in the choice of Io's name: Io—"the wanderer" (Greek iōn, "going")—has an indirect influence on the ionosphere of Jupiter.

Although approximate diameters and spectroscopic characteristics of the

Montage of Jupiter's four Galilean moons—(left to right) Io, Europa, Ganymede, and Callisto—imaged individually by the Galileo spacecraft, 1996–97. The images are scaled proportionally and arranged in order of the moons' increasing distance from Jupiter. NASA/JPL/Caltech

Galilean moons had been determined from Earth-based observations, it was the Voyager missions that indelibly established these four bodies as worlds in their own right. The Galileo mission provided a wealth of additional data. Before Voyager it was known that Callisto and Ganymede are both as large as or larger than the planet Mercury; that they and Europa have surfaces covered with water ice; that Io's orbit is surrounded by a torus of atoms and ions that include sodium, potassium, and sulfur; and that the inner two Galilean moons have mean densities much greater than those of the outer two. This density gradient from Io to Callisto resembles that found in the solar system itself and seems to result from the same cause. The density values suggest that Io and Europa have a rocky composition similar to that of the Moon,

whereas roughly 50 percent of Ganymede and Callisto must be made of a much less dense substance, water ice being the obvious candidate.

CALLISTO

The icy surface of this satellite is so dominated by impact craters that there are no smooth plains like the dark maria observed on the Moon. In other words, there seem to be no areas on Callisto where upwelling of material from subsequent internal activity has obliterated any of the record of early bombardment. This record was formed by impacting debris (comet nuclei and asteroidal material) primarily during the first 500 million years after the formation of the solar system in much the same way that the craters on the Moon were produced.

The unmodified appearance of the surface is consistent with the absence of a differentiated interior. Evidently no tidally induced global heating and consequent melting occurred on Callisto, unlike the other three Galilean moons. The Galileo spacecraft revealed that craters smaller than 10 km (6 miles) are hidden by drifts of fine, dark material resembling a mixture of clay minerals.

In addition to the predominant water ice, solid carbon dioxide is present on the surface, and an extremely tenuous carbon dioxide atmosphere is slowly escaping into space. Other trace surface constituents are hydrogen peroxide, probably produced from the ice by photochemical reactions driven by solar ultraviolet radiation; sulfur and sulfur compounds, probably coming from Io; and organic compounds that may have been delivered by cometary impacts. Callisto has a weak magnetic field induced by Jupiter's field that may imply the existence of a layer of liquid water below its icy crust.

GANYMEDE

Unlike Callisto, Ganymede, an equally icy satellite, reveals distinct patches of dark and light terrain. This contrast is reminiscent of the Moon's surface, but the answer to which terrain came first—dark or light—is exactly reversed. In contrast to the Moon, the dark regions on Ganymede are the older areas, showing the heaviest concentration of craters. The light regions are younger, revealing a complex pattern of parallel and intersecting ridges and grooves in addition to unusually bright impact craters typically surrounded by systems of rays. This manifestation of active crustal movement and resurfacing is accompanied by clear evidence of internal differentiation. Unlike Callisto, Ganymede has an iron-rich core and a permanent magnetic field that is strong enough to create its own magnetosphere and auroras. The trace components identified in Ganymede's icy surface include a smaller amount of the same claylike dust found on Callisto and the same traces of solid carbon dioxide, hydrogen peroxide, and sulfur compounds, plus evidence for molecular oxygen and ozone trapped in the ice.

EUROPA

The surface of Europa is totally different from that of Ganymede or Callisto, despite the fact that the infrared spectrum of this object indicates that it, too, is covered with ice. There are few impact craters on Europa—the number per unit area is comparable to that on the continental regions of Earth, indicating that the surface is relatively recent. Some scientists think the surface is so young that significant resurfacing is still taking place on the satellite. This resurfacing evidently consists of the outflow of water from the interior to form an instant frozen ocean.

Models for the differentiated interior suggest the presence of an iron-rich core surrounded by a silicate mantle surmounted by an icy crust some 150 km (90 miles) thick. This moon possesses both induced and intrinsic magnetic fields. Slightly mottled regions on the surface have been found to contain salt deposits, suggesting evaporation of water from a reservoir below the crust. Europa's frozen surface is crisscrossed with dark and bright stripes and curvilinear ridges and grooves. Spatter cones along some of the grooves again suggest fluid eruptions from below. The relief is extremely low, with ridge heights perhaps a few hundred metres at most. Europa thus has the smoothest surface of any solid body examined in the solar system thus far. Traces of sulfur, sulfur compounds, hydrogen peroxide, and organic compounds have been identified on the surface.

The major open question is whether there is a global ocean of liquid water beneath Europa's ice, warmed by the release of tidal energy in Europa's interior. The possibility of such an ocean arose from Voyager data, and high-resolution Galileo images suggested fluid activity near the surface. In addition, explanation of Europa's induced magnetic field appears to require an interior, electrically conducting fluid medium, implying a salt-containing liquid water layer at some depth beneath the surface ice. If this ocean and its required source of heat exist, the possible presence of at least microbial life-forms must be admitted.

Io

Seen through a telescope from Earth, Io appears reddish orange, while the other moons are neutral in tint. Io's infrared spectrum shows no evidence of the absorption characteristics of water ice. Scientists expected Io's surface to look different from those of Jupiter's other moons, but the Voyager images revealed a landscape even more unusual than anticipated.

Volcanic fissures, instead of impact craters, dot the surface of Io. Nine volcanoes were observed in eruption when the two Voyager spacecraft flew by in 1979, while the closer encounters by Galileo indicated that as many as 300 volcanic vents may be active at a given time. The silicate lava emerging from the vents is extremely hot (about 1,900 K [3,000 °F, 1,630 °C]), resembling primitive lavas on early Earth. This unprecedented level of activity makes Io the most tectonically active object in the solar system. The surface of the satellite is continually and completely replaced by this volcanism in just a few thousand years. Various forms (allotropes) of sulfur appear to be responsible for the black, orange, and red areas on the moon's surface, while solid sulfur dioxide is probably the main constituent of the white areas. Sulfur dioxide was detected as a gas near one of the active volcanic plumes by Voyager's infrared spectrometer and was identified as a solid in ultraviolet and infrared spectra obtained from Earth-orbital and ground-based observations. These identifications provide sources for the sulfur and oxygen ions observed in the Jovian magnetosphere and prove that Io's volcanic activity is the source of its torus of particles.

The energy for this volcanic activity requires a special explanation, since radioactive heating is inadequate for a body as small as Io. The favoured explanation is based on the observation that orbital resonances with the other Galilean satellites perturb Io into a more eccentric orbit than it would assume if only Jupiter controlled its motion. The resulting tides developed by the gravitational contest over Io between the other satellites and Jupiter release enough energy to account for the observed volcanism. The interior contains a dense, iron-rich core, which probably produces a magnetic field. The interactions of Io with Jupiter's magnetosphere and ionosphere are so complex, however, that it has been difficult to distinguish the satellite's own field from the current-produced fields in its vicinity.

Other Satellites

The only other Jovian moon that was close enough to the trajectories of the Voyager spacecraft to allow surface features to be seen was Amalthea, a small, potato-shaped moon that is named for a figure in Greek mythology associated with the infant Jupiter.

Amalthea circles Jupiter once every 11 hours 57 minutes (0.498 Earth day) at a distance of 181,000 km (112,500 miles) in a nearly circular orbit that lies within half a degree of Jupiter's equatorial plane. Photographs transmitted by the Voyager 1 and 2 spacecraft in 1979 and confirmed by the Galileo orbiter in the late 1990s show that Amalthea is an irregular rocky body measuring 262 × 146 × 134 km (163 × 91 × 83 miles). Like the Moon, which always keeps the same face toward Earth, Amalthea rotates at the same rate that it revolves around Jupiter and thus keeps the same face toward the planet. Amalthea's long axis always points toward Jupiter.

By measuring the gravitational influence of Amalthea on the Galileo spacecraft, scientists determined that the moon has such a remarkably low density—0.9 gram per cubic cm—that it could float in water. Evidently, Amalthea is highly porous, perhaps as a result of collisions that repeatedly shattered its rocky interior. Low densities ascribed to this same cause also have been observed for some of the inner moons of Saturn.

Amalthea has a dark, reddish surface marked by impact craters. The leading hemisphere (that facing the direction of motion) is some 30 percent brighter than the trailing one, presumably as a result of bombardment by small meteoroids that have entered the Jovian system. The red colour probably results from contamination by particles of sulfur and sulfur compounds that are continually shed by the nearby volcanically active satellite Io. The largest impact crater on Amalthea is Pan, which has a diameter of about 90 km (55 miles).

In addition to providing new images of Amalthea, the Galileo orbiter was able to view the effect of impacts on Thebe and Metis. These two moons are also tidally locked, keeping the same face oriented toward Jupiter and, like Amalthea, are some 30 percent brighter on their leading sides.

Before the turn of the 21st century, eight outer moons were known, comprising two distinct orbital families. The more distant group—made up of Ananke, Carme, Pasiphae, and Sinope— has retrograde orbits around Jupiter. The closer group—Leda, Himalia, Lysithea, and Elara—has prograde orbits. (In the case of these moons, retrograde motion is in the direction opposite to Jupiter's spin and motion around the Sun, which are counterclockwise as viewed from above Jupiter's north pole, whereas prograde, or direct, motion is in the same direction.) In 1999 astronomers began a concerted effort to find new Jovian satellites using highly sensitive electronic detectors that allowed them to detect fainter—and hence smaller—objects. When in the next few years they discovered a host of additional outer moons, they recognized that the two-family division was an oversimplification. There must be well more than 100 small fragments orbiting Jupiter that can be classified into several different groups according to their orbits. Each group apparently originated from an individual body that was captured by Jupiter and then broke up. The captures could have occurred near the time of Jupiter's formation when the planet was itself surrounded by a nebula that could slow down objects that entered it. These small moons may be related to the Trojan asteroids.

THE RING

As the Pioneer 10 spacecraft sped toward its closest approach to Jupiter in 1974, it detected a sudden decrease in the density of charged particles roughly 125,000 km (78,000 miles) from Jupiter, just inside the orbit of its innermost moon, Metis. This led to the suggestion that a moon or a ring of material might be orbiting the planet at this distance. The existence of a ring was verified in 1979 by the first Voyager spacecraft when it crossed the planet's equatorial plane, and the second spacecraft recorded additional pictures, including a series taken in the shadow of the planet looking back at the ring toward the direction of the Sun. The ring was many times brighter from this perspective. Evidentally most of the ring particles scatter light forward much better than in the reverse direction (toward Earth). It was therefore no surprise that Earth-based observations failed to discover the ring before Voyager. The forward scattering implies that most of the particles are very small, in the micrometre size range, rather like the motes of dust seen in a sunbeam on Earth or the fine particles on a car windshield, which show the same optical effect.

The ring exhibits a complex structure that was elucidated by images obtained

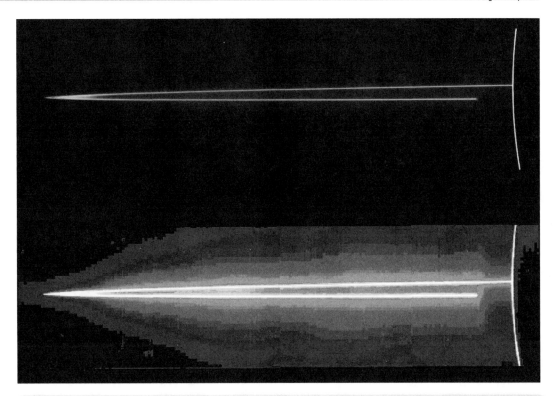

Two versions of a nearly edge-on view of Jupiter's thin main ring in mosaic images made by the Galileo spacecraft on November 8, 1996. In each image, Jupiter's limb is defined by the bright arc at the far right, which is sunlight scattered by small particles in the planet's upper atmosphere. The nearer arm of the ring abruptly disappears close to Jupiter where it passes into the planet's shadow. NASA/JPL

with the Galileo spacecraft in 1996–97. It consists of four principal components: an outer gossamer ring that fades into invisibility beyond the orbital radius of the satellite Thebe (222,000 km); an inner gossamer ring bounded by the orbit of Amalthea (181,000 km); the main ring, about 30 km (18 miles) thick, that extends inward from the orbits of Adrastea (129,000 km [80,156 miles]) and Metis (128,000 km [79,535 miles]) to an inner edge at 123,000 km (76,428 miles); and a toroidal halo of particles with a thickness of 20,000 km (12,427 miles) that extends from the main ring inward to 92,000 km.

The presence of micrometre-size particles in the ring requires a source, and the association of the ring boundaries with the four moons makes the source clear. The ring particles are generated by impacts on these moons (and on still smaller bodies within the main ring) by micrometeoroids, cometary debris, and possibly volcanically produced material from Io. Some of the finest particles are electrically charged and respond to the rocking motion of the Jovian magnetic field as the planet rotates.

ORIGIN OF
THE JOVIAN SYSTEM

Explaining the origin of Jupiter and its satellites is part of the problem of explaining the origin of the solar system. Current thinking favours the gradual development of the Sun and planets from a huge cloud of gas and dust containing gravitational instabilities that caused the cloud to collapse.

Early History of Jupiter

Given the planet's large proportion of hydrogen and its huge mass, it has been traditional to assume that Jupiter formed by condensation from the primordial solar nebula. This hypothesis implies that the elements should all be present on Jupiter in the same proportions that they occur in the Sun. However, the most recent evidence indicates that the elemental proportions on Jupiter differ from the solar values.

Current models for Jupiter's origin suggest instead that a solid core of about 10 Earth masses formed first as a result of the accretion of icy planetesimals. This core would have developed an atmosphere of its own as the planetesimals released gases during accretion. As the mass of the core increased, it would have become capable of attracting gases from the surrounding solar nebula, thus accumulating the huge hydrogen-helium envelope that constitutes Jupiter's atmosphere and fluid mantle. The accumulating envelope would have mixed with the outgassed atmosphere from the core. Thus, the presently observed enrichment of the most abundant heavy elements in this envelope, compared with solar values, reflects the concentration of such elements in the core.

The mass spectrometer on the Galileo probe showed that these heavy elements are enriched by the same factor of about three. For this enrichment to include volatile substances like argon and molecular nitrogen requires that the icy planetesimals must have formed at temperatures of 30 K (-400 °F, -240 °C) or less. Just how this happened remains a puzzle, and its solution may ultimately help explain the presence of giant planets that have been detected very close to their stars in other planetary systems.

Early History
of the Satellites

The inner eight moons of Jupiter are commonly thought to have originated in much the same way as the planet itself. Just as the primordial solar nebula is believed to have broken up into accreting planetesimals, which became the planets, and a central condensation, which became the Sun, the accumulation of material into a protoplanetary cloud at Jupiter's orbit ultimately led to the formation of the planet and its inner moons. The analogy goes further. The high temperature of the forming Jupiter apparently prevented volatile substances from condensing at the distances of the innermost moons. Hence, Ganymede and Callisto, the most distant of the inner eight moons, represent the volatile-rich outer bodies in this system.

The origin of the numerous small outer moons, with their orbits of high eccentricities and inclinations, is thought to be quite different. They are members of the population of irregular satellites in the solar system and are most likely captured objects. Their ultimate origin, however, remains unclear. The parent bodies of these moons may have first formed in the outer nebula of Jupiter, strayed away, and then been recaptured; alternately, they may have formed independently in the solar nebula itself and then been captured. In either case, the capture process apparently caused the parent bodies to break up, forming the debris observed today as the outer irregular moons. Ongoing studies of these objects and their possible relatives among the Trojan asteroids may provide the answer to their origin.

CHAPTER 4

SATURN

In the night sky Saturn is easily visible to the unaided eye as a nontwinkling point of light, and, when viewed in even a small telescope, the planet girded with its magnificent rings is arguably the most sublime object in the solar system. Saturn is designated by the symbol ♄.

Saturn's name comes from the Roman god of agriculture, who is equated with the Greek deity Cronus, one of the Titans and the father of Zeus (the Roman god Jupiter). As the farthest of the planets known to ancient observers, Saturn also was noted to be the slowest-moving. At a distance from the Sun that is 9.5 times as far as Earth's, Saturn takes nearly 30 Earth years to make one solar revolution. The Italian astronomer Galileo in 1610 was the first to observe Saturn with a telescope. Although he saw a strangeness in Saturn's appearance, the low resolution of his instrument did not allow him to discern the true nature of the planet's rings.

Saturn is the second largest planet of the solar system in mass and size and the sixth in distance from the Sun. It occupies almost 60 percent of Jupiter's volume but has only about one-third of its mass and the lowest mean density—about 70 percent that of water—of any known object in the solar system. Hypothetically, Saturn would float in an ocean large enough to hold it. Both Saturn and Jupiter resemble stars in that their bulk chemical composition is dominated by hydrogen. Also, as is the case for Jupiter, the tremendous pressure in Saturn's deep interior maintains the hydrogen there in a fluid metallic state.

Saturn's structure and evolutionary history, however, differ significantly from those of its larger counterpart. Like the other giant, or Jovian, planets—Jupiter, Uranus, and Neptune—Saturn has extensive systems of moons (natural satellites) and rings, which may provide clues to its origin and evolution as well as to those of the solar system. Saturn's moon Titan is distinguished from all other moons in the solar system by the presence of a significant atmosphere, one that is denser than that of any of the terrestrial planets except Venus.

The greatest advances in knowledge of Saturn, as well as of most of the other planets, have come from deep-space probes. Four spacecraft have visited the Saturnian system—Pioneer 11 in 1979, Voyagers 1 and 2 in the two years following, and, after an almost quarter-century hiatus, Cassini-Huygens beginning in 2004. The first three missions were short-term flybys, but Cassini went into orbit around Saturn for several years of investigations, while its Huygens probe parachuted through the atmosphere of Titan and reached its surface, becoming the first spacecraft to land on a moon other than Earth's.

BASIC ASTRONOMICAL DATA

Saturn orbits the Sun at a mean distance of 1,427,000,000 km (887 million miles). Its proximity to Earth is never less than about 1.2 billion km (746 million miles), and its phase angle—the angle that it makes with the Sun and Earth—never exceeds about 6°. Saturn seen from the vicinity of Earth thus always appears nearly fully illuminated, a limitation to observation finally overcome by the side-lit and backlit views enabled by deep-space probes.

Like Jupiter and most of the other planets, Saturn has a regular orbit—that is, its motion around the Sun is prograde (in the same direction that the Sun rotates) and has a small eccentricity (noncircularity) and inclination to the ecliptic, the plane of Earth's orbit. Unlike Jupiter, however, Saturn's rotational axis is tilted substantially—by 26.7°—to its orbital plane. The tilt gives Saturn seasons, as on Earth, but each season lasts more than seven years. Another result is that Saturn's rings, which lie in the plane of its equator, are presented to observers on Earth at opening angles ranging from 0° (edge on) to nearly 30°. The view of Saturn's rings cycles over a 30-year period. Earth-based observers can see the rings' sunlit northern side for about 15 years, then, in an analogous view, the sunlit southern side for the next 15 years. In the short intervals when Earth crosses the ring plane, the rings are all but invisible.

Saturn has no single rotation period. Cloud motions in its massive upper atmosphere trace out a variety of periods, which are as short as about 10 hours 10 minutes near the equator and increase with some oscillation to about 30 minutes longer at latitudes higher than 40°. Scientists have determined the rotation period of Saturn's deep interior from that of its magnetic field, which is presumed to be rooted in the planet's metallic-hydrogen outer core. Direct measurement of the field's rotation is difficult because the field is highly symmetrical around the rotational axis. Radio outbursts from Saturn, which appear related to small irregularities in the magnetic field, show a period of 10 hours 39.4 minutes at the time of the Voyager encounters; this value was taken to be the magnetic field rotation period.

PLANETARY DATA FOR SATURN	
mean distance from Sun	1,427,000,000 km (9.5 AU)
eccentricity of orbit	0.054
inclination of orbit to ecliptic	2.5°
Saturnian year (sidereal period of revolution)	29.44 Earth years
visual magnitude at mean opposition	0.7
mean synodic period*	378.10 Earth days
mean orbital velocity	9.7 km/sec
equatorial radius**	60,268 km
polar radius**	54,364 km
mass	5.685×10^{26} kg
mean density	0.69 g/cm³
equatorial gravity**	896 cm/sec²
polar gravity**	1,214 cm/sec²
equatorial escape velocity**	35.5 km/sec
polar escape velocity**	37.4 km/sec
rotation period (magnetic field)	10 hr 39 min 24 sec (Voyager era); about 10 hr 46 min (Cassini-Huygens mission)
inclination of equator to orbit	26.7°
magnetic field strength at equator	0.21 gauss
number of known moons	at least 47
planetary ring system	3 major rings comprising myriad component ringlets; several less-dense rings

*Time required for the planet to return to the same position in the sky relative to the Sun as seen from Earth.

**Calculated for the altitude at which 1 bar of atmospheric pressure is exerted.

A quarter century later, however, some measurements made by Cassini indicated that the field was rotating with a period 6–7 minutes longer. It is believed that the solar wind is responsible for some of the difference between the two measurements of the rotational period. The time differences between the rotation periods of Saturn's clouds and of its interior have been used to estimate wind velocities. Other radio bursts with periods of about 10 hours 10 minutes originate with lightning in Saturn's atmosphere.

Because the four giant planets have no solid surface in their outer layers, by convention the values for the radius and gravity of these planets are calculated at the level at which one bar of atmospheric pressure is exerted. By this measure, Saturn's equatorial diameter is 120,536 km (74,898 miles). In comparison, its polar diameter is only 108,728 km (67,560 miles), or 10 percent smaller, which makes Saturn the most oblate (flattened at the poles) of all the planets in the solar system. Its oblate shape is apparent even in a small telescope. Even though Saturn rotates slightly slower than Jupiter, it is more oblate because its rotational acceleration cancels a larger fraction of the planet's gravity at the equator. The equatorial gravity of the planet, 896 cm (29.4 feet) per second per second, is only 74 percent of its polar gravity. Saturn is 95 times as massive as Earth but occupies a volume 766 times greater. Its mean density of 0.69 g/cm^3 (0.4 oz/in^3) is thus only some 12 percent of Earth's. Saturn's equatorial escape velocity—the velocity needed for an object, which includes individual atoms and molecules, to escape the planet's gravitational attraction at the equator without having to be further accelerated—is nearly 36 km per second (80,000 miles per hour) at the one-bar level, compared with 11.2 km per second (25,000 miles per hour) for Earth. This high value indicates that there has been no significant loss of atmosphere from Saturn since its formation.

THE ATMOSPHERE

Viewed from Earth, Saturn has an overall hazy yellow-brown appearance. The surface that is seen through telescopes and in spacecraft images is actually a complex of cloud layers. Like the other giant planets, Saturn's atmospheric circulation is dominated by zonal (east-west) flow. This manifests itself as a pattern of lighter and darker cloud bands similar to Jupiter's, although Saturn's bands are more subtly coloured and are wider near the equator. So low in contrast are the features in the cloud tops that it was not until the Voyager flyby encounters that Saturn's atmospheric circulation could be studied in any detail.

When defined with respect to the rotation of its magnetic field, virtually all of Saturn's atmospheric flows, or winds, are to the east—in the direction of rotation. Measured against the slower magnetic rotation rate observed by Cassini, the eastward flows are even more pronounced. The equatorial zone at latitudes below 20° shows a particularly active eastward flow having a maximum velocity close to 500 metres per second (1,800 km [1,100 miles] per hour). This feature is analogous to one on Jupiter but extends twice as wide in latitude and moves four times faster. By contrast, the highest winds on Earth occur in tropical cyclones, where in extreme cases sustained velocities may exceed 67 metres per second (240 km [150 miles] per hour).

The zonal flows are remarkably symmetrical about Saturn's equator; that is, each one at a given northern latitude usually has a counterpart at a similar southern latitude. Strong eastward flows—those having eastward relative velocities in excess of 100 metres per second (360 km [225 miles] per hour)—are seen at 46° N and S and at about 60° N and S. Westward flows, which are nearly stationary in the magnetic field's frame of reference, are seen at 40°, 55°, and 70° N and S. After the Voyager encounters, improvements in Earth-based instrumentation allowed observations of Saturn's clouds at distance. Made over many years, these tended to agree with the detailed Voyager observations of the zonal flows and thus corroborated their stability over time. Some high-resolution observations of Saturn's atmosphere showed a large drop in the velocity of the equatorial jet from 1996 to 2002. Analysis of data from the Cassini orbiter, however, suggests that any such velocity drop is confined to superficial layers of the atmosphere.

The general north-south symmetry suggests that the zonal flows may be connected in some fashion deep within the interior. Theoretical modeling of a deep-convecting fluid planet such as Saturn indicates that differential rotation tends to occur along cylinders aligned about the planet's mean rotation axis. Saturn's atmosphere thus may be built of a series of coaxial cylinders aligned north-south, each rotating at a unique rate, which give rise to the zonal jets seen at the surface. The continuity of the cylinders may be broken at a point where they intersect a major discontinuity within Saturn, such as the core.

Saturn's atmosphere shows many smaller-scale features similar to those found in Jupiter's, such as red, brown, and white spots, bands, eddies, and vortices, that vary over a fairly short time. However, in addition to having a much blander appearance, Saturn's atmosphere is less active than Jupiter's on a small scale. A spectacular exception occurred during September–November 1990, when a large, light-coloured storm system appeared near the equator, expanded to a size exceeding 20,000 km (12,400 miles), and eventually spread around the equator before fading. Storms similar in impressiveness to this "Great White Spot" (so named in analogy with Jupiter's Great Red Spot) have been observed at about 30-year intervals dating back to the late 19th century. This is close to Saturn's orbital period of 29.4 years, which suggests that these storms are seasonal phenomena.

Initial analysis of data from the Voyager spacecraft indicated that the planet's atmosphere is 91 percent molecular hydrogen by mass and is thus the most hydrogen-rich atmosphere in the solar system. Helium, which is measured indirectly, makes up another 6 percent and is less abundant relative to hydrogen compared with a gas having the composition of the Sun. If hydrogen, helium, and other elements were present in the same proportions as in the Sun's atmosphere, Saturn's atmosphere would be about 71 percent hydrogen and 28 percent helium by mass. According to some models, helium may have settled out of Saturn's outer layers, but more-recent research has suggested that the Voyager analysis underestimated the helium fraction in Saturn's atmosphere, which may lie closer to the value in the Sun.

Other major molecules observed in Saturn's atmosphere are methane and ammonia, which are two to five times more abundant relative to hydrogen than in a gas of solar composition. Hydrogen sulfide and water are suspected to be major constituents of the deeper atmosphere but have not yet been detected. Minor molecules that have been detected spectroscopically from Earth include phosphine, carbon monoxide, and germane. Such molecules would not be present in detectable amounts in a hydrogen-rich atmosphere in chemical equilibrium. They may be nonequilibrium products of reactions at high pressure and temperature in Saturn's deep atmosphere well below the observable clouds. A number of nonequilibrium hydrocarbons are observed in Saturn's stratosphere: acetylene, ethane, and, possibly, propane and methyl acetylene. All of the latter may be produced by photochemical effects

Astronomers on Earth have analyzed the refraction (bending) of starlight and radio waves from spacecraft passing through Saturn's atmosphere to gain information on atmospheric temperature over depths corresponding to pressures of one-millionth of a bar to 1.3 bars. At pressures below 1 millibar, the temperature is roughly constant at about 140 to 150 K (-208 to -190 °F, -133 to -123 °C). A stratosphere, where temperatures steadily decline with increasing pressure, extends downward from 1 to 60 millibars, at which level the coldest temperature in Saturn's atmosphere, 82 K (-312 °F, -191 °C), is reached. At higher pressures (deeper levels) the temperature increases once again. This region is analogous to the lowest layer of Earth's atmosphere, the troposphere, in which the increase of temperature with pressure follows the thermodynamic relation for compression of a gas without gain or loss of heat. The temperature is 135 K (-217 °F, -138 °C) at a pressure of 1 bar, and it continues to increase at higher pressures.

Saturn's visible layer of clouds is formed from molecules of minor compounds that condense in the hydrogen-rich atmosphere. Although particles formed from photochemical reactions are seen suspended high in the atmosphere at levels corresponding to pressures of 20–70 millibars, the main clouds commence at a level where the pressure exceeds 400 millibars, with the highest cloud deck thought to be formed of solid ammonia crystals. The base of the ammonia cloud deck is predicted to occur at a depth corresponding to about 1.7 bars, where the ammonia crystals dissolve into the hydrogen gas and disappear abruptly. Nearly all information about deeper cloud layers has been obtained indirectly by constructing chemical models of the behaviour of compounds expected to be present in a gas of near solar composition following the temperature-pressure profile of Saturn's atmosphere. The bases of successively deeper cloud layers occur at 4.7 bars (ammonium hydrosulfide crystals) and at 10.9 bars (water-ice crystals with aqueous ammonia droplets). Although all of the clouds mentioned above would be colourless in the pure state, the actual clouds of Saturn display various shades of yellow, brown, and red. These colours are apparently produced by chemical impurities; phosphorus-containing molecules are a prime candidate.

Even at the extremely high pressures found deeper in Saturn's atmosphere, the minimum atmospheric temperature of 82 K is too high for molecular hydrogen to exist as a gas and a liquid together in equilibrium. Thus, there is no distinct boundary between the higher atmosphere, where the hydrogen behaves predominantly as a gas, and the deeper atmosphere, where it resembles a liquid. Unlike the tropopause on Earth, Saturn's troposphere does not terminate at a solid surface but apparently extends tens of thousands of kilometres below the visible clouds, reaching temperatures of thousands of kelvins and pressures in excess of one million bars.

THE MAGNETIC FIELD AND MAGNETOSPHERE

Saturn's magnetic field resembles that of a simple dipole, or bar magnet, its north-south axis aligned to within 1° of Saturn's rotation axis with the centre of the magnetic dipole at the centre of the planet. The polarity of the field, like Jupiter's, is opposite that of Earth's present field—i.e., the field lines emerge in Saturn's northern hemisphere and reenter the planet in the southern hemisphere, then that magnetic moment is about 600 times Earth's, whereas Jupiter's magnetic moment is 20,000 times Earth's.

Saturn's magnetosphere is the teardrop-shaped region of space around the planet where the behaviour of charged particles, which come mostly from the Sun, is dominated by the planet's magnetic field rather than by interplanetary magnetic fields. The rounded side of the teardrop extends sunward, forming a boundary, or magnetopause, with the outflowing solar wind at a distance of about 20 Saturn radii (1,200,000 km [750,000 miles]) from the centre of the planet but with substantial fluctuation due to variations in the pressure from the solar wind. On the opposite side of Saturn, the magnetosphere is drawn out into an immense magnetotail that extends to great distances.

Saturn's inner magnetosphere, like the magnetospheres of Earth and Jupiter, traps a stable population of highly energetic charged particles, mostly protons, traveling in spiral paths along magnetic field lines. These particles form belts around Saturn similar to the Van Allen belts of Earth. Unlike the cases of Earth and Jupiter, Saturn's charged-particle population is substantially depleted by absorption of the particles onto the surfaces of solid bodies that orbit within the field lines. Voyager data showed that "holes" exist in the particle populations on field lines that intersect the rings and the orbits of moons within the magnetosphere.

Saturn's moons Titan and Hyperion orbit at distances close to the magnetosphere's minimum dimensions, and they occasionally cross the magnetopause and travel outside Saturn's magnetosphere. Energetic charged particles trapped in Saturn's outer magnetosphere collide with neutral atoms in Titan's upper atmosphere and energize them, causing erosion of the atmosphere. A halo of such energetic atoms was observed by the Cassini orbiter.

Saturn possesses ultraviolet auroras produced by the impact of energetic particles from the magnetosphere onto atomic and molecular hydrogen in Saturn's polar atmosphere. Ultraviolet images of Saturn taken by the Earth-orbiting Hubble Space Telescope in the late 1990s and early 21st century succeeded in capturing the auroral rings around the poles. These gave vivid evidence of the high symmetry of Saturn's magnetic field and revealed details of the way the auroras respond to the solar wind and the Sun's magnetic field.

THE INTERIOR

Saturn's low mean density is direct evidence that its bulk composition is mostly hydrogen. Under the conditions found within the planet, hydrogen behaves as a liquid rather than a gas at pressures above about one kilobar, corresponding to a depth of 1,000 km (600 miles) below the clouds; there the temperature is roughly 1,000 K (1,340 °F, 730 °C). Even as a liquid, molecular hydrogen is a highly compressible material, and to achieve Saturn's mean density of 0.69 g/cm^3 (0.4 oz/in^3) requires pressures above one megabar. This occurs at a depth of 20,000 km (12,500 miles) below the clouds, or about one-third of the distance to the planet's centre.

Information about the interior structure of Saturn is obtained from studying its gravitational field, which is not spherically symmetrical. The rapid rotation and low mean density that lead to distortion of the planet's physical shape also distort the shape of its gravitational field. The shape of the field can be measured precisely from its effects on the motion of spacecraft in the vicinity and on the shape of some of the components of

Saturn's rings. The degree of distortion is directly related to the relative amounts of mass concentrated in Saturn's central regions as opposed to its envelope. Analysis of the distortion shows that Saturn is substantially more centrally condensed than Jupiter and therefore contains a significantly larger amount of material denser than hydrogen near its centre. Saturn's central regions contain about 50 percent hydrogen by mass, while Jupiter's contain approximately 67 percent hydrogen.

At a pressure of roughly two megabars and a temperature of about 6,000 K (10,300 °F, 5,730 °C), the fluid molecular hydrogen is predicted to undergo a major phase transition to a fluid metallic state, which resembles a molten alkali metal such as lithium. This transition occurs at a distance about halfway between Saturn's cloud tops and its centre. Evidence from the planet's gravitational field shows that the central metallic region is considerably denser than would be the case for pure hydrogen mixed only with solar proportions of helium. Excess helium that settled from the planet's outer layers might account partly for the increased density. In addition, Saturn may contain a quantity of material denser than both hydrogen and helium with a total mass as much as 30 times that of Earth, but its precise distribution cannot be determined from available data. A rock and ice mixture of about 10–20 Earth masses is likely to be concentrated in a dense central core.

The calculated electrical conductivity of Saturn's outer core of fluid metallic hydrogen is such that if slow circulation currents are present—as would be expected with the flow of heat to the surface accompanied by gravitational settling of denser components—there is sufficient dynamo action to generate the planet's observed magnetic field. Saturn's field thus is produced by essentially the same mechanism that produces Earth's field. According to the dynamo theory, the deep field—that part of the field in the vicinity of the dynamo region near the core—may be quite irregular. On the other hand, the external part of the field that can be observed by spacecraft is quite regular, with a dipole axis that is nearly aligned with the rotation axis. Theories have been proposed that magnetic field lines are made more symmetrical to the rotational axis before they reach the surface by their passing through a nonconvecting, electrically conducting region that is rotating with respect to the field lines. The striking change observed in the magnetic field rotation period over the past 25 years, mentioned above, may be related to the action of deep electric currents involving the conducting core.

On average, Saturn radiates about twice as much energy into space than it receives from the Sun, primarily at infrared wavelengths between 20 and 100 micrometres (0.0008 and 0.004 inch). This difference indicates that Saturn, like Jupiter, possesses a source of internal heat. Kilogram for kilogram of mass, Saturn's internal energy output at present is similar to Jupiter's. But Saturn is less massive than Jupiter and so had less total energy content at the time both planets were formed. For it still to be radiating at Jupiter's level means that its energy apparently is coming at least partially from a different source.

A calculation of thermal evolution shows that Saturn could have originated with a core of 10–20 Earth masses built up from the accretion of ice-rich planetesimals. On top of this, a large amount of gaseous hydrogen and helium from the original solar nebula would have accumulated by gravitational collapse. It is thought that Jupiter underwent a similar process of origin but that it captured an even greater amount of gas. On both planets the gas was heated to high temperatures—several tens of thousands of kelvins—in the course of the capture. Jupiter's present internal energy output can then be understood as the residual cooling of an initially hot planet over the age of the solar system, some 4.6 billion years. For Saturn, application of such a mechanism predicts that the energy output of the planet should have dropped below the presently observed value about two billion years ago. It has been theorized that helium has been precipitating from solution in hydrogen and that its gradual sinking has liberated additional gravitational energy. As the helium separates out into droplets in the metallic phase of hydrogen and "rains" into deeper

levels, potential energy is converted into the kinetic energy of droplet motion. Friction then damps this motion and converts it into heat, which is radiated into space, thus prolonging Saturn's internal heat source. (It is thought that this process also has occurred—although to a much more limited extent—in Jupiter, which has a warmer interior and thus allows more helium to stay in solution.) The Voyagers' detection of a substantial depletion of helium in Saturn's atmosphere originally was taken as a vindication of this theory, but it has since been opened to question.

SATURN'S RINGS AND MOONS

Although Saturn's rings and moons may seem to constitute two groups of quite different entities, they form a single complex system of objects whose structures, dynamics, and evolution are intimately linked. The orbits of the innermost known moons fall within or between the outermost rings, and new moons continue to be found embedded in the ring structure. Indeed, the ring system itself can be considered to consist of myriad tiny moons—ranging from mere dust specks to car- and house-sized pieces—in their own individual orbits around Saturn. Because of the difficulty in distinguishing between the largest ring particles and the smallest moons, determining a precise number of moons for Saturn may not be possible.

THE RING SYSTEM

In 1610 Galileo's first observations of Saturn with a primitive telescope prompted him to report: Saturn is not a single star, but is a composite of three, which almost touch each other, never change or move relative to each other, and are arranged in a row along the zodiac, the middle one being three times larger than the lateral ones. Two years later he was perplexed to find that the image in his telescope had become a single object; Earth had crossed Saturn's ring plane, and, viewed edge on, the rings had essentially disappeared. Later observations showed Galileo that the curious lateral appendages had returned. Apparently he never deduced that the appendages were in fact a disk encircling the planet.

The Dutch scientist Christiaan Huygens, who began studying Saturn with an improved telescope in 1655, eventually deduced the true shape of the rings and the fact that the ring plane was inclined substantially to Saturn's orbit. He believed, however, that the rings were a single solid disk with a substantial thickness. In 1675 the Italian-born French astronomer Gian Domenico Cassini's discovery of a large gap—now known as the Cassini division—within the disk cast doubt on the possibility of a solid ring, and the French mathematician and scientist Pierre-Simon Laplace published a theory in 1789 that the rings were made up of many smaller components. In 1857 the Scottish physicist James Clerk Maxwell demonstrated mathematically that the rings could be stable only if they comprised a very large number of small particles, a deduction confirmed about 40 years later by the American astronomer James Keeler.

Today it is known that, while Saturn's rings are enormous, they are also extremely thin. The major rings have a diameter of 270,000 km (170,000 miles), yet their thickness does not exceed 100 metres (330 feet), and their total mass comprises only about 3×10^{19} kg (6.6×10^{19} pounds), about the mass of Saturn's moon Mimas. The entire ring system spans nearly 1,000,000 km (600,000 miles) when the faint outer rings are included.

Like the rings of the other giant planets, Saturn's major rings lie within the classical Roche limit. This distance, which for the idealized case is 2.44 Saturn radii (147,000 km [91,300 miles]), represents the closest distance to which a fairly large moon can approach the centre of its more-massive planetary parent before it is torn apart by tidal forces. Conversely, small bodies within the Roche limit are prevented by tidal forces from aggregating into larger objects. The limit applies only to objects held together by gravitational attraction; it does not restrict the stability of a relatively small body for which molecular cohesion is more important than the tidal forces tending to pull it apart. Thus, small moons (and artificial satellites) with sizes in the range of tens of kilometres or less can persist indefinitely within the Roche limit.

Although the individual particles that make up Saturn's rings cannot be seen directly, their size distribution can be deduced from their effect on the scattering of light and radio signals propagated through the rings from stars and spacecraft. This analysis reveals a broad and continuous spectrum of particle sizes, ranging from centimetres to several metres, with larger objects being significantly fewer in number than smaller ones. This distribution is consistent with the result expected from repeated collision and shattering of initially larger objects. In some parts of the rings, where collisions are apparently more frequent, even smaller (dust-sized) grains are present, but these have short lifetimes owing to a variety of loss mechanisms. Clouds of the smaller grains apparently acquire electric charges, interact with Saturn's magnetic field, and manifest themselves in the form of moving, wedge-shaped spokes that extend radially over the plane of the rings. Although spokes were observed frequently during the Voyager encounters, they were not seen during Cassini's initial orbits, possibly an indication of the effect of a different Sun angle on the production of charged grains. Larger bodies dubbed ring moons, on the order of several kilometres in diameter, may exist embedded within the major rings, but only a few have been detected. There is evidence that transient "rubble pile" moons are continually created and destroyed by the competing effects of gravity, collisions, and varying orbital speed within the dense rings.

The rings strongly reflect sunlight, and a spectroscopic analysis of the reflected light shows the presence of water ice. It is thus conceivable that the major rings were produced by the breakup of a moon the size and composition of Mimas. Because the rings are known to be irreversibly spreading due to collisions between particles and because there is no known mechanism for confining them indefinitely in their present configuration, many planetary scientists suspect that the postulated ring-forming breakup happened relatively recently, perhaps only some tens of millions of years ago.

The main ring system shows structures on many scales, ranging from the three broad major rings—named C, B, and A (in order of increasing distance from Saturn)—that are visible from Earth down to myriad individual component ringlets having widths on the order of kilometres. The structures have provided scientists a fertile field for investigating gravitational resonances and the collective effects of many small particles orbiting in close proximity. Although many of the structures have been explained theoretically, a large number remain enigmatic, and a complete synthesis of the system is still lacking. Because Saturn's ring system may be an analogue of the original disk-shaped system of particles out of which the planets formed, an understanding of its dynamics and evolution has implications for the origin of the solar system itself.

The structure of the rings is broadly described by their optical depth as a function of distance from Saturn. Optical depth is a measure of the amount of electromagnetic radiation that is absorbed in passing through a medium—e.g., a cloud, the atmosphere of a planet, or a region of particles in space. It thus serves as an indicator of the average density of the medium. A completely transparent medium has an optical depth of 0; as the density of the medium increases, so does the numerical value. Optical depth depends on the wavelength of radiation as well as on the type of medium. In the case of Saturn's rings, radio wavelengths of several centimetres and longer are largely unaffected by the smallest ring particles and thus encounter smaller optical depths than visible wavelengths and shorter.

The B ring is the brightest, thickest, and broadest of the rings. It extends from 1.52 to 1.95 Saturn radii and has optical depths between 0.4 and 2.5, the precise values dependent on both distance from Saturn and wavelength of light. (Saturn's equatorial radius is 60,268 km [37,449 miles].) It is separated visually from the outer major ring, the A ring, by the Cassini division, the most prominent gap in the major rings. Lying between 1.95 and 2.02 Saturn radii and not devoid of particles, the Cassini division exhibits complicated variations in optical depth, with an average value of 0.1. The A ring extends from 2.02 to 2.27 Saturn radii and has optical depths of 0.4 to 1.0. Interior to

the B ring lies the third major ring, the C ring (sometimes known as the crepe ring), at 1.23 to 1.52 Saturn radii, with optical depths near 0.1.

Interior to the C ring at 1.11 to 1.23 Saturn radii lies the extremely tenuous D ring, which has no measurable effect on starlight or radio waves passing through it and is visible only in reflected light. Exterior to the A ring lies the narrow F ring at 2.33 Saturn radii. The F ring is a complicated structure that, according to Cassini observations, may be a tightly wound spiral. Between the A and F rings, distributed along the orbit of the inner moon Atlas, is a tenuous band of material probably shed by the moon. Still farther out is the tenuous G ring, with an optical depth of only 0.000001; lying at about 2.8 Saturn radii, it was originally detected by its influence on charged particles in Saturn's magnetosphere, and it is faintly discernible in Voyager images. Cassini images taken in 2008 revealed the presence of a small moon in the G ring that was named Aegaeon and is about 0.5 km (0.3 mile) across. This moon may be one of several parent bodies of the G ring. The outermost known ring, the extremely broad and diffuse E ring, extends from 3 to 8 Saturn radii. Cassini observations have verified that the E ring is composed of ice particles originating from geysers (a form of ice volcanism, or cryovolcanism) at a thermally active region—a hot spot—near the south pole of the moon Enceladus. Those rings of Saturn that lie outside the A ring are analogous to

Jupiter's rings in that they are composed mostly of small particles continuously shed by moons.

Numerous gaps occur in the distribution of optical depth in the major ring regions. Some of the major gaps have been named after famous astronomers who were associated with studies of Saturn. In addition to the Cassini division, they include the Colombo, Maxwell, Bond, and Dawes gaps (1.29, 1.45. 1.47, and 1.50 Saturn radii, respectively), within the C ring; the Huygens gap (1.95 Saturn radii), at the outer edge of the B ring; the Encke gap (2.21 Saturn radii), a gap in the outer part of the A ring; and the Keeler gap (2.26 Saturn radii), almost at the outer edge of the A ring. Of these gaps, only Encke was known prior to spacecraft exploration of Saturn.

Following the Voyager visits, scientists theorized that particles can be cleared from a region to form a gap by the gravitational effects of a moon about 10 km (6 miles) in size orbiting within the gap region. In 1990 one such moon, Pan, was discovered within the Encke gap in Voyager images and was recorded again in Cassini images. The anticipated corresponding moon, Daphnis, within the Keeler gap was found in Cassini images in 2005. Similar moons may exist within the Huygens and Maxwell gaps.

Other theories indicate that a gap can also be cleared in a ring region that is in orbital resonance with a moon whose orbit is substantially internal or external to the ring. The condition for resonance is that the orbital periods of the moon and the ring particles be a ratio of whole numbers. When this is the case, a given ring particle will always make close approaches to the moon at the same points in its orbit, and gravitational perturbations to the particle's orbit will build up over time, eventually forcing the particle out of precise resonance. If the moon orbits outside the ring, it receives angular momentum from the resonant ring particles and, in turn, launches a tightly wound spiral density wave in the ring, which ultimately clears a gap if the resonance is strong enough.

The boundary region at the outer edge of the B ring and the inner edge of the Cassini division is in a 2:1 resonance with Mimas, meaning that the orbital period of Mimas is twice that of the ring particles located at that radius. As predicted from such a resonance, the boundary is not perfectly circular but shows deviations in radius that result in a two-lobed shape. Although the location of this boundary clearly shows the influence of the resonance in sculpting the inner edge of the Cassini division, the remainder of the division's structure is not fully understood. Similarly, the outer edge of the A ring is in a 7:6 resonance with the co-orbital moons Janus and Epimetheus and is scalloped with seven lobes. Effects of other resonances of this kind are seen throughout the ring system, but many similar features cannot be so explained. In general, the number of known moons and resonances falls far short of what is needed to account for the countless thousands of ringlets and other fine structure in Saturn's ring system.

MOONS

Saturn possesses more than 60 known moons. (A table summarizing data for Saturn's moons appears in Appendix B, "Moons of Saturn.") Of the first 18 discovered, all but the much more distant moon Phoebe orbit within about 3.6 million km (2.2 million miles) of Saturn. Nine are more than 100 km (60 miles) in radius and were discovered telescopically before the 20th century; the others were found in an analysis of Voyager images in the early 1980s. Several additional inner moons—tiny bodies with radii of 3–4 km (1.9–2.5 miles)—were discovered in Cassini spacecraft images beginning in 2004. All of the inner moons are regular, having prograde, low-inclination, and low-eccentricity orbits with respect to the planet. The eight largest are thought to have formed along Saturn's equatorial plane from a protoplanetary disk of material, in much the same way as the planets formed around the Sun from the primordial solar nebula.

A second, outer group of moons lies beyond about 11 million km (6.8 million miles). They are irregular in that all of their orbits have large eccentricities and inclinations; about two-thirds revolve around Saturn in a retrograde fashion—they move opposite to the planet's

rotation. Except for Phoebe, they are less than about 20 km (12 miles) in radius. Some were discovered from Earth beginning in 2000 as the result of efforts to apply new electronic detection methods to the search for fainter—and hence smaller—objects in the solar system; others were found by Cassini. These outer bodies appear to be not primordial moons but rather captured objects or their fragments.

THEIR ORBITS AND ROTATION

The orbital and rotational dynamics of Saturn's moons have unusual and puzzling characteristics, some of which are related to their interactions with the rings. For example, the three small moons Janus, Epimetheus, and Pandora orbit near the outer edge of the main ring system and are thought to have been receiving angular momentum, amounting to a minuscule but steady outward push, from ring particles through collective gravitational interactions. The effects of this process would be to reduce the spreading of the rings caused by collisions between ring particles and to drive these moons to ever larger orbits. Because of the small size of the moons, scientists have found it difficult to find a mechanism by which this process could have endured over the age of the solar system without driving the moons far beyond their current positions. The sharpness of the outer edge of the main ring system and the present orbits of such inner moons as Atlas are puzzling, and they appear to support the idea that the current ring system is much younger than Saturn itself.

Pandora and its nearest neighbour moon, Prometheus, have been dubbed shepherd moons because of their influence on ring particles. During Voyager 1's flyby, the two bodies were discovered orbiting on either side of the narrow F ring, which itself had been found only a year earlier by Pioneer 11. The moons' gravitational interactions with the F ring produce a "shepherding" effect, in which the ring's constituent particles are kept confined to a narrow band. Prometheus, the inner shepherd, transmits angular momentum to the ring particles, pushing the ring outward and itself inward, while Pandora, the outer shepherd, receives angular momentum from the ring particles, pushing the ring inward and itself outward. Cassini obtained a spectacular video record of this process, in which complex wavelike bands of particles are drawn out from the F ring as the shepherds pass it. (The term *shepherd* often is used to describe any moon that constrains the extent of a ring through gravitational forces. Consequently, in this expanded sense, moons such as Janus and Epimetheus, whose ring effects are described in the paragraph above, and gap-creating moons such as Pan also qualify as shepherds.)

Janus and Epimetheus are co-orbital moons—they share the same average orbit. Every few years they make a close approach, interacting gravitationally in such a way that one transmits angular momentum to the other, which forces the latter into a slightly higher orbit and the former into a slightly lower orbit. At the next close approach, the process repeats in the opposite direction. Tethys and Dione also have their own co-orbital satellites, but, because Tethys and Dione are much more massive than their co-orbiters, there is no significant exchange of angular momentum. Instead, Tethys's two co-orbiters, Telesto and Calypso, are located at the stable Lagrangian points along Tethys's orbit, leading and following Tethys by 60°, respectively, analogous to the Trojan asteroids in Jupiter's orbit. Dione's Trojan-like companions, Helene and Polydeuces, lead and follow it by 60°, respectively, on average.

Several pairs of moons are in stable dynamic resonances—i.e., the members of each pair pass one another in their orbits in a periodic fashion, interacting gravitationally in a way that preserves the regularity of these encounters. In such a resonance the orbital periods of a pair of moons are related to each other approximately in the ratio of small whole numbers. For example, the orbital periods of Hyperion and the nearer Titan, at 21.28 at 15.94 days, respectively, are in the ratio 4:3, which means that Titan completes four orbits around Saturn in the time that it takes Hyperion to complete three. Titan and Hyperion always pass most closely at Hyperion's apoapse, the farthest point of its elliptical orbit.

Because Titan has more than 50 times the mass of Hyperion and always transmits the most momentum to the smaller moon at the same points along its orbit, Hyperion is forced by these periodic "shoves" into a relatively elongated (eccentric) orbit. Analogously, the moon pairs Dione and Enceladus and Tethys and Mimas have orbital periods in the ratio 2:1.

Because resonances between pairs of moons can force orbital eccentricities to relatively large values, they are potentially important in the geologic evolution of the bodies concerned. Ordinarily, tidal interactions between Saturn and its nearer moons—the cyclic deformations in each body caused by the gravitational attraction of the other—tend to reduce the eccentricity of the moons' orbits as well as to brake their spins in such a way that they rotate at the same rate as they revolve around Saturn. This state, called synchronous rotation, is common in the solar system, being the case, for example, for Earth's Moon and several of Jupiter's nearer moons. For a moon that rotates with respect to its planet, the internal deformation is dynamic; it travels cyclically around the moon and generates heat by internal friction. Once a moon is in synchronous rotation, it always keeps the same hemisphere facing the planet and the same hemispheres forward and rearward in its orbit; the deformation no longer travels but remains stationary in the moon's reference frame, and frictional heating does not occur. However,

even a moon in synchronous rotation experiences tidal interaction if it is forced into an eccentric orbit by resonance; as it travels alternately farther from and closer to its planet, the ensuing dynamic deformation heats its interior. The most dramatic example of such a moon is Jupiter's Io.

Although calculations indicate that the present tides on Saturn's moons are not particularly significant as a heating mechanism, this may not have been true in the past. Furthermore, the hot "tiger-stripe" region of Enceladus is the present-day source of the icy material for the diffuse E ring in which it orbits. The cause of the region's thermal activity remains to be deduced, but it is likely to be related to some form of tidal deformation.

Hyperion is a spectacular exception to the rule in which tidal interactions force moons into synchronous rotation. Hyperion's orbital eccentricity and highly nonspherical shape, which is unusual for a body as large as it is, have led to a complicated interaction between its spin and orbital angular momentum. The outcome of this interaction is a behaviour that is described mathematically as chaotic. Although the fleeting Voyager encounters found Hyperion to be rotating nonsynchronously with a period of about 13 days, chaos theory applied to Voyager data and subsequent Earth-based observations of the moon shows that it is actually tumbling in an essentially unpredictable manner. Hyperion is the only

Saturn's impact-scarred moon Hyperion, in a photograph taken by the Cassini spacecraft during a close approach on September 26, 2005. Hyperion's interior may be a loose agglomeration of ice blocks interspersed with voids, which would account for its low mean density (half that of water ice) and would explain its unusual "spongy" appearance in Cassini images. NASA/JPL/Space Science Institute

object known in the solar system to be in chaotic rotation.

TITAN

Titan is the largest moon of Saturn and the only moon in the solar system known to have clouds and a dense atmosphere. It was discovered telescopically in 1655 by the Dutch scientist Christiaan Huygens—the first planetary satellite to be discovered after the four Galilean moons of Jupiter. The moon is named for the Titans of Greek mythology, which include Cronus (equated with the Roman god Saturn) and his 11 siblings. In an Earth-based telescope, Titan appears as a nearly featureless brownish red globe, its surface permanently veiled by a thick haze. It is larger than the planet Mercury and more massive than Pluto, and, in significant ways, it resembles a planet more than it does a typical moon.

Titan orbits Saturn at a mean distance of 1,221,850 km (759,220 miles), taking 15.94 Earth days for one revolution. It rotates once on its axis for each revolution—i.e., its rotation is synchronous—so that it always keeps the same face toward Saturn and always leads with the same face in its orbit. The diameter of the solid body of Titan is 5,150 km (3,200 miles), only about 120 km (75 miles) less than that of Jupiter's moon Ganymede, the largest moon in the solar system. If its hundreds of kilometres of atmosphere are included, however, Titan far exceeds Ganymede in size. Titan's relatively low mean density of 1.88 g/cm³ (1.1 oz/in³) implies that its interior is a mixture of rocky and icy materials, the latter probably including ammonia mixed with water and methane and possibly including liquid layers, covered by a solid, mostly water-ice crust. A rocky core may lie at the centre and extend to perhaps 80 percent of the total radius. In its bulk properties, Titan resembles other large icy moons of the outer solar system, such as Jupiter's Ganymede and Callisto and Neptune's largest moon, Triton.

Titan's Atmosphere

Titan's atmosphere was first detected spectroscopically in 1944 by the Dutch American astronomer Gerard P. Kuiper, who found evidence of the absorption of sunlight by methane. However, studies of the refraction (bending) of radio waves in the atmosphere carried out during Voyager 1's flyby in 1980 showed that methane molecules must make up only a few percent of the total number of molecules in the atmosphere and that the predominant molecules are not detectable in visible-light spectra. Comparison of infrared and radio data from Voyager revealed that the atoms and molecules making up the atmosphere have a mean molecular weight of 28.6 atomic mass units. Thus, Voyager correctly identified the most plausible major constituent to be molecular nitrogen (mean molecular weight 28), although some atomic argon (mean molecular weight 36) could also be present.

Other constituents detected by Voyager in Titan's atmosphere via their absorption of ultraviolet light from the Sun were molecular hydrogen and many carbon-bearing molecules, believed to be produced by solar ultraviolet light acting on methane and nitrogen at high altitudes. These include carbon monoxide, carbon dioxide, and the organic gases ethane, propane, acetylene, ethylene, hydrogen cyanide, diacetylene, methyl acetylene, cyanoacetylene, and cyanogen, all observed in trace amounts.

Structure

Titan's atmosphere is similar to Earth's both in the predominance of nitrogen gas and in surface pressure, which is about 1.5 bars, or 50 percent higher than sea-level pressure on Earth. The moon's atmosphere is much colder, however, having a temperature at the surface of 94 K (-290 °F, -179 °C), and it contains no free oxygen. A troposphere analogous to Earth's extends from Titan's surface to an altitude of 42 km (26 miles), where a minimum temperature of 71 K (-332 °F, -202 °C) is reached. Clouds of nitrogen are not present, apparently because temperatures are always above the condensation point of nitrogen. Initial data from the Cassini-Huygens spacecraft, which began exploring the Saturnian system in 2004, show that methane is indeed a minor, but very important, atmospheric constituent, possibly playing a role analogous to that of water vapour in Earth's troposphere.

Near Titan's surface, about 5 percent of the atmospheric molecules are methane, the fraction decreasing with altitude. (For comparison, Earth's lower atmosphere contains about 1 percent water vapour on average.) When Cassini first encountered Titan, it observed a large outburst of methane cumulus clouds over Titan's south polar region. There also is indirect evidence that methane "rain" occasionally precipitates near the surface. In contrast to water on Earth, however, a liquid methane ocean does not exist on Titan, because it would require an atmospheric mixing ratio of 12 percent, contrary to observation.

Titan has a thin atmospheric layer of roughly constant temperature above the troposphere, followed by an extensive stratosphere ranging from 50 to 200 km (30 to 120 miles) in altitude, where temperatures steadily increase with altitude to a maximum of 160 to 180 K (-172 to -136 °F, -113 to -93 °C). Studies of the refraction of starlight in Titan's upper atmosphere show that temperatures remain in this range up to an altitude of 450 km (280 miles), and spacecraft observations of the transmission of solar ultraviolet light give similar values at even higher altitudes.

Titan's Haze

Titan's veiling haze is probably composed of an aerosol of complex organic solids that are continuously produced by solar ultraviolet light falling on the nitrogen-methane atmosphere. These small particles absorb solar radiation and account for the deep brownish red

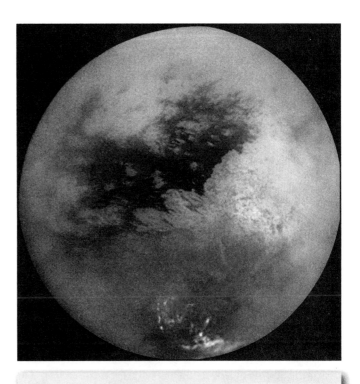

Saturn's moon Titan, in a mosaic of nine images taken by the Cassini spacecraft on Oct. 26, 2004, and processed to reduce the veiling effects of the moon's atmosphere. The view is centered slightly south of the equator, with north toward the top. The continent-sized region Xanadu Regio shows as the large bright patch on the right, while bright methane clouds appear near Titan's south pole. NASA/JPL/Space Science Institute

tint. Extraordinarily pervasive throughout Titan's atmosphere, they are substantially dense even at altitudes as high as 300 km (200 miles) and pressures below one millibar. The Huygens entry probe observed haze particles as it descended through the troposphere, down to an altitude of about 30 km (20 miles). Particle sizes probably lie in the range of 0.1 micrometre (0.000004 inch). There is evidence that they undergo seasonal changes in density, becoming thicker in Titan's summer hemisphere, which suggests that they are a form of natural "smog" formed by the action of solar radiation. Solar heating of the particle layers creates a temperature inversion layer in Titan's stratosphere, preventing the smog layer from dissipating by convection.

The haze particles are thought to settle slowly through the atmosphere and accumulate on Titan's surface. The amount produced throughout the history of Titan is calculated to be the equivalent of a continuous layer of organic solids covering the entire surface to a depth of at least hundreds of metres. Titan's atmospheric chemistry and the presence of complex organic compounds suggests that the moon may be a laboratory for studying the types of organic molecules and the chemical processes that led to the origin of life on Earth four billion years ago.

Titan's nitrogen-rich atmosphere is thought to be not primordial but rather a secondary atmosphere like Earth's. It probably arose from photochemical dissociation of ammonia—an abundant ice in the outer solar system—into molecular nitrogen and hydrogen. The ability of a large moon such as Titan to subsequently retain a substantial atmosphere for billions of years depends on a delicate balance between surface gravity, atmospheric molecular mass, and solar heating. The higher the force of attraction between the moon and an atmospheric molecule, the longer the molecule is retained. On the other hand, the hotter the atmosphere, the more likely it is that the molecule will be lost to space. Jupiter's Galilean moons and Earth's Moon are too warm to have retained any abundant gases, but cold Titan and warm but sufficiently massive Earth both have retained the nitrogen molecule. Neither Titan nor Earth has retained the lighter hydrogen molecule.

The Surface

Little was known about Titan's surface before the Cassini-Huygens mission. Because the moon's haze is partially transparent to near-infrared light, earlier telescopic studies exploiting this property were able to show that the surface is not uniform. Images taken in near-infrared wavelengths by the Hubble Space Telescope in 1994 revealed a bright continent-sized region, later named Xanadu Regio, on Titan's leading face. This region was also discerned from Earth and from the Cassini spacecraft at radar wavelengths, which can penetrate the haze.

As the Cassini spacecraft orbited Saturn, it made numerous observations during a series of close flybys of Titan beginning in late 2004. On Jan. 14, 2005, the Huygens entry probe became the first spacecraft to land on a planetary surface in the outer solar system, carrying out various physical and chemical measurements of Titan's atmosphere and transmitting high-resolution images as it descended by parachute. The Cassini-Huygens mission revealed that Titan's surface is quite young by planetary standards, with only a few large impact craters observed. Titan's surface, like Earth's, is sculpted by wind and probably also rain (in the form of liquid methane). "River" channels coated with dark hydrocarbon deposits are common, sometimes running along faults and sometimes with extensive tributary systems. Features dubbed "cat scratches"—long, dark, east-west features hundreds of kilometres in length—may be dunes of dark particulate matter. Despite expectations of lakes and even oceans on Titan's surface, however, no surface liquids have been detected unequivocally.

MIMAS

Mimas is the smallest and innermost of the major regular moons of Saturn. It was discovered in 1789 by the English astronomer William Herschel and named for one of the Giants (Gigantes) of Greek mythology.

Mimas measures about 400 km (250 miles) in diameter and revolves around the planet in a prograde, near-circular orbit at a mean distance of 185,520 km (115,277 miles). Because of tidal interactions with Saturn, the moon rotates synchronously with its orbital motion, always keeping the same hemisphere toward Saturn and always leading with the same hemisphere in orbit.

The mean density of Mimas is only 1.1 times that of water, and its surface shows characteristics of water frost. For these reasons, Mimas is believed to be composed principally of ice. Its surface is bright and heavily marked with deep, bowl-shaped impact craters. The depth of the craters appears to be a consequence of the low surface gravity, which apparently is not strong enough to cause slumping. In spite of Mimas's small size, it shows some evidence of resurfacing, possibly resulting from a partial melting of the icy crust. Its most noteworthy feature is a 130-km- (80-mile-) diameter crater named Herschel, which is near the centre of the leading hemisphere. The crater's outer walls are 5 km (3 miles) high, its floor 10 km (6 miles) deep, and the central peak 6 km (4 miles) high. Herschel is one of the largest impact structures, relative to the size of the body, known in the solar system.

Mimas is in an orbital resonance with the more distant Saturnian moon Tethys—its 22.6-hour circuit of Saturn is half that of Tethys—and the two bodies always make their closest approach to each other on the same side of Saturn. Clearly this resonance is not accidental.

In general terms, it could have arisen from a gradual process, such as the slowing of Saturn's rotation because of tidal friction, that—due to conservation of momentum—expanded the orbits of both moons, Mimas's more than Tethys's, over geologic time. Mimas also is in orbital resonance with a number of observed structures in Saturn's ring system. The inner edge of the Cassini division, a prominent gap of lowered particle density in the main rings, has an orbital period close to one-half of that of Mimas, and this gap is thought to be formed at least in part by resonant interactions of ring particles with the moon. Other ring orbits that are in resonance with Mimas display bending waves, tightly wound spiral waves of ring material displaced upward or downward from the ring plane.

ENCELADUS

The second nearest of the major regular moons of Saturn and the brightest of all its moons is Enceladus. It was discovered in 1789 by the English astronomer William Herschel and named for one of the Giants (Gigantes) of Greek mythology.

Enceladus measures about 500 km (310 miles) in diameter and orbits Saturn in a prograde, nearly circular path at a mean distance of 238,020 km (147,899 miles). Its average density is only 30 percent greater than that of water, which indicates that it is at least half water ice.

View of Enceladus from Voyager 2, showing crater-free portions of the surface, possibly indicative of resurfacing by liquid water from the interior. B.A. Smith/National Space Science Data Center

The surface of Enceladus reflects more light than newly fallen snow. Voyager images showed few large craters; the presence of smooth, crater-free areas and extensive ridged plains gave convincing evidence that fairly recent internal activity, possibly within the last 100 million years, has caused widespread melting and resurfacing. Spectral data from Cassini show that Enceladus's surface is almost pure water ice.

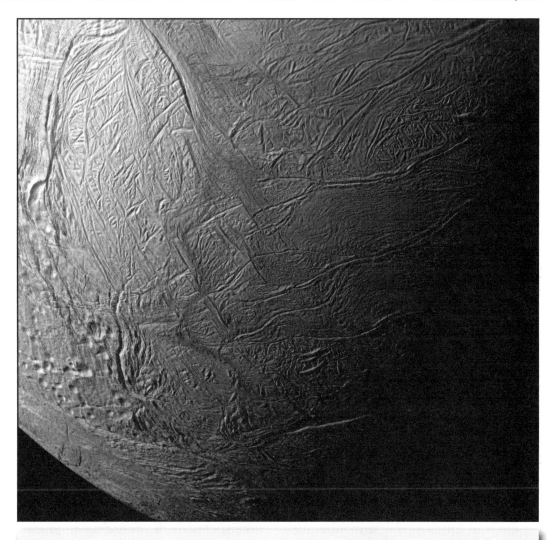

Saturn's moon Enceladus; photograph taken by the Cassini spacecraft, 2008. NASA

Little was known about Enceladus until the flyby of the U.S. spacecraft Voyager 2 in 1981. Approaching as close as 87,140 km (54,146 miles), the spacecraft returned images revealing that Enceladus is complex geologically, its surface having undergone five distinct evolutionary periods. Additional observations by the Cassini spacecraft, which began a series of close flybys of Enceladus (some less than 200 km [125 miles] away) in 2005, confirmed that portions of the moon are geologically active today, with extremely high heat flow (far hotter than predicted from solar heating alone) and associated eruptions of water vapour and ice from geysers (a form of ice volcanism, or cryovolcanism) especially apparent in its south polar region. The moon's south polar hot spot is at a temperature of 140 K (-208 °F, -133 °C); the region also exhibits enigmatic geologic structures dubbed "tiger stripes." Several craterless areas may be only 100 million years old, suggesting that parts of the surface melted and refroze in the recent geologic past and that Enceladus may have multiple active areas. Enceladus's current activity is responsible for Saturn's E ring, a tenuous ring of micrometre-sized particles of water ice condensed from vapour ejected by the geysers. The particles are densest near Enceladus's orbit and are analogous to the cloud of orbiting particles ejected from Jupiter's volcanically active moon Io. The orbital lifetimes of the E ring particles are very short, perhaps only 10,000 years, but they are resupplied continually by cryovolcanic eruptions. The water-ice particles that form the E ring are being expelled from Enceladus at the rate of about 1,000 metric tons per year. As is the case with Europa, the existence of possible liquid water on Enceladus makes it a promising environment for life.

Enceladus's 33-hour trip around Saturn is one-half that of the more distant moon Dione; the two bodies are thus associated in an orbital resonance. Under certain circumstances, such a resonance can lead to large amounts of tidal heating of the inner of the involved moons, but it remains to be shown in detailed calculations how this mechanism could generate enough heating to account for continuing activity within Enceladus.

TETHYS

Tethys is remarkable for a fissure that wraps around the greater part of its circumference. It was discovered in 1684 by the Italian-born French astronomer Gian Domenico Cassini and named for a Titan in Greek mythology.

Tethys has a diameter of 1,060 km (659 miles), and its density of 1.0 g/cm³ (0.58 oz/in³)—the same as that of water—indicates that it is composed essentially of pure water ice. It revolves around Saturn in a prograde, circular orbit at a distance of 294,660 km (183,090 miles), which is within the planet's broad, tenuous E ring. It is involved in an orbital resonance with the nearer moon Mimas such that Tethys completes one 45-hour orbit for every two of Mimas. Tethys rotates synchronously with its orbital period, keeping the same face toward Saturn and the same face forward in its orbit. It is accompanied by two tiny moons, Telesto and Calypso (named for daughters of Titans), that maintain gravitationally stable positions along its orbit, analogous to Jupiter's Trojan asteroids.

Image of Tethys, showing Ithaca Chasma, from the Cassini-Huygens spacecraft. NASA/JPL/ Space Science Institute

Telesto precedes Tethys by 60°; Calypso follows by 60°.

Tethys shows little evidence of internal activity. Tethys's most impressive feature is Ithaca Chasma, a giant crack several kilometres deep that extends along three-quarters of the moon's circumference and accounts for 5–10 percent of its surface. Because the ridges around the feature are heavily cratered, scientists have theorized that the chasm was produced early in the moon's geologic history, when the water that composes its interior froze and expanded. A second notable feature is the crater Odysseus, which measures 400 km (250 miles) across and has a large central peak. The density of impact craters on Tethys is high, suggesting that the surface is ancient. Nevertheless, the surface is highly reflective, especially on Tethys's leading face, which is not typical of geologically old surfaces. Planetary scientists suspect that this distribution of surface brightness is affected by the deposition of micrometre-sized ice particles from Saturn's E ring, in which Tethys is well-embedded. Cited as evidence is the observation that many of the craters on Tethys have bright floors, whereas the craters on Saturn's moon Hyperion, which orbits relatively far from Tethys and the E ring, tend to have dark floors.

DIONE

Dione was discovered by the Italian-born French astronomer Gian Domenico Cassini in 1684 and named for a daughter of the Titan Oceanus in Greek mythology.

Dione has a diameter of 1,120 km (696 miles) and revolves around Saturn in a prograde, nearly circular orbit at a mean distance of 377,400 km (234,500 miles), which is within the outer part of Saturn's tenuous E ring. It is accompanied in its orbit by two much smaller moons, Helene and Polydeuces (also named for Greek mythological figures). Helene, which has a diameter of about 30 km (20 miles),

maintains a gravitationally stable position 60° ahead of Dione. Polydeuces has less than half the diameter of Helene and follows Dione by 60°, though with large deviations from its mean position. The orbits of these tiny companion moons can be compared to those of Jupiter's Trojan asteroids.

Tidal interactions with Saturn have slowed Dione's rotation so that it now turns synchronously with its orbital motion, always keeping the same hemisphere toward the planet and always leading with the same hemisphere in orbit. The surface of Dione shows great brightness contrasts, with the trailing hemisphere generally darker than the leading one. On average, however, Dione is highly reflective, which indicates a surface composed of large amounts of geologically fresh water ice. The moon's low density, which is 1.5 times that of water, is consistent with a bulk composition of about equal amounts of ice and rock. Dione is heavily covered in places with impact craters; their density and distribution of sizes suggests a geological age close to four billion years. In other areas, however, the crater density is lower, which suggests that the moon may have experienced substantial ice melting and resurfacing. It is also possible that Dione's surface is continually coated by new ice particles deposited from the E ring.

Most of Dione's craters are found on the bright, leading hemisphere. The opposite hemisphere is broken by many bright linear features that form a polygonal network. Some of these bright features are associated with linear troughs and ridges and may have been caused by episodic tectonic activity. Wispy features seen in Voyager spacecraft images had been thought to be deposits of recondensed volatile material that erupted from Dione's interior along linear fractures. Higher-resolution images from the Cassini spacecraft, however, show no evidence of such activity. The asymmetry of the moon's surface is not understood, although there is evidence of a major impact near the centre of the linear network on the trailing hemisphere.

Like many objects in orbit around Saturn, Dione is involved in an orbital resonance; i.e., its 66-hour trip around Saturn is twice that of the nearer moon Enceladus. This relationship has been proposed as a source of the dramatic tidal heating seen in Enceladus, but the details of this mechanism have not been worked out.

RHEA

Rhea is Saturn's second largest moon, after Titan. It was discovered in 1672 by the Italian-born French astronomer Gian Domenico Cassini and named for a Titan of Greek mythology.

Rhea has a diameter of 1,528 km (949 miles) and revolves around Saturn in a prograde, nearly circular orbit at a mean distance of 527,040 km (327,490 miles) and with an orbital period of about 4.52 Earth days. Rhea's density, which is 1.3

times that of water, indicates that the moon is composed mostly of water ice. In addition, infrared spectral observations show a surface composed mainly of water frost. Like most of Saturn's other major moons, Rhea rotates synchronously with its orbital period, keeping the same hemisphere toward Saturn and the same hemisphere forward in its orbit.

Rhea's surface is highly reflective overall, although large regional variations are apparent. Rhea resembles Saturn's moon Iapetus in size and density, but the distribution of its surface brightness is opposite to that of Iapetus and less extreme. In the latter regard it more resembles its neighbouring moon Dione—its leading hemisphere is bright and heavily cratered, whereas its trailing hemisphere is darker with bright wispy streaks, a paucity of craters, and evidence of resurfacing.

At Saturn's distance from the Sun, frozen water and other volatile substances are so cold that they behave mechanically like rock and can retain impact craters. Consequently, Rhea's bright cratered side strongly resembles the extensively cratered highlands of Mercury or of Earth's Moon. Rhea is in fact the most heavily cratered of Saturn's moons, and the reflective properties of its surface indicate that it is highly porous, like the Moon's impact-pulverized debris layer, or regolith. Bright streaks have been observed on the darker, trailing side of Rhea. It remains to be determined whether the streaks are caused by tectonic activity (faulting) or by the escape of volatiles such as water or methane through fissures and their precipitation on the surface. The leading side of Rhea as it orbits Saturn has a remarkable bright crater with extensive bright rays extending over much of the hemisphere, rather like the spectacular rayed lunar crater Tycho.

HYPERION

Hyperion is notable in that it has no regular rotation period but tumbles in an apparently random fashion in its orbit. Hyperion was discovered in 1848 by the American astronomers William Bond and George Bond and independently by the English astronomer William Lassell. It was named for one of the Titans of Greek mythology.

Hyperion orbits Saturn once every 21.3 Earth days in the prograde direction at a distance of 1,481,100 km (920,300 miles), between the orbits of the moons Titan and Iapetus. Hyperion's orbit is unusual in that it is somewhat eccentric (elongated) yet inclined less than a half degree from the plane of Saturn's equator. The nearer moon Titan makes four circuits of Saturn for every three of Hyperion (i.e., their orbits are in a 4:3 dynamic resonance), and the two moons approach each other most closely when Hyperion is at the farthest point in its orbit. Under these conditions, Titan, which is the much more massive body, gives Hyperion periodic gravitational nudges that force it into a relatively eccentric orbit. Another peculiarity of Hyperion is its nonspherical shape, which

is sometimes described as resembling a thick hamburger patty. Measuring 370 × 280 × 225 km (230 × 174 × 140 miles), it is the largest known moon with such a pronounced irregular shape. Its reflectance of 30 percent, which is moderately high, is consistent with the presence of some water frost on its surface. Hyperion has a reddish hue that resembles the colour of the enigmatic dark areas on the more distant moon Iapetus. Hyperion's mean density is only about half that of water ice, suggesting that the moon's interior may be a loose agglomeration of ice blocks interspersed with voids. This structure may account for the remarkable "spongy" appearance of parts of Hyperion's cratered surface in images from the Cassini spacecraft.

Because of Hyperion's shape and eccentric orbit, it does not maintain a stable rotation about a fixed axis. Unlike any other known object in the solar system, Hyperion rotates chaotically, changing its rotational characteristics over timescales as short as a month. According to theory, Hyperion can rotate in a seemingly regular manner over intervals as long as a few thousand years, followed by equally long intervals of completely chaotic tumbling, its rotation state at any specified time being completely unpredictable.

IAPETUS

Iapetus, the outermost of Saturn's major regular moons, is extraordinary because of its great contrast in surface brightness.

It was discovered by the Italian-born French astronomer Gian Domenico Cassini in 1671 and named for one of the Titans of Greek mythology.

Iapetus has a radius of 718 km (446 miles) and orbits Saturn once every 79.3 Earth days at a distance of 3,561,300 km (2,212,900 miles). Its bulk density of 1.0 grams per cubic cm implies that it must be made mostly of ices. The closer moons of Saturn orbit within roughly one degree of Saturn's equatorial plane, but, at Iapetus's orbit and beyond, the gravitational influence of Saturn's equatorial bulge becomes less important, permitting larger orbital inclinations. It has

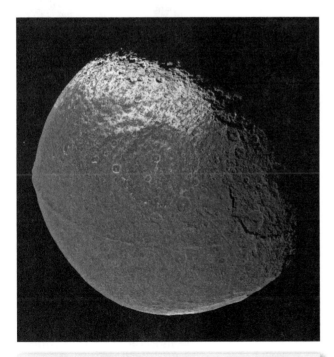

Image of Iapetus from the Cassini-Huygens spacecraft. NASA/JPL/Space Science Institute

been suggested that Iapetus's 15° average inclination is a relic of the tilt of the long-vanished gaseous disk from which Saturn's major regular moons formed.

Tidal interactions with Saturn have synchronized the rotation of Iapetus with its orbital period. As a result, the moon always keeps the same face to Saturn and always leads with the same face in its orbital motion. Remarkably, the leading hemisphere is extremely dark, reflecting only a few percent of the sunlight falling on it, whereas the trailing hemisphere is as much as 10 times a better reflector. The reflectance at the poles is higher still. Iapetus displays the greatest variation in brightness of any object known in the solar system. Cassini himself wrote that, as Iapetus traveled in its orbit, he could observe it on one side of Saturn but not on the other, and he speculated correctly about the reason for this discrepancy.

Although the U.S. Voyager spacecraft flybys revealed impact craters only on Iapetus's bright trailing side, subsequent higher-resolution Cassini spacecraft images show craters on the leading side as well. The surface material on the bright side is very nearly pure water ice, possibly mixed with other ices. The material coating the surface of the dark side, which has a reddish hue, appears to be an opaque layer of complex organic molecules mixed with iron-bearing minerals that have been altered by water. The reflectivity difference is caused by dark material composed of particles that originated elsewhere in the Saturnian system collecting on the moon's leading hemisphere and absorbing more sunlight, which heats up this region enough to cause significant sublimation of water ice over geologic time. The water vapour then condenses onto the trailing hemisphere and freezes.

The Cassini spacecraft imaged a remarkable narrow ridge encircling much of Iapetus's equator. Models suggest that it was formed by motions of a thin, active ice lithosphere when deeper layers of the moon were warm. On the other hand, the moon's observed impact basins and other topography generally require a thicker lithosphere. Possibly most of the features were formed when temperatures within the moon were changing rapidly during its first few million years of existence.

PHOEBE

Phoebe is a midsized irregular moon of Saturn, discovered by the American astronomer William Henry Pickering in 1899 on photographic plates and named for a Titan in Greek mythology.

Roughly spherical and about 220 km (136 miles) in diameter, Phoebe has a mean distance from Saturn of about 12,952,000 km (8,050,000 miles), which is several times farther than any of Saturn's other major moons; it takes about 1.5 Earth years to complete one trip around Saturn. Its orbit is significantly eccentric, retrograde, and steeply

Image of Phoebe from the Cassini-Huygens spacecraft. NASA/JPL/Space Science Institute

inclined to the plane of Saturn's rings and regular moons.

Phoebe's surface shows large differences in reflectivity but is very dark overall. Infrared spectral observations reveal the presence of water-ice particles mixed with dark material resembling the carbon-rich material seen on primitive C-class asteroids. Some of the moon's craters show evidence of alternating surface layers of bright and dark material. Phoebe has a mean density roughly 1.6 times that of pure water ice, higher than the density of most of Saturn's icy major moons. This finding and Phoebe's irregular orbital properties suggest to some scientists that the moon did not form in orbit around Saturn but was captured after having formed in a more distant orbit from the Sun, where temperatures and carbon-oxygen chemistry were different.

OBSERVATIONS OF SATURN FROM EARTH

Even under the best telescopic viewing conditions possible from Earth's surface, features on Saturn smaller than a few thousand kilometres cannot be resolved. Thus, the great detail exhibited in the rings and atmosphere was largely unknown prior to spacecraft observations. Even the A ring's Encke gap, reported in 1837 by the German astronomer Johann Franz Encke, was considered dubious for well over a century until it was confirmed in 1978 by the American astronomer Harold Reitsema, who used measurements of an eclipse of the moon Iapetus by the rings to improve on normal Earth-based resolution.

Modern research on Saturn from Earth's vicinity relies on a variety of special telescopic techniques. Infrared spectroscopy of the rings, atmosphere, and moons has yielded considerable information about their composition and thermal balance. Spatial resolution of the

rings and atmospheric structures on the scale of kilometres is obtained by observing light from bright stars that pass behind the planet as seen from Earth. Such an instance occurred in 1989, when both Saturn and Titan occulted the bright star 28 Sagittarii, allowing astronomers to observe ring and atmospheric structures at a level of detail not seen since the Voyager encounters. The 1990 appearance of the Great White Spot in Saturn's atmosphere was successfully observed not only with surface-based telescopes but also with the Hubble Space Telescope above the distorting effect of Earth's atmosphere. In 1995, when Earth passed through the ring plane, the edge-on viewing geometry permitted a direct determination of the ring thickness and a precise measurement of the rate of precession of Saturn's rotational axis.

SPACECRAFT EXPLORATION

The first spacecraft to visit Saturn, the U.S. Pioneer 11, was one of a pair of probes launched in the early 1970s to Jupiter. Though a retargeting was not part of the original objective, mission scientists took advantage of Pioneer 11's close encounter with Jupiter's gravitational field to alter the spacecraft's trajectory and send it on to a successful flyby of Saturn. In 1979 Pioneer 11 passed through Saturn's ring plane at a distance of only 38,000 km (24,000 miles) from the A ring and flew within 21,000 km (13,000 miles) of its atmosphere.

The twin spacecraft that followed, the U.S. Voyagers 1 and 2, were launched initially toward Jupiter in 1977. They carried much more elaborate imaging equipment and were specifically designed for multiple-planet flybys and for accomplishing specific scientific objectives at each destination. Like Pioneer 11, Voyagers 1 and 2 used Jupiter's mass in gravity-assist maneuvers to redirect their trajectories to Saturn, which they encountered in 1980 and '81, respectively. Together the two spacecraft returned tens of thousands of images of Saturn and its rings and moons.

The Cassini-Huygens spacecraft was launched in 1997 as a joint project of the space agencies of the United States, Europe, and Italy. It followed a complicated trajectory involving gravity-assist flybys of Venus (twice), Earth, and Jupiter that brought it to the Saturnian system in mid-2004. Weighing almost six metric tons when loaded with propellants, the interplanetary craft was one of the largest, most expensive, and most complex built to that time. It comprised a Saturn orbiter, Cassini, designed to carry out studies of the planet, rings, and moons for several years, and a probe, Huygens, that descended by parachute through Titan's atmosphere to a solid-surface landing in early 2005. For about three hours during its descent and from the surface, Huygens transmitted measurements and images to Cassini, which relayed them to scientists on Earth.

CHAPTER 5

URANUS

Beyond Saturn is Uranus, the seventh planet in distance from the Sun and the least massive of the solar system's four giant, or Jovian, planets, which also include Jupiter, Saturn, and Neptune. At its brightest, Uranus is just visible to the unaided eye as a blue-green point of light. It is designated by the symbol ♅

Uranus is named for the personification of heaven and the son and husband of Gaea in Greek mythology. It was discovered in 1781 with the aid of a telescope, the first planet to be found that had not been recognized in prehistoric times. Uranus actually had been seen through the telescope several times over the previous century but dismissed as another star. Its mean distance from the Sun is nearly 2.9 billion km (1.8 billion miles), more than 19 times as far as is Earth, and it never approaches Earth more closely than about 2.7 billion km (1.7 billion miles). Its relatively low density (only about 1.3 times that of water) and large size (four times the radius of Earth) indicate that, like the other giant planets, Uranus is composed primarily of hydrogen, helium, water, and other volatile compounds; also like its kin, Uranus has no solid surface. Methane in the Uranian atmosphere absorbs the red wavelengths of sunlight, giving the planet its blue-green colour.

Most of the planets rotate on an axis that is more or less perpendicular to the plane of their respective orbits around

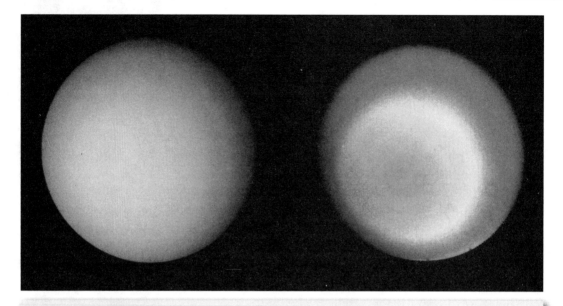

Two views of the southern hemisphere of Uranus, produced from images obtained by Voyager 2 on Jan. 17, 1986. Uranus shows the banded cloud structure common to the four giant planets (right). Small ring-shaped features in the right image are artifacts arising from dust in the spacecraft's camera. Jet Propulsion Laboratory/NASA

the Sun. But Uranus's axis lies almost parallel to its orbital plane, which means that the planet spins nearly on its side, its poles taking turns pointing toward the Sun as the planet travels in its orbit. In addition, the axis of the planet's magnetic field is substantially tipped relative to the rotation axis and offset from the planet's centre. Uranus has more than two dozen moons, five of which are relatively large, and a system of narrow rings.

Uranus has been visited by a spacecraft only once—by the U.S. Voyager 2 probe in 1986. Before then, astronomers had known little about the planet, since its distance from Earth makes the study of its

visible surface difficult even with the most powerful telescopes available. Earth-based attempts to measure a property as basic as the planetary rotation period had produced widely differing values, ranging from 24 to 13 hours, until Voyager 2 finally established a 17.24-hour rotation period for the Uranian interior. Since Voyager's encounter, advances in Earth-based observational technology have added to knowledge of the Uranian system.

BASIC ASTRONOMICAL DATA

At Uranus's distance from the Sun, the planet takes slightly more than 84 Earth years, essentially an entire human life span, to complete one orbit. The eccentricity of its orbit is low—that is, its orbit deviates little from a perfect circle—and the inclination of the orbit to the ecliptic—the plane of Earth's orbit and nearly the plane of the solar system in general—is less than 1°. Low orbital eccentricity and inclination are characteristic of the planets of the solar system, with the notable exceptions of Mercury and Pluto. Scientists believe that collisions and gaseous drag removed energy from the orbits while the planets were forming and so reduced the eccentricities and inclinations to their present values. Thus, Uranus formed with the other planets soon after the birth of the Sun nearly 4.6 billion years ago.

Uranus and its neighbour Neptune, the next planet outward from the Sun, are nearly twins in size. Measured at the level of the atmosphere at which the pressure is one bar (equivalent to Earth's sea-level pressure), Uranus's equatorial radius of 25,559 km (15,882 miles) is 3.2 percent greater than that of Neptune. But Uranus has only 85 percent the mass of Neptune and thus is significantly less dense. The difference in their bulk densities—1.285 and 1.64 grams per cubic cm, respectively—reveals a fundamental difference in composition and internal structure. Although Uranus and Neptune are significantly larger than the terrestrial planets, their radii are less than half those of the largest planets, Jupiter and Saturn.

Because Uranus's spin axis is not perfectly parallel to the ecliptic, one of its poles is directed above the ecliptic and the other below it. (The terms *above* and *below* refer to the same sides of the ecliptic as Earth's North and South poles, respectively.) According to international convention, the north pole of a planet is defined as the pole that is above the ecliptic regardless of the direction in which the planet is spinning. In terms of this definition, Uranus spins clockwise, or in a retrograde fashion, about its north pole, which is opposite to the prograde spin of Earth and most of the other planets. When Voyager 2 flew by Uranus in 1986, the north pole was in darkness, and the Sun was almost directly overhead at the south pole. In 42 years, or one-half the Uranian year, the Sun will have moved to a position nearly overhead at the north pole. The prevailing theory is that the severe tilt arose during the final stages of planetary accretion when bodies comparable in size to the present planets collided in a series of violent events that knocked Uranus on its side. An alternate theory is that a Mars-sized moon, orbiting Uranus in a direction opposite to the planet's spin, eventually crashed into the planet and knocked it on its side.

Uranus's rotation period of 17.24 hours was inferred when Voyager 2 detected radio wave emissions with that period coming from charged particles trapped in the planet's magnetic field. Subsequent direct measurements of the field showed that it is tilted at an angle of

58.6° relative to the rotation axis and that it turns with the same 17.24-hour period. Because the field is thought to be generated in the electrically conducting interior of the planet, the 17.24-hour period is assumed to be that of the interior. The relatively fast rotation causes an oblateness, or flattening of the planet's poles, such that the polar radius is about 2.3 percent smaller than the equatorial radius. Winds in the atmosphere cause cloud markings on the visible surface to rotate around the planet with periods ranging from 18 hours near the equator to slightly more than 14 hours at higher latitudes.

PLANETARY DATA FOR URANUS	
mean distance from Sun	2,870,990,000 km (19.2 AU)
eccentricity of orbit	0.0461
inclination of orbit to ecliptic	0.774°
Uranian year (sidereal period of revolution)	84.01 Earth years
visual magnitude at mean opposition	5.5
mean synodic period*	369.66 Earth days
mean orbital velocity	6.81 km/s
equatorial radius**	25,559 km
polar radius**	24,973 km
mass	8.684×10^{25} kg
mean density	1.285 g/cm³
gravity**	869 cm/s²
escape velocity**	21.3 km/s
rotation period (magnetic field)	17 hr 14 min (retrograde)
inclination of equator to orbit	97.86°
magnetic field strength at equator	0.23 gauss
tilt angle of magnetic axis	58.6°
offset of magnetic axis	0.31 of Uranus's radius
number of known moons	27
planetary ring system	10 known rings

*Time required for the planet to return to the same position in the sky relative to the Sun as seen from Earth.

**Calculated for the altitude at which 1 bar of atmospheric pressure is exerted.

THE ATMOSPHERE

Molecular hydrogen and atomic helium are the two main constituents of the Uranian atmosphere. Hydrogen is detectable from Earth in the spectrum of sunlight scattered by the planet's clouds. The ratio of helium to hydrogen was determined from the refraction (bending) of Voyager 2's radio signal by the atmosphere as the spacecraft passed behind the planet. Helium was found to make up 15 percent of the total number of hydrogen molecules and helium atoms, a proportion that corresponds to 26 percent by mass of the total amount of hydrogen and helium. These values are consistent with the values inferred for the Sun and are greater than those inferred for the atmospheres of Jupiter and Saturn. It is assumed that all four giant planets received the same proportions of hydrogen and helium as the Sun during their formation but that, in the cases of Jupiter and Saturn, some of the helium has settled toward their centres. The processes that cause this settling have been shown in theoretical studies not to operate on less-massive planets like Uranus and Neptune.

Methane absorbs strongly at near-infrared wavelengths, and it dominates that part of the spectrum of reflected light even though the number of methane molecules is only 2.3 percent of the total. Astronomers determined this estimate of methane abundance using Voyager 2's radio signals that probed to atmospheric depths at which the methane-to-hydrogen ratio is likely to be constant. If this constancy is characteristic of the planet as a whole, the carbon-to-hydrogen ratio of Uranus is 24 times that of the Sun. (Methane [CH_4] comprises one atom of carbon and four of hydrogen.) The large value of the carbon-to-hydrogen ratio suggests that the elements oxygen, nitrogen, and sulfur also are enriched relative to solar values. These elements, however, are tied up in molecules of water, ammonia, and hydrogen sulfide, which are thought to condense into clouds at levels below the part of the atmosphere that can be seen. Earth-based radio observations reveal a curious depletion of ammonia molecules in the atmosphere, perhaps because hydrogen sulfide is more abundant and combines with all the ammonia to form cloud particles of ammonium hydrosulfide. Voyager's ultraviolet spectrometer detected traces of acetylene and ethane in very low abundances. These gases are by-products of methane, which dissociates when ultraviolet light from the Sun strikes the upper atmosphere.

On average, Uranus radiates the same amount of energy as an ideal, perfectly absorbing surface at a temperature of 59.1 kelvins (K; -353 °F, -214 °C). This radiation temperature is equal to the physical temperature of the atmosphere at a pressure of about 0.4 bar. Temperature decreases with decreasing pressure—i.e., with increasing altitude—throughout this portion of the atmosphere to the 70-millibar level, where it is about 52 K (-366 °F,

-221 °C), the coldest temperature in Uranus's atmosphere. From this point upward the temperature rises again until it reaches 750 K (890 °F, 480 °C) in the exosphere—the top of the atmosphere at a distance of 1.1 Uranian radii from the planetary centre—where pressures are on the order of a trillionth of a bar. The cause of the high exospheric temperatures remains to be determined, but it may involve a combination of ultraviolet absorption, electron bombardment, and inability of the gas to radiate at infrared wavelengths.

Voyager 2 measured the horizontal variation of atmospheric temperature in two broad altitude ranges, at 60–200 millibars and 500–1,000 millibars. In both ranges the pole-to-pole variation was found to be small—less than 1 K (1.8 °F, 1 °C)—despite the fact that one pole was facing the Sun at the time of the flyby. This lack of global variation is thought to be related to the efficient horizontal heat transfer and the large heat-storage capacity of the deep atmosphere.

Although Uranus appears nearly featureless to the eye, extreme-contrast-enhanced images from Voyager 2 and more-recent observations from Earth reveal faint cloud bands oriented parallel to the equator. The same kind of zonal flow dominates the atmospheric circulation of Jupiter and Saturn, whose rotational axes are much less tilted than Uranus's axis and thus whose seasonal changes in solar illumination are much different. Apparently, rotation of the planet itself and not the distribution of absorbed sunlight controls the cloud patterns. Rotation manifests itself through the Coriolis force, an effect that causes material moving on a rotating planet to appear to be deflected to either the right or the left depending on the hemisphere—northern or southern—being considered. In terms of cloud patterns, therefore, Uranus looks like a tipped-over version of Jupiter or Saturn.

The wind is the motion of the atmosphere relative to the rotating planet. At high latitudes on Uranus, this relative motion is in the direction of the planet's rotation. At equatorial latitudes the relative motion is in the opposite direction. Uranus is like Earth in this regard. On Earth these directions are called east and west, respectively, but the more general terms are prograde and retrograde. The winds that exist on Uranus are several times stronger than on Earth. The wind is 720 km (450 miles) per hour prograde at a latitude of 55° S and 400 km (250 miles) per hour retrograde at the equator. Neptune's equatorial winds are also retrograde, but those of Jupiter and Saturn are prograde. No satisfactory theory exists to explain these differences.

Uranus has no large spots like Jupiter's long-lived Great Red Spot or the Great Dark Spot observed on Neptune by Voyager 2 in 1989. Voyager's measurements of the wind profile on Uranus came from just four small spots whose visual contrast was no more than 2 or 3 percent relative to the surrounding atmosphere. Because the giant planets have no solid surfaces, the spots must represent atmospheric storms. For reasons that are not clear, Uranus seems to have the smallest number of storms of any of the giant planets.

THE MAGNETIC FIELD
AND MAGNETOSPHERE

Like the other giant planets, Uranus has a magnetic field that is generated by convection currents in an electrically conducting interior. The dipole field, which resembles the field of a small but intense bar magnet, has a strength of 0.23 gauss in its equatorial plane at a distance of one Uranian equatorial radius from the centre. The polarity of the field is oriented in the same direction as Earth's present field—i.e., an ordinary magnetic compass would point toward the counterclockwise rotation pole, which for Earth is the North Pole. The dipole axis is tilted with respect to the planet's rotation axis at an angle of 58.6°, which greatly exceeds that for Earth (11.5°), Jupiter (9.6°), and Saturn (less than 1°). The magnetic centre is displaced from the planet's centre by 31 percent of Uranus's radius (nearly 8,000 km [5,000 miles]). The displacement is mainly along the rotation axis toward the north pole.

The magnetic field is unusual not only because of its tilt and offset but also because of the relatively large size of its small-scale components. This "roughness" suggests that the field is generated at shallow depths within the planet, because small-scale components of a field die out rapidly above the electrically conducting region. Thus, the interior of

Uranus must become electrically conducting closer to the surface than on Jupiter, Saturn, and Earth. This inference is consistent with what is known about Uranus's internal composition, which must be mostly water, methane, and ammonia in order to match the average density of the planet. Water and ammonia dissociate into positive and negative ions—which are electrically conducting—at relatively low pressures and temperatures. As on Jupiter, Saturn, and Earth, the field is generated by fluid motions in the conducting layers, but on Uranus the layers are not as deep.

As is the case for the other planets that have magnetic fields, Uranus's field repels the solar wind, the stream of charged particles flowing outward from the Sun. The planetary magnetosphere—a huge region of space containing charged particles that are bound to the magnetic field—surrounds the planet and extends downwind from it. On the upwind side, facing the Sun, the magnetopause—the boundary between the magnetosphere and the solar wind—is 18 Uranian radii (460,000 km [286,000 miles]) from the centre of the planet.

The particles trapped within the Uranian magnetosphere comprise protons and electrons, which indicate that the planet's upper atmosphere is supplying most of the material. There is no evidence of helium, which might originate with the solar wind, or of heavier ions, which might come from the Uranian moons. Because the largest Uranian moons orbit within the magnetosphere, they absorb some of the trapped particles. The particles behave as if they were attached to the magnetic field lines, so that those lines intersecting a moon in its orbit have fewer trapped particles than neighbouring field lines.

As is the case for Jupiter and Saturn, charged particles from the Uranian magnetosphere impinge on the upper atmosphere and produce auroras. Auroral heating can just barely account for the high temperature of Uranus's exosphere.

THE INTERIOR

Although Uranus has a somewhat lower density than Jupiter, it has a higher proportion of elements heavier than hydrogen and helium. Jupiter's greater mass (by a factor of 22) leads to a greater gravitational force and thus greater self-compression than for Uranus. This additional compression adds to Jupiter's bulk density. If Uranus were made of the same proportions of material as Jupiter, it would be considerably less dense than it is.

Different models proposed for the Uranian interior assume different ratios of rock (silicates and metals), ices (water, methane, and ammonia), and gases (essentially hydrogen and helium). At the high temperatures and pressures within the giant planets, the "ices" will in fact be liquids. To be consistent with the bulk density data, the mass of rock plus ice must constitute roughly 80 percent of the total mass of Uranus, compared with 10 percent for Jupiter and 2 percent for a mixture of the Sun's composition. In all models Uranus is

a fluid planet, with the gaseous higher atmosphere gradually merging with the liquid interior. Pressure at the centre of the planet is about five megabars.

Scientists have obtained more information about the interior by comparing a given model's response to centrifugal forces, which arise from the planet's rotation, with the response of the actual planet measured by Voyager 2. This response is expressed in terms of the planet's oblateness. By measuring the degree of flattening at the poles and relating it to the speed of rotation, scientists can infer the density distribution inside the planet. For two planets with the same mass and bulk density, the planet with more of its mass concentrated close to the centre would be less flattened by rotation. Before the Voyager mission, it was difficult to choose between models in which the three components—rock, ice, and gas—were separated into distinct layers and those in which the ice and gas were well mixed. From the combination of large oblateness and comparatively slow rotation for Uranus measured by Voyager, it appears that the ice and gas are well mixed and a rocky core is small or nonexistent.

The fact that the mixed model of Uranus fits observations better than the layered model may reveal information on the planet's formation. Rather than indicating a process in which Uranus formed from a rock-ice core that subsequently captured gas from the solar nebula, the mixed model seems to favour one in which large, solid objects were continually captured into a giant planet that already contained major amounts of the gaseous component.

Unlike the other three giant planets, Uranus does not radiate a substantial amount of excess internal heat. The total heat output is determined from the planet's measured infrared emissions, while the heat input is determined from the fraction of incident sunlight that is absorbed—i.e., not scattered back into space. For Uranus the ratio of the two is between 1.00 and 1.14, which means that its internal energy source supplies, at most, 14 percent more energy than the planet receives from the Sun. (The equivalent ratios for the other giant planets are greater than 1.7.) The small terrestrial planets—Mercury, Venus, Earth, and Mars—generate relatively little internal heat; the heat flow from Earth's interior, for example, is only about a ten-thousandth of what it receives from the Sun.

It is not clear why Uranus has such a low internal heat output compared with the other Jovian planets. All the planets should have started warm, since gravitational energy was transformed into heat during planetary accretion. Over the age of the solar system, Earth and the other smaller objects have lost most of their heat of formation. Being massive objects with cold surfaces, however, the giant planets store heat well and radiate poorly. Therefore, they should have retained large fractions of their heat of formation, which should still be escaping today. Chance events (such as collisions with large bodies) experienced by some planets but not others at the time of their formation and the resulting differences in internal structure are one explanation proposed to explain differences among the giant planets such as the anomalous heat output of Uranus.

URANUS'S MOONS AND RINGS

Uranus's 27 known moons are accompanied by at least 10 narrow rings. Each of the countless particles that make up the rings can be considered a tiny moon in its own orbit. In general, the rings are located closest to the planet, some small moons orbit just outside the rings, the largest moons orbit beyond them, and other small moons orbit much farther out. The orbits of the outermost group of moons are eccentric (elongated) and highly inclined to Uranus's equatorial plane. The other moons and the rings are essentially coplanar with the equator.

MOONS

Uranus's five largest moons range from about 240 to 800 km (150 to 500 miles) in radius. All were discovered telescopically from Earth, four of them before the 20th century. Ten small inner moons were found by Voyager 2 in 1985–86. They are estimated to be between about 10 and 80 km (6 and 50 miles) in radius, and they orbit the planet at distances between 49,800 and 86,000 km (31,000 and 53,500 miles). The innermost moon, Cordelia, orbits just inside the outermost rings,

Lambda and Epsilon. An 11th tiny inner moon, Perdita, photographed by Voyager near the orbit of Belinda remained unnoticed in the images until 1999 and was not confirmed until 2003. Two additional inner moons, one near Belinda's orbit, Cupid, and the other near Puck's, Mab, were discovered in observations from Earth in 2003. All 18 of the above are regular, having prograde, low-inclination, and low-eccentricity orbits with respect to the planet.

Nine small outer moons in roughly the same size range as the Voyager finds were discovered from Earth beginning in 1997. These are irregular satellites, having highly elliptical orbits that are inclined at large angles to the planet's equator; all but one also orbit in the retrograde direction. Their mean distances from the planet lie between 4 million and 21 million km (2.5 million and 13 million miles), which is 7–36 times the distance of the outermost known regular moon, Oberon. The irregular moons likely were captured into orbits around Uranus after the planet formed. The regular moons probably formed in their equatorial orbits at the same time that the planet formed.

The four largest moons—Titania, Oberon, Umbriel, and Ariel, in order of decreasing size—have densities of 1.4–1.7 grams per cubic cm. This range is only slightly greater than the density of a hypothetical object that would be obtained by cooling a mixture of solar composition and removing all the gaseous components. The object that remained would be 60 percent ice and

Titania, the largest moon of Uranus, in a composite of images taken by Voyager 2 as it made its closest approach to the Uranian system on Jan. 24, 1986. In addition to many small bright impact craters, there can be seen a large ring-shaped impact basin in the upper right of the moon's disk near the terminator (day-night boundary) and a long, deep fault line extending from near the centre of the moon's disk toward the terminator. Titania's neutral gray colour is representative of the planet's five major moons as a whole. NASA/JPL

40 percent rock. In contrast to these four is Miranda, the fifth largest Uranian moon, but only half the size of Ariel or Umbriel. Like the smaller moons of Saturn, Miranda has a density (1.2 g/cm³ [0.7 oz/in³]) that is slightly below the solar composition value, which indicates a higher ice-to-rock ratio.

Water ice shows up in the surface spectra of the five major moons. Because the reflectivities of the moons are lower than that of pure ice, the obvious implication is that their surfaces consist of dirty water ice. The composition of the dark component is unknown, but, at wavelengths other than those of water, the surface spectra seem evenly dark, indicating a neutral gray colour and thus ruling out material such as iron-bearing minerals, which would impart a reddish tinge. One possibility is carbon, originating from inside the moons in question or from Uranus's rings, which could have released methane gas that later decomposed to produce solid carbon when bombarded by charged particles and solar ultraviolet light.

Two observations indicate that the surfaces of the major moons are porous and highly insulating. First, the reflectivity increases dramatically at opposition, when the observer is within 2° of the Sun as viewed from the planet. Such so-called opposition surges are characteristic of loosely stacked particles that shadow each other except in this special geometry, in which the observer is in line with the source of illumination and can see the light reflecting directly back out of the spaces between the particles. Second, changes in surface temperatures seem to follow the Sun during the day with no appreciable lag due to thermal inertia. Again, such behaviour is characteristic of porous surfaces that block the inward flow of heat.

Virtually all of what is known about the distinctive surface characters of Uranus's major moons comes from Voyager 2, which sped past them in a few hours and imaged only their sunlit southern hemispheres. Oberon and particularly Umbriel display dense populations of large impact craters, similar to the highlands of Earth's Moon and many of the oldest terrains in the solar system. In fact, Umbriel is also the most heavily and uniformly cratered of the major Uranian moons, an indicator that its surface experienced little reworking by tectonic activity in the past. In contrast, Titania and Ariel have far fewer large craters (in the range of 50–100 km [30–60 miles] in diameter) but have comparable numbers in the smaller size ranges. The large craters are thought to date back to the early history of the solar system more than four billion years ago, when large planetesimals still existed, whereas the smaller ones are thought to reflect more recent events including, perhaps, the impacts of objects knocked loose from other moons in the Uranian system. Thus, the surfaces of Titania and Ariel must be younger than those of Oberon and Umbriel. These differences, which do not follow an obvious pattern with respect to either the moons' distances from Uranus or their sizes, are largely unexplained.

Volcanic deposits observed on the major moons are generally flat, with lobed edges and surface ripples characteristic of fluid flow. Some of the deposits are bright, while some are dark. Because of the very low temperatures expected for the outer solar system, the erupting fluid was probably a water-ammonia mixture with a melting point well below that of pure water ice. Brightness differences could indicate differences in the composition of the erupting fluid or in the history of the surface. Riftlike canyons seen on the major moons imply extension and fracturing of their surfaces.

MIRANDA

Miranda is the innermost and smallest of the five major moons of Uranus and, topographically, the most varied of the group. It was discovered in telescopic photographs of the Uranian system in 1948 by the Dutch American astronomer Gerard P. Kuiper, who named it after a character in William Shakespeare's play *The Tempest*. Miranda revolves around Uranus once every 1.413 days in a nearly circular orbit at a mean distance of 129,800 km (80,654 miles) from the centre of the planet. Slightly nonspherical in shape, it has a mean diameter of about 470 km (290 miles).

Because of the trajectory that the U.S. Voyager 2 spacecraft followed in its flyby of Uranus in 1986 (in order for it to be redirected to Neptune), the probe had the opportunity to study Miranda more closely than any other Uranian moon. Photographs from Voyager revealed that Miranda's surface is a bizarre patchwork of winding valleys, parallel grooves, fault scarps, and cratered highlands. The basic surface is heavily cratered, but it is interrupted by three lightly cratered regions that astronomers have named coronae

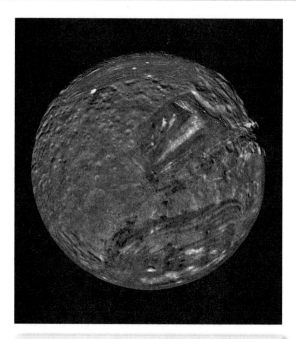

Miranda in a mosaic of images obtained by Voyager 2 on Jan. 24, 1986. In this south polar view, old, heavily cratered terrain is interspersed with large sharp-edged patches of young, lightly cratered regions characterized by parallel bright and dark bands, scarps, and ridges. The patches, called coronae, appear to be unique to Miranda among all the bodies of the solar system. U.S. Geological Survey/NASA/JPL

(but which are not geologically related to surface features of Venus of the same name). These are fairly squarish, roughly the length of one Miranda radius on a side, and are surrounded by parallel bands that curve around the edges. The boundaries where the coronae meet the cratered terrain are sharp. The coronae are unlike any features found elsewhere in the solar system. Whether they reflect a heterogeneous origin for the moon, a giant impact that shattered it, or a unique pattern of eruptions from its interior is not known.

Miranda's canyons are the most spectacular, some being as much as 80 km (50 miles) wide and 15 km (9 miles) deep. The rupturing of the crust was caused by an expansion in the volume of the moons, inferred to be in the range of 1–2 percent, except for Miranda, for which the expansion is thought to be 6 percent. Miranda's expansion could be explained if all the water making up its interior was once liquid and then froze after the crust had formed. Freezing under low pressure, the water would have expanded and thereby stretched and shattered the surface. The presence of liquid water on the surface at any stage of the moon's history seems unlikely.

Miranda's topographic variation was a surprise because the moon was thought too small—being only a third the diameter of its much less topographically diverse siblings Titania and Oberon—to have experienced the extensive tectonic activity needed to fashion this varied terrain. It remains to be determined whether this activity resulted from extrinsic forces, such as one or more shattering collisions in the moon's early history, or intrinsic ones, such as eruptions from its interior caused by past tidal heating (as now occurs on Jupiter's volcanically active moon Io).

ARIEL

The second nearest of the five major moons of Uranus is Ariel. It was discovered in 1851 by William Lassell, an English astronomer, and bears the name of characters in Alexander Pope's poem *The Rape of the Lock* and William Shakespeare's play *The Tempest.*

Ariel revolves around Uranus at a mean distance of 191,240 km (118,830 miles) from the centre of the planet, taking 2.52 days to complete one orbit. Like the other large Uranian moons, Ariel rotates synchronously with its orbital

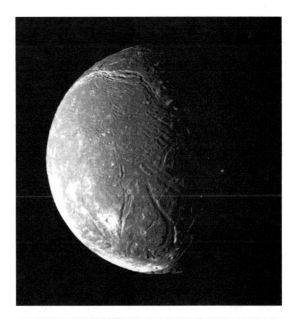

Ariel, one of the five major moons of Uranus, in a mosaic image made from the most detailed photographs taken by Voyager 2 on Jan. 24, 1986, during its flight through the Uranian system. Jet Propulsion Laboratory

period, keeping the same face toward the planet and the same face forward in its orbit. The moon's mean diameter is about 1,160 km (720 miles). Its density is about 1.67 g/cm³ (0.97 oz/in³).

Photographs taken by the U.S. Voyager 2 spacecraft during its flyby of the Uranian system in 1986 show that Ariel's surface is crisscrossed with scarps and long valley-like formations. Some of the latter are partially filled with materials that may have upwelled from the moon's interior as a result of tectonic activity in the past. In a few cases, ice appears to have spread out from the valleys across broad plains, much like glacier flows on Earth. These features and the paucity of large impact craters suggest that Ariel has the youngest surface of all of Uranus's major moons.

Umbriel, the third nearest and darkest of Uranus's five major moons, in an image made by Voyager 2 on Jan. 24, 1986. NASA/JPL

UMBRIEL

Umbriel is the third nearest of the five major moons of Uranus and the one having the darkest and oldest surface of the group. Its discovery is attributed to the English astronomer William Lassell in 1851, although the English astronomer William Herschel, who discovered Uranus and its two largest moons, may have glimpsed it more than a half century earlier. Umbriel was named by Herschel's son, John, for a character in Alexander Pope's poem *The Rape of the Lock*.

It orbits Uranus once every 4.144 days at a mean distance of 265,970 km (165,270 miles). Umbriel has a diameter of 1,170 km (727 miles) and a density of about 1.4 g/cm³ (0.81 oz/in³).

The only images of Umbriel's surface have come from the U.S. Voyager 2 spacecraft's flyby encounter with the Uranian system in 1986. These show that Umbriel is distinct from the other major moons of Uranus in having no evidence of past tectonic activity, as shown by the presence of many large impact craters. The most notable feature of the hemisphere imaged by Voyager is a bright ring, dubbed Wunda, that appears to line the floor of a crater 40 km (25 miles) across.

TITANIA

Titania is the largest of the moons of Uranus. It was first detected telescopically in 1787 by William Herschel, who had discovered Uranus itself six years earlier. Titania was named by William's son, John Herschel, for a character in William Shakespeare's play *A Midsummer Night's Dream.*

Titania orbits at a mean distance of 435,840 km (270,820 miles) from the centre of Uranus, which makes it the second outermost of the planet's major moons. Its orbital period is 8.706 days, as is its rotational period. It is thus in synchronous rotation, keeping the same face toward the planet and the same face forward in its orbit. Its diameter is 1,578 km (980 miles), and it has a density of about 1.71 g/cm³ (1 oz/in³).

Titania was observed close up on only one occasion, when the U.S. Voyager 2 spacecraft swiftly flew through the Uranian system in 1986. Spacecraft images show its surface to have many bright impact craters up to 50 km (30 miles) in diameter, but few large ones, along with trenches and a deep fault line extending roughly 1,600 km (1,000 miles). These and other related features strongly suggest the occurrence of internal geologic processes in the moon's ancient past.

OBERON

The outermost of the five major moons of Uranus and the second largest is Oberon, which was discovered in 1787 by William Herschel. As with Titania, it was also named by William's son for a character in William Shakespeare's play *A Midsummer Night's Dream.*

The mean distance of Oberon from the centre of Uranus is about 582,600 km (362,000 miles), and its orbital period is 13.46 days. Like all of Uranus's large moons, Oberon rotates synchronously with its orbital period, keeping the same hemisphere toward the planet and the same hemisphere forward in its orbit. The moon has a diameter of 1,522 km (946 miles) and a density of 1.63 g/cm³ (0.94 oz/in³).

Photographic images transmitted by the U.S. Voyager 2 spacecraft when it flew past the Uranian system in 1986 revealed that Oberon's surface is old and that a few of the numerous bright craters appear to have been flooded by some kind of dark material that upwelled from the moon's interior.

THE RING SYSTEM

The rings of Uranus were the first to be found around a planet other than Saturn. The American astronomer James L. Elliot and colleagues discovered the ring system from Earth in 1977, nine years before the Voyager 2 encounter, during a stellar occultation by Uranus—i.e., when the planet passed between a star and Earth, temporarily blocking the star's light. Unexpectedly, they observed the star to dim briefly five times at some considerable distance above Uranus's atmosphere both before and after the planet occulted the star. The dips in brightness indicated that the planet was encircled by five narrow rings. Later Earth-based observations revealed four additional rings. Voyager 2 detected a 10th ring and found indications of others. Outward from Uranus, the 10 are named 6, 5, 4, Alpha, Beta, Eta,

Gamma, Delta, Lambda, and Epsilon. The cumbersome nomenclature arose as the new rings were found in places that did not fit the original nomenclature.

The rings are narrow and fairly opaque. Observed widths are the product (more precisely, the integral) of the radial distance and the fraction of starlight blocked. The fact that the equivalent widths are generally less than the observed widths indicates that the rings are not completely opaque. Combining the brightness of the rings observed in Voyager images with the equivalent widths from occultations shows that the ring particles reflect less than 5 percent of the incident sunlight. Their nearly flat reflectance spectrum means that the particles are basically gray in colour. Ordinary soot, which is mostly carbon, is the closest terrestrial analogue. It is not known whether the carbon comes from darkening of methane by particle bombardment or is intrinsic to the ring particles.

The scattering effects on Voyager's radio signal propagated through the rings to Earth revealed that the rings consist of mostly large particles, objects greater than 140 cm (4.6 feet) across. Scattering of sunlight when Voyager was on the far side of the rings and aiming its camera back toward the Sun also revealed small dust particles in the micrometre size range. Only a small amount of dust was found in the main rings. Most of the microscopic particles were instead distributed in the spaces between the main rings, which suggests that the rings are losing mass as a result of collisions. The

lifetime of the dust in orbit around Uranus is limited by drag exerted by the planet's extended atmosphere and by the radiation pressure of sunlight; the dust particles are driven to lower orbits and eventually fall into the Uranian atmosphere. The calculated orbital lifetimes are so short—1,000 years—that the dust must be rapidly and continually created. Uranus's atmospheric drag appears to be so large that the present rings themselves may be short-lived. If so, the rings did not form with Uranus, and their origin and history are unknown.

Collisions between the tightly packed ring particles would naturally lead to an increase in the radial width of the rings. As with the rings of Saturn, moons more massive than the rings can halt this spreading through shepherding. Voyager 2 found that the innermost two moons, Cordelia and Ophelia, orbit on either side of the Epsilon ring at exactly the right radii required for shepherding. Shepherds for the other rings were not observed, perhaps because the moons are too small to be seen in the Voyager images. Small moons may also be reservoirs that supply the dust leaving the ring system.

THE DISCOVERY OF URANUS

Uranus was discovered by the English astronomer William Herschel, who had undertaken a survey of all stars down to eighth magnitude—i.e., those about five times fainter than stars visible to the naked eye. On March 13, 1781, he found "a curious either nebulous star or perhaps a comet," distinguished from the stars by its clearly visible disk. Its lack of any trace of a tail and its slow motion led within months to the conclusion that the object was a planet, rather than a comet or an asteroid, moving in a nearly circular orbit well beyond Saturn. Observations of the new planet during the next 65 years revealed discrepancies in its orbital motion—evidence of gravitational forces on Uranus that were not due to any other known planet, which ultimately led to the discovery of yet more distant Neptune in 1846.

Herschel suggested naming his new discovery Georgium Sidus (Latin: "Georgian Planet") after his patron, King George III of England, while the French favoured the name Herschel. The planet was eventually named according to the tradition of naming planets for the gods of Greek and Roman mythology; Uranus is the father of Saturn, who is in turn the father of Jupiter.

SPACECRAFT EXPLORATION

Although the missions of the twin Voyager 1 and 2 spacecraft originally called for flybys of only Jupiter and Saturn, the timing of Voyager 2's launch allowed for a change to its trajectory so that it could be retargeted to Uranus and Neptune for an extended mission, which ultimately was carried out. After more than eight years in space, Voyager 2 sped through the Uranian system on Jan. 24, 1986. Its instruments provided an accurate determination of the masses and radii of the planet and its major moons, detected Uranus's magnetic field and determined its strength and orientation, and measured the planet's interior rotation rate. Images of the Uranian system, which totaled more than 8,000, revealed for the first time the weather patterns in the planet's atmosphere and the surface characteristics of the moons. In addition to Voyager's discoveries of new moons, a ring, and dust bands between the rings, it provided details of ring structure at scales not achievable from Earth.

Yet, despite these achievements, Voyager left many unanswered questions that only another spacecraft mission or a major advance in Earth-based observational technology would be able to address. As of 2009, no missions to Uranus are planned.

CHAPTER 6

NEPTUNE

The third most massive planet of the solar system and the eighth planet from the Sun is Neptune. Because of its great distance from Earth, it cannot be seen with the unaided eye. With a small telescope, it appears as a tiny, faint blue-green disk. It is designated by the symbol ♆.

Neptune is named for the Roman god of the sea, who is identified with the Greek deity Poseidon, a son of the Titan Cronus (the Roman god Saturn) and a brother of Zeus (the Roman god Jupiter). It is the second planet to have been found by means of a telescope. Its discovery in 1846 was a remarkable combination of the application of solid Newtonian physics and a belief in a numerological scheme that later proved to be scientifically unfounded. Neptune's orbit is almost perfectly circular; as a result, its distance from the Sun varies comparatively little over its nearly 164-year period of revolution. Although the dwarf planet Pluto's mean distance from the Sun is greater than Neptune's, its orbit is so eccentric (elongated) that for about 20 years of each revolution Pluto is actually nearer the Sun than is Neptune.

Neptune is almost four times the size of Earth but slightly smaller than Uranus, which makes it the smallest in diameter of the four giant, or Jovian, planets. It is more massive than Uranus, however, having a density roughly 25 percent higher. Like the other giant planets, Neptune consists primarily of hydrogen, helium, water, and other volatile compounds, along with rocky material, and it has no solid surface. It receives less than half as much sunlight as Uranus, but heat escaping from its interior makes Neptune slightly warmer than Uranus. The heat liberated may also be responsible for the storminess in Neptune's atmosphere, which exhibits the fastest winds seen on any planet in the solar system.

Neptune has 13 moons (natural satellites), only two of which had been discovered before the Voyager 2 spacecraft flew past the planet in 1989, and a system of rings, which had been unconfirmed until Voyager's visit. As is the case for Uranus, most of what astronomers know about Neptune, including its rotation period and the existence and characteristics of its magnetic field and magnetosphere, was learned from a

PLANETARY DATA FOR NEPTUNE	
mean distance from Sun	4,498,250,000 km (30.1 AU)
eccentricity of orbit	0.0086
inclination of orbit to ecliptic	1.77°
Neptunian year (sidereal period of revolution)	163.72 Earth years
visual magnitude at mean opposition	7.8
mean synodic period*	367.49 Earth days
mean orbital velocity	5.48 km/sec
equatorial radius**	24,764 km
polar radius**	24,340 km
mass	1.02×10^{26} kg
mean density	1.64 g/cm³
gravity**	1,115 cm/sec²
escape velocity**	23.5 km/sec
rotation period (magnetic field)	16 hr 7 min
inclination of equator to orbit	29.6°
magnetic field strength at equator (mean)	0.14 gauss
tilt angle of magnetic axis	46.8°
offset of magnetic axis	0.55 of Neptune's radius
number of known moons	13
planetary ring system	6 rings, one containing several arcs

*Time required for the planet to return to the same position in the sky relative to the Sun as seen from Earth.

**Calculated for the altitude at which one bar of atmospheric pressure is exerted.

single spacecraft encounter. In recent years new knowledge of the Neptunian system has come as a result of advances in Earth-based observational technology.

BASIC ASTRONOMICAL DATA

Neptune's orbital period of 163.72 years means that by mid-2010 it will have circled the Sun only once since its discovery in September 1846. Consequently, astronomers expect to be making refinements in calculating its orbital size and shape well into the 21st century. Voyager 2's encounter with Neptune resulted in a small upward revision of the planet's estimated mean distance from the Sun, which is now thought to be 4,498,250,000 km (2,795,083,000 miles). Its orbital eccentricity of 0.0086 is the second lowest of the planets; only Venus's orbit is more circular. Neptune's rotation axis is tipped toward its orbital plane by 29.6°, somewhat larger than Earth's 23.4°. As on Earth, the axial tilt gives rise to seasons on Neptune, and, because of the circularity of Neptune's orbit, the seasons (and the seasons of its moons) are of nearly equal length, each nearly 41 years in duration.

Neptune's rotation period was established when Voyager 2 detected radio bursts associated with the planet's magnetic field and having a period of 16.11 hours. This value was inferred to be the rotation period at the level of the planet's interior where the magnetic field is rooted. Neptune's equatorial diameter measured at the one-bar pressure level (the pressure of Earth's atmosphere at sea level) is 49,528 km (30,775 miles), which is only about 3 percent shy of the diameter of Uranus. Because of a flattening of the poles caused by the planet's relatively fast rotation, Neptune's polar diameter is 848 km (527 miles) less than its diameter at the equator. Although Neptune occupies a little less volume than Uranus, owing to its greater density—1.64 grams per cubic cm, compared with about 1.3 for Uranus—Neptune's mass is 18 percent higher.

THE ATMOSPHERE

Like the other giant planets, Neptune's outer atmosphere is composed predominantly of hydrogen and helium. Near the one-bar pressure level in the atmosphere, these two gases contribute nearly 98 percent of the atmospheric molecules. Most of the remaining molecules consist of methane gas. Hydrogen and helium are nearly invisible, but methane strongly absorbs red light. Sunlight reflected off Neptune's clouds therefore exits the atmosphere with most of its red colours removed and so has a bluish cast. Although Uranus's blue-green colour is also the result of atmospheric methane, Neptune's colour is a more vivid, brighter blue, presumably an effect of the presence of an unidentified atmospheric gas.

The temperature of Neptune's atmosphere varies with altitude. A minimum temperature of about 50 kelvins (K; –370 °F, –223 °C) occurs at a pressure near 0.1 bar. The temperature increases with decreasing pressure—i.e., with increasing

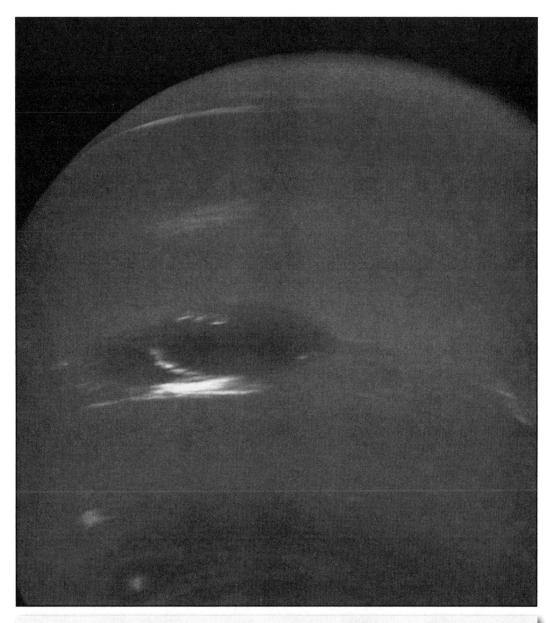

Clouds in Neptune's atmosphere, photographed by Voyager 2 in August 1989. Accompanying the Great Dark Spot (centre left) are bright, wispy clouds thought to comprise methane ice crystals. At higher southern latitudes lies a smaller, eye-shaped dark spot with a light core (bottom left). Just above that spot is a bright cloud dubbed Scooter. Each of these cloud features was seen to travel eastward but at a different rate, the Great Dark Spot moving the slowest. *JPL/NASA*

altitude—to about 750 K (890 °F, 480 °C) at a pressure of a hundred-billionth of a bar, which corresponds to an altitude of 2,000 km (1,240 miles) as measured from the one-bar level, and it remains uniform above that altitude. Temperatures also increase with increasing depth below the 0.1-bar level to about 7,000 K (12,000 °F, 6,700 °C) near the centre of the planet, where the pressure may reach five megabars. The total amount of energy radiated by Neptune is equivalent to that of a nonreflecting sphere of the same size with a uniform temperature of 59.3 K (-353 °F, -214 °C). This temperature is called the effective temperature.

Neptune is more than 50 percent farther from the Sun than is Uranus and so receives less than half the sunlight of the latter. Yet the effective temperatures of these two giant planets are nearly equal. Uranus and Neptune each reflect— and hence also must absorb—about the same proportion of the sunlight that reaches them. As a result of processes not fully understood, Neptune emits more than twice the energy that it receives from the Sun. The added energy is generated in Neptune's interior. Uranus, by contrast, has little energy escaping from its interior.

At the one-bar reference level, the mean temperature of Neptune's atmosphere is roughly 74 K (-326 °F, -199 °C). Atmospheric temperatures are a few degrees warmer at the equator and poles than at mid-latitudes. This is probably an indication that air currents are rising near mid-latitudes and descending near the equator and poles. This vertical flow may extend to great heights within the atmosphere. A more vertically confined horizontal wind system exists near the cloud tops. As with the other giant planets, Neptune's atmospheric circulation exhibits zonal flow—the winds are constrained to blow generally along lines of constant latitude (east-west) and are relatively invariable with time. Winds on Neptune range from about 100 metres per second (360 km [220 miles] per hour) in an easterly direction (prograde, or in the same direction as the planet's spin) near latitude 70° S to as high as 700 metres per second (2,520 km [1,570 miles] per hour) in a westerly direction (retrograde, or opposite to the planet's spin) near latitude 20° S.

The high winds and relatively large amount of escaping internal heat may be responsible for the turbulence observed in Neptune's visible atmosphere by Voyager 2. Two large dark ovals were clearly visible in Voyager images of Neptune's southern hemisphere. The largest, called the Great Dark Spot because of its similarity in latitude and shape to Jupiter's Great Red Spot, is comparable to Earth in size. It was near this storm system that the highest wind speeds were measured. Jupiter's Great Red Spot has been seen in Earth-based telescopes for more than 300 years. Neptune's Great Dark Spot was expected by analogy to be similarly long-lived. Scientists thus were surprised by its absence from images of Neptune obtained by the Earth-orbiting Hubble Space Telescope in 1991, only two years after the Voyager flyby, just as they were by the appearance of a comparable dark spot in Neptune's northern hemisphere in 1994. Bright cloud features seen in the Voyager images are even more transient. They may be methane ice clouds created by strong upward motions of pockets of methane gas to higher, colder altitudes in the atmosphere, where the gas then condenses to ice crystals.

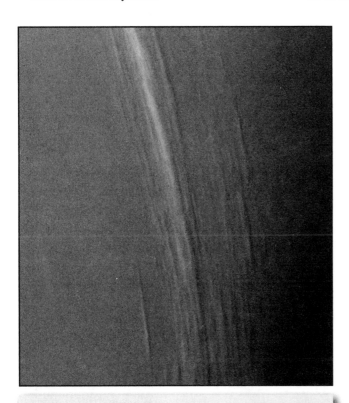

Clouds in Neptune's northern hemisphere, as observed by the Voyager 2 spacecraft in August 1989. NASA/JPL/Caltech

Neptune is the only giant planet to display cloud shadows cast by high dispersed clouds on a lower, more continuous cloud bank. The higher clouds, probably composed of methane ice crystals, are generally located 50–100 km (30–60 miles) above the main cloud deck, which may be composed of ice crystals of ammonia or hydrogen sulfide. Like the other giant planets, Neptune is thought to possess cloud layers at deeper levels, below those visible to Voyager's remote sensing instruments, but their composition is dependent on the relative amounts of gases composed of compounds of sulfur and nitrogen. Clouds of water ice are expected to occur at depths within Neptune's atmosphere where the pressure exceeds 100 bars.

THE MAGNETIC FIELD AND MAGNETOSPHERE

Neptune, like most of the other planets in the solar system, possesses an internally generated magnetic field, first detected in 1989 by Voyager 2. Like Earth's magnetic field, Neptune's field can be represented approximately by that of a dipole (similar to a bar magnet), but its polarity is essentially opposite to that of Earth's present field. A magnetic compass on Neptune would point toward south instead of north. Earth's field is thought to be generated by electric currents flowing in its liquid iron core, and electric currents flowing within the outer cores of liquid metallic hydrogen in Jupiter and Saturn may similarly be the source of their magnetic fields. The magnetic fields of Earth, Jupiter, and Saturn are relatively well centred within the respective planets and aligned within about 12° of the planetary rotation axes. Uranus and Neptune, by contrast, have magnetic fields that are tilted from their rotation axes by almost 59° and 47°, respectively. Furthermore, the fields are not internally well centred. Uranus's field is offset by 31 percent of the planet's radius. Neptune's field, having an offset of 55 percent of the radius, is centred in a portion of the interior that is actually closer to the cloud tops than to the planetary centre. The unusual configurations of the magnetic fields of Uranus and Neptune have led scientists to speculate that these fields may be generated in processes occurring in the upper layers of the planetary interiors.

The magnetic field of Neptune (and of the other planets) is approximately apple-shaped, with the stem end and the opposite end oriented in the directions of the magnetic poles. The solar wind, a stream of electrically charged particles that flows outward from the Sun, distorts that regular shape, compressing it on the sunward side of the planet and stretching it into a long tail in the direction away from the Sun. Trapped within the magnetic field are charged particles, predominantly protons and electrons.

The region of space dominated by Neptune's magnetic field and charged particles is called its magnetosphere. Because of the high tilt of Neptune's magnetic field, the particles trapped in the magnetosphere are repeatedly swept past the orbits of the moons and rings. Many of these particles may be absorbed by the moons and ring material, effectively emptying from the magnetosphere a large fraction of its charged particle content. Neptune's magnetosphere is populated with fewer protons and electrons per unit volume than that of any other giant planet. Near the magnetic poles, the charged particles in the magnetosphere can travel along magnetic field lines into the atmosphere. As they collide with gases there, they cause those gases to fluoresce, resulting in classical, albeit weak, auroras.

INTERIOR STRUCTURE AND COMPOSITION

Although Neptune has a mean density slightly less than 30 percent of Earth's, it is the densest of the giant planets. This implies that a larger percentage of Neptune's interior is composed of melted ices and molten rocky materials than is the case for the other giant planets.

The distribution of these heavier elements and compounds is poorly known. Voyager 2 data suggest that Neptune is unlikely to have a distinct inner core of molten rocky materials surrounded by an outer core of melted ices of methane, ammonia, and water. The relatively slow rotation of 16.11 hours measured by Voyager was about one hour longer than would be expected from such a layered interior model. Scientists have concluded that the heavier compounds and elements, rather than being centrally condensed, may be spread almost uniformly throughout the interior. In this respect, as in many others, Neptune resembles Uranus far more than it does the larger giants Jupiter and Saturn.

The large fraction of Neptune's total heat budget derived from the planet's interior may not necessarily imply that Neptune is hotter at its centre than Uranus. Multiple stratified layers in the deep Uranian atmosphere may serve to insulate the interior, trapping within the planet the radiation that more readily escapes from Neptune. Images of Uranus from Earth as Uranus approaches an equinox and thus as the Sun begins to illuminate the equatorial regions more directly seem to show an increasingly active atmosphere. This may imply that discrete atmospheric activity on both Uranus and Neptune is more dependent on solar radiation than on the relative amounts of heat escaping from the interior.

NEPTUNE'S
MOONS AND RINGS

Neptune has at least 13 moons and six known narrow rings. Each of the myriad particles that constitute the rings can be considered a tiny moon in its own orbit.

The four moons nearest the planet orbit within the ring system, where at least some of them may interact gravitationally with the ring particles, keeping them from spreading out.

MOONS

Prior to Voyager 2's encounter, Neptune's only known moons were Triton, discovered visually through a telescope in October 1846 by English astronomer William Lassell shortly after the discovery of Neptune, and Nereid, discovered in telescopic photographs more than a century later in 1949 by American astronomer Gerard Kuiper. In 1989, Voyager's observations added six previously unknown moons to Neptune's system. All are less than half of Triton's distance from Neptune and are regular moons—i.e., they travel in prograde, nearly circular orbits that lie near Neptune's equatorial plane. These moons are probably synchronous rotators; that is, their rotational and orbital periods are the same.

In 2002–03, five additional tiny moons, estimated to be about 15–30 km (9–18 miles) in radius, were discovered in Earth-based observations. These are irregular, having highly eccentric orbits that are inclined at large angles to the planet's equator; three also orbit in the retrograde direction. Their mean distances from Neptune lie roughly between 15 million and 48 million km (9 million and 30 million miles), well outside the orbit of Nereid.

Each of Neptune's moons are named after figures in Greek mythology usually connected with Poseidon (the Roman god Neptune) or with water. Of Voyager's six discoveries, all but Proteus orbit Neptune in less time than it takes the planet to rotate. Hence, to an observer positioned near Neptune's cloud tops, these five would appear to rise in the west and set in the east. Voyager observed two of its discoveries, Proteus and Larissa, closely enough to detect both their size and approximate shape. Both bodies are irregular in shape and appear to have heavily cratered surfaces. The sizes of the other four are estimated from a combination of distant images and their brightnesses, based on the assumption that they reflect about as much light as Proteus and Larissa—about 7 percent. The other five moons are much smaller, each having a mean radius of less than 100 km (60 miles).

Following are slightly more in-depth profiles of Neptune's three largest moons: Triton, Proteus, and Nereid.

Triton

Triton is the largest of Neptune's moons, whose unusual orbital characteristics suggest that it formed elsewhere in the solar system and was later captured by Neptune. Triton was named after a merman in Greek mythology who was the son of the sea god Poseidon (the Roman god Neptune).

Triton is unique among the large moons of the solar system in that it moves in a retrograde orbit—i.e., one that is opposite the direction of Neptune's rotation. Its mean orbital distance is about 354,800 km (220,500 miles) from the planet. Also unusual for a large moon is Triton's orbital inclination—the plane of its orbit is tilted more than 157° to Neptune's equator. (The orbits of the other large moons in the solar system are inclined less than about 5° to their planet's equator.) Triton rotates once on its axis every 5.877 days, which is the same time that it takes to revolve around Neptune. As a result of this synchronous rotation, the moon always keeps the same face toward Neptune and leads with the same face in its orbit. Each of Triton's seasons, like those of Neptune, lasts nearly 41 years, or one-fourth of Neptune's orbital period. Triton's orbital tilt and its axial tilt of 30° with respect to Neptune's orbit combine in such a way that the moon's poles alternately point toward the Sun, much like the case of Uranus.

Little was known about Triton until 1989, when the U.S. Voyager 2 probe flew within 40,000 km (24,800 miles) of it. As measured by Voyager, Triton is about 2,706 km (1,681 miles) across, which is nearly the diameter of Earth's Moon. Pre-Voyager estimates of Triton's size made from Earth had been based on an erroneously high mass determination and an assumption of low surface reflectivity. Triton's mass is now known to be only a small fraction of the previously accepted value and its surface to be icy and highly reflective, in contrast to the Moon's dark

Crescents of Neptune and its moon, Triton, photographed by Voyager 2, August 1989. NASA/JPL

surface, which is devoid of water and other volatile components (with the exception of what is interpreted as water ice on the floors of craters near its poles). Triton's low mass is likely a consequence of a predominantly water-ice interior surrounding a denser rocky core. Nevertheless, its mean density of 2.06 g/cm^3 (1.19 oz/in^3) is higher than that measured for any of the satellites of Saturn or Uranus and is surpassed

among large satellites only by the Moon and Jupiter's Io and Europa.

Triton is similar in size, density, and surface composition to the dwarf planet Pluto. Its highly inclined, retrograde orbit suggests that it is a captured object, which perhaps formed originally, like Pluto, as an independent icy planetesimal in the outer solar system. At some point in Neptune's early history, Triton's orbit around the Sun may have carried it too near the giant planet. Gas drag in Neptune's extended atmosphere or a collision with an existing moon of Neptune slowed Triton enough to place it in an elongated orbit, which was also retrograde and highly inclined. Tidal interactions between Triton and Neptune—cyclic deformations in each body caused by the gravitational attraction of the other—eventually would have reshaped its path around Neptune into a circle. The process of Triton's capture and circularization of its orbit would have severely disrupted any previously existing system of moons that had formed along with Neptune from a disk of protoplanetary material. Nereid's radical orbit may be one consequence of this process (although the possibility that Nereid too is a captured object has not been ruled out). Moons that were in orbit between Proteus and Nereid would have been ejected from the Neptunian system, thrown into Neptune itself, or absorbed by the molten Triton. Even those moons orbiting closer to Neptune would not have escaped some disruption. The present orbits of Naiad through Proteus are probably very different from their original orbits, and these moons may be only fragments of the original bodies that formed with Neptune. Subsequent bombardment by Neptune-orbiting debris and by meteoroids from interplanetary space may have further altered their sizes, shapes, and orbits.

Triton's visible surface is covered by methane and nitrogen ices. Spectroscopic studies from Earth also reveal evidence of trace amounts of carbon monoxide and carbon dioxide ices. Even at the remarkably low surface temperature of 38 K (-390 °F, -235 °C) measured by Voyager, a sufficient amount of frozen nitrogen sublimes (passes from a solid directly to a gas) to form a tenuous atmosphere having a near-surface pressure less than 0.00002 bar. During the Voyager flyby, a polar ice cap presumably composed of nitrogen ice deposited the prior winter covered most of Triton's southern hemisphere. At that time Triton was nearly three-fourths of the way through its 41-year southern springtime. Equatorward of the polar cap, much of the terrain had the appearance of a cantaloupe rind, consisting of dimples crisscrossed with a network of fractures.

Within the polar cap region, numerous darker streaks provide evidence of surface winds. At least two of the streaks, and perhaps dozens, are the result of active geyserlike plumes seen erupting during the Voyager 2 flyby. Nitrogen gas, escaping through vents in the overlying ice, carries entrained dust particles to heights of about 8 km (5 miles), where the dust is then transported downwind as far as 150 km (90 miles). The energy sources and mechanisms for driving these plumes are not yet well understood, but their preference for latitudes illuminated vertically by the Sun has led to the conclusion that incident sunlight is an important factor.

Near the equator on the Neptune-facing side of Triton exist at least two, and perhaps several, frozen lakelike features with terraced edges. The terracing is probably the result of multiple epochs of melting, each successive melt involving a somewhat smaller patch of ice. Some of the terrace cliffs rise more than 1 km (0.6 mile) high. Even at Triton's low surface temperature, nitrogen or methane ice is not strong enough to support structures of that height without slumping. Scientists assume that the underlying material in these structures is water ice, which is much more rocklike at low temperatures, although no direct evidence for it is seen in Triton's spectra. A thin veneer of nitrogen or methane ice could effectively hide the spectral signature of water ice.

The process from capture to circular orbit may have taken more than one billion years, during which time the enormous tidal deformations experienced by Triton most likely melted its entire interior. The molten body would have undergone differentiation, the denser material sinking into a core region and the more-volatile materials rising to the surface. It is thought that Triton's surface cooled faster than its interior and formed a thick outer layer of predominantly water ice.

PROTEUS AND NEREID

Proteus is the second largest moon of Neptune and is named after the prophetic, shape-changing old man of the sea in Greek mythology. It was one of the moons discovered by Voyager 2 in 1989. With a mean radius of about 208 km (129 miles), Proteus is a little larger than Nereid, with a mean radius of about 170 km (106 miles). Because Proteus is so near to Neptune, however, scientists on Earth had been unable to detect it in the planet's glare.

Nereid is the third largest known moon of Neptune. It is named after the numerous daughters, called Nereids, of the sea god Nereus in Greek mythology.

Nereid has a diameter of about 340 km (210 miles). It revolves around Neptune with a period of just over 360 days in a highly elliptical orbit—the most eccentric of any known moon—that is inclined by more than 7° to the planet's equator. Its mean distance from Neptune is 5,513,400 km (3,425,900 miles), which is about 15 times farther from Neptune than the next closest known moon, Triton. Nereid is exceedingly faint, making observations with even the largest Earth-based telescopes very difficult. Thus, little is known about it, but reflectivity data returned by the U.S. Voyager 2 space probe in 1989 suggest a surface composition of ices and silicates. Nereid's odd orbit supports the hypothesis that its sibling Triton is an object that was captured by Neptune's gravity and whose billion-year-long "settling-in" process severely disrupted Neptune's original system of moons. On the other hand, Nereid itself may be a captured object that formed elsewhere in the solar system.

Voyager did not observe Nereid at close range, but data from the probe indicate that it has a nearly spherical shape. Voyager detected no large variations in brightness as Nereid rotated. Although the spacecraft was unable to determine a rotation period, the moon's highly elliptical orbit makes it unlikely that it is in synchronous rotation—i.e., that its rotation and orbital periods are equal.

THE RING SYSTEM

Evidence that Neptune has one or more rings arose in the mid-1980s when stellar occultation studies from Earth occasionally showed a brief dip in the star's brightness just before or after the planet passed in front of it. Because dips were seen only in some studies and never symmetrically on both sides of the planet, scientists concluded that any rings present do not completely encircle Neptune but instead have the form of partial rings, or ring arcs.

Images from Voyager 2, however, revealed a system of six rings, each of which in fact fully surrounds Neptune. The putative arcs turned out to be bright regions in the outermost ring, named Adams, where the density of ring particles is particularly high. Although rings also encircle each of the other three giant planets, none displays the striking clumpiness of Adams. The arcs are found within a 45° segment of the ring. From leading to trailing, the most prominent are named Courage, Liberté, Egalité 1,

Egalité 2, and Fraternité. They range in length from about 1,000 km (600 miles) to more than 10,000 km (6,000 miles). Although the moon Galatea, which orbits just planetward of the inner edge of Adams, may gravitationally interact with the ring to trap ring particles temporarily in such arclike regions, collisions between ring particles should eventually spread the constituent material relatively uniformly around the ring. Consequently, it is suspected that the event that supplied the material for Adams's enigmatic arcs—perhaps the breakup of a small moon—occurred within the past few thousand years.

The other five known rings of Neptune—Galle, Le Verrier, Lassell, Arago, and Galatea, in order of increasing distance from the planet—lack the nonuniformity in density exhibited by Adams. Le Verrier, which is about 110 km (70 miles) in radial width, closely resembles the nonarc regions of Adams. Similar to the relationship between the moon Galatea and the ring Adams, the moon Despina orbits Neptune just planetward of the ring Le Verrier. Each moon may gravitationally repel particles near the inner edge of its respective ring, acting as a shepherd moon to keep ring material from spreading inward.

Galle, the innermost ring, is much broader and fainter than either Adams or Le Verrier, possibly owing to the absence of a nearby moon that could provide a strong shepherding effect. Lassell consists of a faint plateau of ring

Neptune's ring system, captured by Voyager 2 in two long-exposure backlit images made a few hours after the spacecraft's closest approach to the planet in August 1989. The two brightest rings are Adams, the outermost ring of the system, and Le Verrier. Spreading halfway to Adams from Le Verrier is the diffuse ring Lassell, whose somewhat brighter outer edge constitutes the ring Arago. The innermost ring, Galle, appears as a faint diffuse band between Le Verrier and the overexposed crescent of Neptune. Adams's bright arcs are absent from the combined image because they were on the opposite side of the planet when the separate photographs were taken. JPL/NASA

material that extends outward from Le Verrier about halfway to Adams. Arago is the name used to distinguish a narrow, relatively bright region at the outer edge of Lassell. Galatea is the name generally used to refer to a faint ring of material spread all along the orbit of the moon Galatea.

None of Neptune's rings were detected from scattering effects on Voyager's radio signal propagating through the rings, which indicates that they are nearly devoid of particles in the centimetre size range or larger. The fact that the rings were most visible in Voyager images when backlit by sunlight implies that they are largely populated by dust-sized particles, which scatter light forward much better than back toward the Sun and Earth. Their chemical makeup is not known, but, like the rings of Uranus, the surfaces of Neptune's ring particles (and possibly the particles in their entirety) may be composed of radiation-darkened methane ices.

The suspected youthfulness of Adams's ring arcs and the arguments offered can be extended to Neptune's rings in general. The present rings are narrow, and scientists have found it difficult to explain how the orbits of the known moons can effectively confine the natural radial spreading of the rings. This has led many to speculate that Neptune's present rings may be much younger than the planet itself, perhaps substantially less than a million years. The present ring system may be markedly different from any that existed a million years ago. It is even possible that the next spacecraft to visit Neptune's rings will find a system greatly evolved from the one Voyager 2 imaged in 1989.

NEPTUNE'S DISCOVERY

Neptune is the only giant planet that is not visible without the aid of a telescope. Having an apparent magnitude of 7.8, it is approximately one-fifth as bright as the faintest stars visible to the unaided eye. Hence, it is fairly certain that there were no observations of Neptune prior to the use of telescopes. Galileo is credited as the first person to view the heavens with a telescope in 1609. His sketches from a few years later, the first of which was made on Dec. 28, 1612, suggest that he saw Neptune when it passed near Jupiter but did not recognize it as a planet.

Prior to the discovery of Uranus by the English astronomer William Herschel in 1781, the consensus among scientists and philosophers alike was that the planets in the solar system were limited to six—Earth plus those five planets that had been observed in the sky since ancient times. Knowledge of a seventh planet almost immediately led astronomers and others to suspect the existence of still more planetary bodies. Additional impetus came from the mathematical curiosity known as Bode's law.

Some astronomers were so impressed by the seeming success of Bode's law in explaining the distances of Ceres and Uranus that they proposed the name Ophion for the large planet that the law told them must lie beyond Uranus, at a distance of 38.8 AU.

In addition to this scientifically unfounded prediction, observations of Uranus provided actual evidence for the existence of another planet. Uranus was not following the path predicted by Newton's laws of motion and the gravitational forces exerted by the Sun and the known planets. Furthermore, more than

20 recorded prediscovery sightings of Uranus dating back as far as 1690 disagreed with the calculated positions of Uranus for the respective time at which each observation was made. It appeared possible that the gravitational attraction of an undiscovered planet was perturbing the orbit of Uranus.

In 1843 the British mathematician John Couch Adams began a serious study to see if he could predict the location of a more distant planet that would account for the strange motions of Uranus. Adams communicated his results to the astronomer royal, George B. Airy, at Greenwich Observatory, but they apparently were considered not precise enough to begin a reasonably concise search for the new planet. In 1845 Urbain-Jean-Joseph Le Verrier of France, unaware of Adams's efforts in Britain, began a similar study of his own.

By mid-1846 the English astronomer John Herschel, son of William Herschel, had expressed his opinion that the mathematical studies under way could well lead to the discovery of a new planet. Airy, convinced by Herschel's arguments, proposed a search based on Adams's calculations to James Challis at Cambridge Observatory. Challis began a systematic examination of a large area of sky surrounding Adams's predicted location. The search was slow and tedious because Challis had no detailed maps of the dim stars in the area where the new planet was predicted. He would draw charts of the stars he observed and then compare them with the same region several nights later to see if any had moved.

Le Verrier also had difficulty convincing astronomers in his country that a telescopic search of the skies in the area he predicted for the new planet was not a waste of time. On Sept. 23, 1846, he communicated his results to the German astronomer Johann Gottfried Galle at the Berlin Observatory. Galle and his assistant Heinrich Louis d'Arrest had access to detailed star maps of the sky painstakingly constructed to aid in the search for new asteroids. Galle and d'Arrest identified Neptune as an uncharted star that same night and verified the next night that it had moved relative to the background stars.

Although Galle and d'Arrest have the distinction of having been the first individuals to identify Neptune in the night sky, credit for its "discovery" arguably belongs to Le Verrier for his calculations of Neptune's direction in the sky. At first the French attempted to proclaim Le Verrier as the sole discoverer of the new planet and even suggested that the planet be named after him. The proposal was not favourably received outside France, both because of Adams's reported contribution and because of the general reluctance to name a major planet after a living individual. Neptune's discovery was eventually credited to both Adams and Le Verrier, although it now appears likely that Adams's contribution was less substantial than earlier believed. It is nevertheless appropriate that the more traditional practice of using names from ancient mythology for planets eventually prevailed.

The discovery of Neptune finally laid Bode's law to rest. Instead of being near the predicted 38.8 AU, Neptune was found to be only 30.1 AU from the Sun. This discrepancy, combined with the lack of any scientific explanation as to why the law should work, discredited it.

LATER OBSERVATIONS FROM EARTH

Earth-based observations of Neptune before Voyager 2's flyby suffered greatly as a consequence of the planet's enormous distance from both Earth and the Sun. Its average orbital radius of 30.1 AU means that the sunlight reaching its moons and its upper atmosphere is barely 0.1 percent as bright as that at Earth. Pre-Voyager telescopic viewing of Neptune through the full thickness of Earth's atmosphere could not resolve features smaller than about one-tenth of Neptune's diameter, even under the best observing conditions. Most such observations concentrated on determining Neptune's size, mass, density, and orbital parameters and searching for moons. In the early 21st century specialized interferometric techniques have routinely improved spatial resolution of distant objects by factors of 10–100 over earlier surface-based observations.

From time to time astronomers reported seeing visual markings in the Neptunian atmosphere, but not until the use of high-resolution infrared charge-coupled device (CCD) cameras in the 1980s could such observations be repeated with enough consistency to permit determination of an approximate rotation period for Neptune. Spectroscopic observations from Earth revealed the presence of hydrogen and methane in the planet's atmosphere. By analogy with the other giant planets, helium was also expected to be present. Infrared and visual studies revealed that Neptune has an internal heat source.

By the mid-1990s the fully operational Hubble Space Telescope (HST) was enabling images and other data concerning Neptune to be collected outside the filtering and distorting effects of Earth's atmosphere. The orbiting infrared Spitzer Space Telescope also succeeded in imaging Neptune with a resolution much higher than those available from Earth's surface in the 1980s. In addition, astronomers have developed techniques for minimizing the effects of atmospheric distortion from Earth-based observation. The most successful of these, known as adaptive optics, continually processes information from infrared star images and applies it nearly instantaneously to correct the shape of the telescope mirror and thereby compensate for the distortion. As a consequence, large Earth-based telescopes now routinely achieve resolutions better than those of the HST. Images of Neptune obtained with adaptive optics allow studies of this distant planet at resolutions approaching those from the Voyager 2 encounter.

SPACECRAFT EXPLORATION

Voyager 2 is the only spacecraft to have encountered the Neptunian system. This spacecraft and its twin, Voyager 1—both launched in 1977—originally were slated to visit only Jupiter and Saturn, but the timing of Voyager 2's launch gave its trajectory the leeway needed for the spacecraft to be redirected, with a gravity assist from Saturn, on extended missions to Uranus and then to Neptune.

Voyager 2 flew past Neptune and its moons on Aug. 24–25, 1989, observing the system almost continuously between June and October of that year. It measured the planet's radius and interior rotation rate and detected its magnetic field, determining that the latter is both highly inclined and offset from the planet's rotation axis. It confirmed that Neptune has rings and discovered six new moons. Neptune previously had been thought too cold to support active weather systems, but Voyager's images of the planet revealed the highest atmospheric winds seen in the solar system and several large-scale storms, one the size of Earth.

Because Neptune was Voyager 2's last planetary destination, mission scientists risked sending the spacecraft closer to it than to any other planet during the mission. Voyager passed about 5,000 km (3,100 miles) above Neptune's north pole. A few hours later it passed within 40,000 km (24,800 miles) of Triton, which allowed it to gather high-resolution images of the moon's highly varied surface as well as precise measurements of its radius and surface temperature.

As of 2009, no future missions to Neptune are planned.

CHAPTER 7

PLUTO, THE KUIPER BELT, AND BEYOND

Neptune is the last planet in the solar system. However, beyond Neptune is not empty space but a plethora of unusual icebound worlds, the Kuiper Belt and its most notable member, the dwarf planet Pluto.

Pluto was formerly regarded as the outermost and smallest planet. It also was considered the most recently discovered planet, having been found in 1930. In August 2006, however, the International Astronomical Union, the organization charged by the scientific community with classifying astronomical objects, voted to remove Pluto from the list of planets and give it the new classification of dwarf planet. The change reflects astronomers' realization that Pluto is a large member of the Kuiper Belt, a collection of debris of ice and rock left over from the formation of the solar system and now revolving around the Sun beyond Neptune's orbit.

Pluto is not visible in the night sky to the unaided eye. Its largest moon, Charon, is close enough in size to the dwarf planet that it has become common to refer to the two bodies as a double system. Pluto is designated by the symbol ♇.

Named for the god of the underworld in Roman mythology (the Greek equivalent is Hades), Pluto is so distant that the Sun's light, which travels about 300,000 km (186,000 miles) per second, takes more than five hours to reach it. An observer standing on Pluto's surface would see the Sun as an extremely bright star in the dark sky, providing Pluto on average 1/1,600 of the amount of sunlight that reaches Earth. Pluto's surface temperature therefore is so cold that common gases such as nitrogen and carbon monoxide exist there as ices.

Because of Pluto's remoteness and small size, the best telescopes on Earth and in Earth's orbit have been able to resolve little detail on its surface. Indeed, such basic information as its radius and mass have been difficult to determine; most of what is known about Pluto has been learned since the late 1970s as an outcome of the discovery of Charon. Pluto has yet to be visited by spacecraft, though the U.S. spacecraft New Horizons departed Earth for the Pluto-Charon system in 2006 and will arrive there in July 2015; many key questions about it and its environs can be answered only by close-up robotic observations.

BASIC DATA FOR PLUTO	
mean distance from Sun	5,910,000,000 km (39.5 AU)
eccentricity of orbit	0.251
inclination of orbit to ecliptic	17.1°
Plutonian year (sidereal period of revolution)	247.69 Earth years
visual magnitude at mean opposition	15.1
mean synodic period*	366.74 Earth days
mean orbital velocity	4.72 km/s
radius	1,172 km
mass	1.2×10^{22} kg
mean density	about 2 g/cm³
mean surface gravity	58 cm/s
escape velocity	1.1 km/s
rotation period (Plutonian sidereal day)	6.3873 Earth days (retrograde)
Plutonian mean solar day**	6.3874 Earth days
inclination of equator to orbit (obliquity)	120°
mean surface temperature	about 40 K (-387 °F, -233 °C)
surface pressure (near perihelion)	about 10^{-5} bar
number of known moons	3

*Time required for Pluto to return to the same position in the sky relative to the Sun as seen from Earth.

**Smallness of deviation from sidereal day is due to Pluto's huge orbit.

BASIC ASTRONOMICAL DATA

Pluto's mean distance from the Sun, about 5.9 billion km (3.7 billion miles or 39.5 AU), gives it an orbit larger than that of the outermost planet, Neptune. Its orbit, compared with those of the planets, is atypical in several ways. It is more elongated, or eccentric, than any of the planetary orbits and more inclined (at 17.1°) to the ecliptic, the plane of Earth's orbit, near which the orbits of most of the planets lie. In traveling its eccentric path around the Sun, Pluto varies in distance from 29.7 AU, at its closest point to the Sun (perihelion), to 49.5 AU, at its farthest point (aphelion). Because Neptune orbits in a nearly circular path at 30.1 AU, Pluto is for a small part of each revolution actually closer to the Sun than is Neptune. Nevertheless, the two bodies will never collide, because Pluto is locked in a stabilizing 3:2 resonance with Neptune—i.e., it completes two orbits around the Sun in exactly the time it takes Neptune to complete three. This gravitational interaction affects their orbits such that they can never pass closer than about 17 AU. The last time Pluto reached perihelion occurred in 1989; for about 10 years before that time and again afterward, Neptune was more distant than Pluto from the Sun.

Observations from Earth have revealed that Pluto's brightness varies with a period of 6.3873 Earth days, which is now well established as its rotation period (or sidereal day). Of the planets,

only Mercury, with a rotation period of almost 59 days, and Venus, with 243 days, turn more slowly. Pluto's axis of rotation is tilted at an angle of 120° from the perpendicular to the plane of its orbit, so that its north pole actually points 30° below the plane. (For comparison, Earth's north polar axis is tilted 23.5° away from the perpendicular, above its orbital plane.) Pluto thus rotates nearly on its side in a retrograde direction; an observer on its surface would see the Sun rise in the west and set in the east.

Compared with the planets, Pluto is also anomalous in its physical characteristics. Pluto has a radius less than half that of Mercury; it is only about two-thirds the size of Earth's Moon. Next to the outer planets—the giants Jupiter, Saturn, Uranus, and Neptune—it is strikingly tiny. When these characteristics are combined with what is known about its density and composition, Pluto appears to have more in common with the large icy moons of the outer planets than with any of the planets themselves. Its closest twin is Neptune's moon Triton, which suggests a similar origin for these two bodies

THE ATMOSPHERE

Although the detection of methane ice on Pluto's surface in the 1970s gave scientists confidence that the body had an atmosphere, direct observation of it had to wait until the next decade. Discovery of its atmosphere was made in 1988 when Pluto passed in front of (or occulted) a star as observed from Earth. The star's light gradually dimmed just before it disappeared behind Pluto, demonstrating the presence of a thin, greatly distended atmosphere. Because Pluto's atmosphere must consist of vapours in equilibrium with their ices, small changes in temperature should have a large effect on the amount of gas in the atmosphere. During the years surrounding Pluto's perihelion in 1989, when Pluto was slightly less cold than average, more of its frozen gases vaporized; the atmosphere was then at or near its thickest, making it a favourable time to study the body. Astronomers estimate a surface pressure in the range of a few to several tens of microbars. At aphelion, when Pluto is receiving the least sunlight, its atmosphere may not be detectable at all.

Observations made during occultations cannot provide direct information about atmospheric composition, but they can allow determination of the ratio of mean molecular weight to temperature. Using reasonable assumptions about the atmospheric temperature, scientists have calculated that each particle—i.e., each atom or molecule—of Pluto's atmosphere has a mean molecular weight of approximately 25 atomic mass units. This implies that significant amounts of gases heavier than methane, which has a molecular weight of 16, must also be present. Molecular nitrogen, with a molecular weight of 28, must in fact be the dominant constituent, because nitrogen ice was discovered on the surface and is

known to be more volatile than methane ice. Nitrogen is also the main constituent of the atmospheres of both Triton and Saturn's largest satellite, Titan, as well as of Earth.

Although ongoing Earth-based observations will add to knowledge about the atmosphere and other aspects of Pluto, major new insights will likely require a close-up visit from a spacecraft. Scientists looked to the U.S. New Horizons spacecraft mission, launched in 2006, to Pluto, Charon, and the outer solar system beyond to provide much of the needed data. The mission plan called for a nine-year flight to the Pluto-Charon system followed by a 150-day flyby for investigation of the surfaces, atmospheres, interiors, and space environment of the two bodies.

THE SURFACE AND INTERIOR

Observations of Pluto show that its colour is slightly reddish, although much less red than Mars or Jupiter's moon Io. Thus, the surface of Pluto cannot be composed simply of pure ices, a conclusion supported by the observed variation in brightness caused by its rotation. Its average reflectivity, or albedo, is 0.55 (i.e., it returns 55 percent of the light that strikes it), compared with 0.1 for the Moon and 0.8 for Triton.

The first crude infrared spectroscopic measurements reveal that Pluto's south polar region is unusually bright. Scientists find such variation in Pluto's surface

Artist's rendering of the New Horizons spacecraft approaching Pluto and its three moons.
NASA/Johns Hopkins University Applied Physics Laboratory/Southwest Research Institute

striking because, with the exception of Saturn's mysterious moon Iapetus, all the other icy bodies in the outer solar system exhibit much more uniform surfaces. Brightness maps based on observations with the Earth-orbiting Hubble Space Telescope reveal some of this heterogeneity, but only visiting spacecraft can provide the spatial resolution needed to make associations between brightness and surface composition or topography.

Pluto-Charon eclipses have allowed astronomers to estimate the masses and radii of the two bodies. From this information their densities have been calculated to fall between 1.92 and 2.06 g/cm^3 (1.11 and 1.19 oz/in^3) for Pluto and between 1.51 and 1.81 g/cm^3 (0.87 and 1.05 oz/in^3) for Charon. These values suggest that both bodies are composed of a significant fraction of materials such as silicate rock and organic compounds denser than water ice (which has a density of 1 g/cm³ [0.58 oz/in³]). It is customary to assume that Pluto, like the icy moons of Jupiter and Saturn, has an inner rocky core surrounded by a thick mantle of water ice. The frozen nitrogen, carbon monoxide, and methane observed on its surface are expected to be in the form of a relatively thin layer, similar to the layer of water on Earth's surface. Such a model, however, requires verification by spacecraft observations.

The surface temperature of Pluto has proved very difficult to measure. Observations made in 1983 from the Earth-orbiting Infrared Astronomical Satellite suggest values in the range of 45 to 58 K (-379 to -355 °F, -228 to -215 °C), whereas measurements from Earth's surface at millimetre wavelengths imply a slightly lower range of 35 to 50 K (-397 to -370 °F, -238 to -223 °C). The temperature certainly must vary over the surface, depending on the reflectivity at a given location and the angle of the noon Sun there. The solar energy falling on Pluto is also expected to decrease by a factor of roughly three as it moves from perihelion to aphelion.

PLUTO'S MOONS

Pluto possesses three known moons. Charon, by far the largest, is fully half the size of Pluto. It revolves around the dwarf planet—more accurately, the two bodies revolve around a common centre of mass—at a distance of about 19,640 km (12,200 miles), equal to about eight Pluto diameters. (By contrast, Earth's Moon is a little more than one-fourth the size of Earth and is separated from the latter by about 30 Earth diameters.)

Charon's period of revolution is exactly equal to the rotation period of Pluto itself; in other words, Charon is in synchronous orbit around Pluto. As a result, Charon is visible from only one hemisphere of Pluto. It remains above the same location on Pluto's surface, never rising or setting (just as do communication satellites in geostationary orbits over Earth). In addition, as with most moons in the solar system, Charon is in a state of synchronous rotation—i.e., it always presents the same face to Pluto.

Charon is somewhat less reflective (has a lower albedo—about 0.35) than Pluto and is more neutral in colour. Its spectrum reveals the presence of water ice, which appears to be the dominant surface constituent. There is no hint of the solid methane that is so obvious on its larger neighbour. The observations to date were not capable of detecting ices of nitrogen or carbon monoxide, but, given the absence of methane, which is less volatile, they seem unlikely to be present. Charon's density implies that the moon contains materials such as silicates and organic compounds that are denser than water ice. The disposition of these materials inside Charon is even more speculative than it is for Pluto.

Scientists have exploited the presence of Charon to reveal several characteristics of Pluto that would not otherwise be known, particularly its mass and size. Much of this information was acquired through the extraordinary coincidence that in 1985, just seven years after Charon's discovery, it began a five-year period of mutual eclipse events with Pluto in which the moon alternately crossed the disk of (transited) and was hidden (was occulted, or was eclipsed) by Pluto, as seen from Earth, every 6.4 days. These events occur when Earth passes through Charon's orbital plane around Pluto, which happens only twice during Pluto's 248-year orbit around the Sun. Careful observations of these events allowed determinations of the radii of Pluto and Charon and of the masses of both bodies that were more precise than heretofore possible. In addition, monitoring the changes in the total brightness of the two bodies as they blocked each other permitted astronomers to estimate their individual overall albedos and even to create maps depicting brightness differences over their surfaces.

Pluto's other two moons, called Hydra and Nix (provisionally designated S/2005 P1 and S/2005 P2, respectively, on their discovery), are much smaller than Charon—about 60 and 50 km (37 and 31 miles) in diameter, respectively, if their surface reflectivity is assumed to be similar to Charon's. They revolve around Pluto outside Charon's path in nearly circular orbits (like Charon) and in the same orbital plane as Charon. Based on preliminary observations, the orbital radius of Hydra is about 64,700

km (40,200 miles); of Nix, 49,400 km (30,700 miles). It appears that for every 12 orbits completed by Charon, Hydra makes about 2 orbits (for a ratio of 6:1 in their orbital periods), while Nix makes nearly 3 orbits (for a 4:1 ratio); this also means that the orbital periods of Hydra and Nix are in a 3:2 ratio. These relationships of the orbital periods, which are approximately in the ratios of small whole numbers, suggest that the small moons are in stable dynamic resonances with Charon and with each other—that is, all three bodies pass one another periodically, interacting via gravity in a way that tends to maintain the regularity of their encounters.

DISCOVERY OF PLUTO AND ITS MOONS

When Pluto was found, it was considered the third planet to be discovered, after Uranus and Neptune, as opposed to the six planets that have been visible in the sky to the naked eye since ancient times. The existence of a ninth planet had been postulated beginning in the late 19th century on the basis of apparent perturbations of the orbital motion of Uranus, which suggested that a more-distant body was gravitationally disturbing it. Astronomers later realized that these perturbations were spurious—the gravitational force from Pluto's small mass is not strong enough to have been the source of the suspected disturbances. Thus, Pluto's discovery was a remarkable coincidence attributable to careful observations rather than to accurate prediction of the existence of a hypothetical planet.

The search for the expected planet was supported most actively at the Lowell Observatory in Flagstaff, Ariz., U.S., in the early 20th century. It was initiated by the founder of the observatory, Percival Lowell, an American astronomer who had achieved notoriety through his highly publicized claims of canal sightings on Mars. After two unsuccessful attempts to find the planet prior to Lowell's death in 1916, an astronomical camera built specifically for this purpose and capable of collecting light from a wide field of sky was put into service in 1929, and a young amateur astronomer, Clyde Tombaugh, was hired to carry out the search. On Feb. 18, 1930, less than one year after he began his work, Tombaugh found Pluto in the constellation Gemini. The object appeared as a dim "star" of the 15th magnitude that slowly changed its position against the fixed background stars as it pursued its 248-year orbit around the Sun. Although Lowell and other astronomers had predicted that the unknown planet would be much larger and brighter than the object Tombaugh found, Pluto was quickly accepted as the expected ninth planet. The symbol invented for it, ♇, stands both for the first two letters of Pluto and for the initials of Percival Lowell.

Charon was discovered in 1978 on images of Pluto that had been recorded photographically at the U.S. Naval Observatory station in Flagstaff, fewer than 6 km (3.7 miles) from the site of

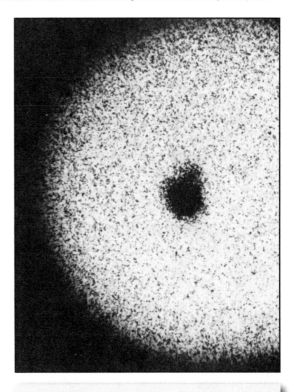

One of the discovery photographs of Pluto's moon Charon, taken at the U.S. Naval Observatory station in Flagstaff, Ariz., in 1978. Charon appears merely as a bulge on the upper right portion of Pluto's silhouette. Official U.S. Navy Photograph

Pluto's discovery. These images were being recorded by James W. Christy and Robert S. Harrington in an attempt to obtain more-accurate measurements of Pluto's orbit. The new satellite was named after the boatman in Greek mythology who ferries dead souls to Hades' realm in the underworld.

Prior to the discovery of Charon, Pluto was thought to be larger and more massive than it actually is; there was no way to determine either quantity directly. Even in the discovery images, Charon appears as an unresolved bump on the side of Pluto, an indication of the observational difficulties posed by the relative nearness of the two bodies, their great distance from Earth, and the distorting effects of Earth's atmosphere. Only near the end of the 20th century, with the availability of the Hubble Space Telescope and Earth-based instruments equipped with adaptive optics that compensate for atmospheric turbulence, did astronomers first resolve Pluto and Charon into separate bodies.

A team of nine astronomers working in the United States discovered Pluto's two small moons, Hydra and Nix, in 2005 via images made with the Hubble Space Telescope during a concerted search for objects traveling around Pluto as small as 25 km (16 miles) in diameter. To confirm the orbits, the astronomers checked Hubble images of Pluto and Charon made in 2002 for surface-mapping studies and found faint but definite indications of two objects moving along the orbital paths calculated from the 2005 images.

THE KUIPER BELT

Pluto is one member of a flat ring of icy small bodies that revolve around the Sun beyond the orbit of the planet Neptune. Named for the Dutch American astronomer Gerard P. Kuiper, it comprises hundreds of millions of objects—presumed leftovers from the formation of the outer planets—whose orbits lie close

to the plane of the solar system. It is thought to be the source of most of the observed short-period comets, particularly those that orbit the Sun in less than 20 years, and for the icy Centaur objects, which have orbits in the region of the giant planets. (Some of the Centaurs may represent the transition from Kuiper Belt objects to short-period comets.)

Although its existence had been assumed for decades, the Kuiper Belt remained undetected until the 1990s, when the prerequisite large telescopes and sensitive light detectors became available. The Irish astronomer Kenneth E. Edgeworth speculated in 1943 that the distribution of the solar system's small bodies was not bounded by the present distance of Pluto. Kuiper developed a stronger case in 1951. Working from an analysis of the mass distribution of bodies needed to accrete into planets during the formation of the solar system, he demonstrated that a large residual amount of small icy bodies—inactive comet nuclei—must lie beyond Neptune.

A year earlier the Dutch astronomer Jan Oort had proposed the existence of a much more distant, spherical reservoir of icy bodies, now called the Oort cloud, from which comets are continually replenished. This distant source adequately accounted for the origin of long-period comets—those having periods greater than 200 years. Kuiper noted, however, that comets with very short periods (20 years or less), which all orbit in the same direction as all the planets around the Sun and close to the plane of the solar system, require a nearer, more flattened source. This explanation, clearly restated in 1988 by the American astronomer Martin Duncan and coworkers, became the best argument for the existence of the Kuiper Belt until its direct detection.

The first Kuiper Belt object (KBO) was discovered in 1992 by the American astronomer David Jewitt and graduate student Jane Luu. Designated 1992 QB1, the body is about 200–250 km (125–155 miles) in diameter, as estimated from its brightness. It moves in a nearly circular orbit in the plane of the planetary system at a distance from the Sun of about 44 AU. This is outside the orbit of Pluto, which has a mean radius of 39.5 AU. The discovery of 1992 QB1 alerted astronomers to the feasibility of detecting other KBOs, and within 12 years more than 800 had been discovered. Most of them lie between 30 and 50 AU from the Sun, and all must be larger than 100 km (60 miles) in diameter to be seen. On the basis of brightness estimates, the sizes of the larger known KBOs approach or exceed that of Pluto's largest moon, Charon, which has a diameter of 1,250 km (780 miles). One KBO, given the name Eris, appears to be twice that diameter—i.e., larger than Pluto itself. Because of their location outside Neptune's orbit (mean radius 30.1 AU), they are also called trans-Neptunian objects.

Two broad groups of KBOs can be distinguished: those in nearly circular stable orbits and those in highly eccentric (elongated) orbits that are much inclined to the plane of the solar system. Most of the latter objects survive only because they are in a stabilizing 3:2 resonance with Neptune—i.e., they complete two orbits around the Sun in the time it takes Neptune to complete three. Pluto is likewise in an eccentric, inclined orbit having a 3:2 resonance with Neptune. Because of its orbital characteristics, composition of ice and rock, and diminutive size compared with the planets (being smaller than Earth's Moon), Pluto is generally considered a very large KBO. In recognition of this kinship, the other KBOs with 3:2 resonances have been dubbed Plutinos ("little Plutos"). A small percentage of KBOs form a third group: those in elongated, inclined orbits that are not in resonance with Neptune. Because of their unstable orbits, they have the potential to be perturbed onto paths either far from the Sun or into the inner solar system, where they may become short-period comets.

An extrapolation of KBO discovery statistics suggests that 100,000 objects with diameters larger than 100 km—and probably many millions more smaller objects down to 1 km (0.6 miles)—exist between 30 and 50 AU. The population may extend farther outward, but at what distance it ends and whether it reaches the innermost boundary of the Oort cloud is not known. Astronomers generally consider the Kuiper Belt to be the outer remnant of the massive protoplanetary disk that existed some 4.5 billion years ago but failed to form large planets beyond the present orbit of Neptune.

ORIGIN OF
PLUTO AND ITS MOONS

Before the discovery of Charon, it was popular to assume that Pluto was a former moon of Neptune that had somehow escaped its orbit. This idea gained support from the apparent similarity of the dimensions of Pluto and Triton and the near coincidence in Triton's orbital period (5.9 days) and Pluto's rotation period (6.4 days). It was suggested that a close encounter between these two bodies when they were both moons led to the ejection of Pluto from the Neptunian system and caused Triton to assume the retrograde orbit that is presently observed.

Astronomers found it difficult to establish the likelihood that all these events would have occurred, and the discovery of Charon provided information that further refuted the theory. Because the revised mass of Pluto is only half that of Triton, Pluto clearly could not have caused the reversal of Triton's orbit. Also, the fact that Pluto has a proportionally large moon of its own makes the escape idea implausible. Current thinking favours the idea that Pluto and Charon instead formed as two independent bodies in the solar nebula, the gaseous cloud from which the solar system condensed. Just as the Moon appears to be deficient in volatile elements relative to Earth as a consequence of its high-temperature origin, so also can the absence of methane on Charon, along with the relatively high densities of both Pluto and Charon, be explained by a similar process.

Astronomers have argued that Pluto's two small moons also are products of the same collision that resulted in the present Charon. The alternative scenario—that they formed independently elsewhere in the outer solar system and were later gravitationally captured by the Pluto-Charon system—does not appear likely given the combination of circular coplanar orbits and multiple dynamic resonances that currently exist for the two small bodies and Charon. Rather, these conditions suggest that material in the ring of debris that was ejected from the collision accreted into all three moons—and possibly into others yet to be found.

This collision scenario implies that at the time the Pluto-Charon system formed, about 4.6 billion years ago, the outer solar nebula contained many icy bodies with the same approximate dimensions as these two. The bodies themselves are thought to have been built up from smaller entities that today would be recognized as the nuclei of comets.

Most of these icy planetesimals were incorporated into the cores of the giant planets during their formation. Many others, however, are thought to have remained as the unconsolidated debris that makes up the Kuiper Belt, which includes the outer part of Pluto's orbit. After more than 1,000 Kuiper Belt objects

PLUTO: PLANET OR DWARF PLANET?

Prior to the removal of Pluto from the official list of planets, astronomers had never established a rigorous scientific definition of a solar system planet, nor had they agreed on a minimum mass, radius, or mechanism of origin for a body to qualify as one. The traditional "instinctive" distinctions between the larger planetary bodies of the solar system, their moons, and small bodies such as asteroids and comets were made when their differences had seemed more profound and clearcut and when the nature of the small bodies as remnant building blocks of the planets was dimly perceived. This early, disjointed conception of the solar system was in some ways analogous to the situation described by the Indian fable of the blind men, each of whom identified a different object after touching a different part of the same elephant. It later became clear that the original groupings of the components of the solar system required reclassification under a set of more-complex, interrelated definitions.

If Pluto had been discovered in the context of the Kuiper Belt rather than as an isolated entity, it might never have been ranked with the eight planets. Indeed, in the decades after Pluto's discovery, some astronomers continued to question its planetary status in view of its small size, icy composition, and anomalous orbital characteristics. Moreover, about the turn of the 21st century, astronomers observed several KBOs that are each roughly the size of Charon and one, named Eris, that is slightly larger than Pluto itself.

Because Pluto was no longer unique in the outer reaches of the solar system, it became incumbent on astronomers either to admit additional members into the planetary ranks or to exclude Pluto. In August 2006 the IAU voted to take the latter course while establishing the category of dwarf planets to recognize the larger members of a given population of objects having similar compositions and origins and occupying the same orbital "neighbourhood." A dwarf planet is smaller than the planet Mercury yet large enough for its own gravity to have rounded its shape substantially. Like the major planets, it orbits the Sun, but unlike major planets, these bodies are not massive enough to have swept up most smaller nearby bodies by gravitational attraction; they thus failed to grow larger. Pluto, Eris, and Ceres met these criterion and were designated dwarf planets.

In June 2008, the IAU created a subcategory within the dwarf planet category, called plutoids, for all dwarf planets that are farther from the Sun than Neptune—that is, bodies that are large KBOs. Pluto and Eris are plutoids; Ceres, because of its location in the asteroid belt, is not. Since then, two more KBOs, Makemake and Haumea, have been designated dwarf planets and plutoids.

(KBOs) were directly observed starting in the early 1990s, astronomers came to the conclusion that Pluto and Charon likely are large members of the Kuiper Belt and that bodies such as Chiron, Neptune's moon Triton, and a number of other icy moons of the outer planets originated as KBOs.

THE OORT CLOUD

Beyond the Kuiper Belt lies the Oort cloud, an immense, roughly spherical cloud of icy small bodies that are inferred to revolve around the Sun at distances typically more than 1,000 times that of the orbit of Neptune, the outermost known major planet. Named for Jan Oort, who demonstrated its existence, the Oort cloud comprises objects that are less than 100 km (60 miles) in diameter and that number perhaps in the trillions, with an estimated total mass 10–100 times that of Earth. Although too distant to be seen directly, it is believed to be the source of most of the historically observed long-period comets—those that take more than 200 years (and usually much longer) to orbit the Sun.

The Estonian astronomer Ernest J. Öpik in 1932 suggested the possible presence of a distant reservoir of comets, arguing that, because comets burn out relatively quickly from their passages through the inner solar system, there must exist a source of "fresh" comets, which steadily replenishes the comet supply. Although these comets have never been in the inner solar system before, they are difficult to distinguish from older long-period comets because, by the time they are first observed, their orbits already have been gravitationally perturbed by the outer planets.

In 1950, Oort showed by statistical arguments that a steady flux of a few "new" comets are observed per year (those that had never been through the solar system before). This flux comes from the fringe of the Oort cloud. He identified it by looking at the distribution of the original values of the total energies of cometary orbits. These energies are in proportion to a^{-1}, with a being the semimajor axis of the cometary orbit. The original value of a refers to the orbit when the comet was still outside of the solar system, as opposed to the osculating orbit, which refers to the arc observed from Earth after it has been modified by the perturbations of the giant planets. Passages through the solar system produce a rather wide diffusion in orbital energies (in a^{-1}). In 1950 Oort accounted for only 19 accurate original orbits of long-period comets. The fact that 10 of the 19 orbits were concentrated in a very narrow range of a^{-1} established that most of them had never been through this diffusion process due to the planets. The mean value of a for these new comets suggested the distance they were coming from—about 10^5 AU. This distance is also the place where perturbations resulting from the passage of nearby stars begin to be felt. The distance coincidence suggested to Oort that stellar perturbations were the mechanism by which comets were sent into the planetary system.

Subsequently, using a much larger number of observed orbits, the American astronomer Brian Marsden calculated that the part of the Oort cloud where new comets originate—the more distant part of the cloud—is between 40,000 and 50,000 AU from the Sun. At such distances, the orbits of the tiny icy bodies can be disrupted and sent inward by either of two processes: the occasional close passage of a star or giant interstellar molecular cloud near the solar system or the gravitational forces, called disk tides, exerted by the mass of the Galaxy's disk. Although the inner part of the Oort cloud, which is thought to begin at about 20,000 AU, does not supply comets, its existence and large mass are predicted by the theory of the origin of the solar system. The Oort cloud must have been created from icy planetesimals that originally accreted in the outer part of the protoplanetary disk and were then scattered far away by the gravity of the incipient giant planets. How far the Oort cloud extends into space is not known, although Marsden's results suggest that it is almost empty beyond 50,000 AU, which is about one-fifth of the distance to the nearest star.

THE HELIOPAUSE

Between the Kuiper Belt and the Oort cloud lies the heliopause, the teardrop-shaped region around the Sun that is filled with solar magnetic fields and the outward-moving solar wind consisting of protons and electrons. Nearer the Sun than the heliopause lies the heliosheath, a region of transition where the solar wind slows to subsonic speeds, that is, slower than the speed with which disturbances travel through the interstellar medium.

The tail of the heliopause is estimated to be between 110 and 170 AU (17 and 26 billion km [10 and 16 billion miles]) from the Sun. Its shape fluctuates and is influenced by a wind of interstellar gas caused by the Sun's motion through space. The orbits of all the major planets, including Earth's, lie well within the heliopause.

No satellite has yet reached the heliopause, although the Voyager 1 and 2 probes launched in 1977 are the closest to it at distances from the Sun of 105 and 85 AU (16 and 13 billion km [10 and 8 billion miles]), respectively. (Voyager 1 and 2 crossed into the heliosheath at distances from the Sun of 94 and 84 AU in 2004 and 2007, respectively.) What is known about the heliopause is deduced by its effects on cosmic-ray particles coming into the solar system after passing through it and by the radio emission generated when material thrown off by the Sun in coronal mass ejections crosses it.

CHAPTER 8

COMETS

In ancient times, the regularity of the sky was a bedrock of stability in a harsh world. The Sun rose and set. The planets moved along the zodiac. However, sometimes, something new and frightening appeared, a star with a tail trailing behind it, a comet. (The word comet comes from the Greek *komētēs*, meaning "hairy one," a description that fits the bright comets noticed by the ancients.) Made of ice, these objects come from the Kuiper Belt and the Oort cloud and develop diffuse gaseous envelopes and often long luminous tails when near the Sun.

BASIC FEATURES

Many comets do not develop tails; moreover, comets are not surrounded by nebulosity during most of their lifetime. The only permanent feature of a comet is its nucleus, which is a small body that may be seen as a stellar image in large telescopes when tail and nebulosity do not exist, particularly when the comet is still far away from the Sun. Two characteristics differentiate the cometary nucleus from a very small asteroid—namely, its orbit and its chemical nature. A comet's orbit is more eccentric; therefore, its distance to the Sun varies considerably. Its material is more volatile. When far from the Sun, however, a comet remains in its pristine state for eons without losing any volatile components because of the deep cold of space. For this reason, astronomers believe that pristine cometary nuclei may represent the oldest and best-preserved material in the solar system.

During a close passage near the Sun, the nucleus of a comet loses water vapour and other more volatile compounds, as well as dust dragged away by the sublimating gases. It is then surrounded by a transient dusty "atmosphere" that is steadily lost to space. This feature is the coma, which gives a comet its nebulous appearance. The nucleus surrounded by the coma makes up the head of the comet. When it is even closer to the Sun, solar radiation usually blows the dust of the coma away from the head and produces a dust tail, which is often rather wide, featureless, and yellowish. The solar wind, on the other hand, drags ionized gas away in a slightly different direction and produces a plasma tail, which is usually narrow with nods and twists and has a bluish appearance.

DESIGNATIONS

In order to classify the chronological appearance of comets, the *Astronomische Nachrichten* ("Astronomical Reports") introduced in 1870 a system of preliminary and final designations that was used until 1995. The preliminary designation classified comets according to their order of discovery, using the year of discovery followed by a lowercase letter in alphabetical order, as in 1987a, 1987b, 1987c, and so forth. Comets were

then reclassified as soon as possible—usually a few years later—according to their chronological order of passage at perihelion (closest distance to the Sun); a Roman numeral was used, as in 1987 I, 1987 II, 1987 III, and so on.

In 1995 the International Astronomical Union (IAU) simplified the designation of comets since the two chronologies of letters and Roman numerals were often the same, and redesignating a comet after its perihelion was confusing. A newly discovered comet is called by the year in which it was discovered, then by a letter corresponding to the half-month of discovery, and finally a number denoting its order in that half-month. For example, Comet Hale-Bopp was 1995 O1. The official designation generally includes the name(s) of its discoverer(s)—with a maximum of three names—preceded by a P/ if the comet is on a periodic orbit of less than 200 years. If a comet has been observed at two perihelions, it is given a permanent number. For example, Halley's Comet is 1P/Halley since it was the first comet determined to be periodic. Comets with longer periods or that will not return to the inner solar system are preceded by a C/.

The discoverer's rule has not always been strictly applied: comets 1P/Halley, 2P/Encke, and 27P/Crommelin have been named after the astronomers who proved their periodic character. In the past, some comets became bright so fast that they were discovered by a large number of persons at almost the same time. They are given an arbitrary impersonal designation such as the Great September Comet (C/1882 R1), Southern Comet (C/1947 X1), or Eclipse Comet (C/1948 V1). Finally, comets may be discovered by an unusual instrument without direct intervention of a specific observer, as in the case of the Earth-orbiting Infrared Astronomical Satellite (IRAS). Its initials are used as if it were a human observer, as in C/1983 H1 IRAS-Araki-Alcock.

EARLY OBSERVATIONS

In ancient times, without interference from streetlights or urban pollution, comets could be seen by everyone. Their sudden appearance was interpreted as an omen of nature that awed people and was used by astrologers to predict flood, famine, pestilence, or the death of kings. The Greek philosopher Aristotle (4th century BCE) thought that the heavens were perfect and incorruptible. The very transient nature of comets seemed to imply that they were not part of the heavens but were merely earthly exhalations ignited and transported by heat to the upper atmosphere. Although the Roman philosopher Seneca (1st century CE) had proposed that comets could be heavenly bodies like the planets, Aristotle's ideas prevailed until the 14th century CE

Finally, during the 16th century, the Danish nobleman Tycho Brahe established critical proof that comets are heavenly bodies. He compared the lack of diurnal parallax of the comet of 1577 with the well-known parallax of the Moon (the diurnal parallax is the apparent change of position in the sky relative to the distant stars due to the rotation of Earth). Tycho deduced that the comet was at least four times farther away than the Moon, establishing for the first time that comets were heavenly bodies.

In 1619, the German astronomer Johannes Kepler still believed in 1619 that comets travel across the sky in a straight line. It was the English physicist and mathematician Isaac Newton who demonstrated in his *Principia* (1687) that, if heavenly bodies are attracted by a central body (the Sun) in proportion to the inverse square of its distance, they must move along a conic section (circle, ellipse, parabola, or hyperbola). Using the observed positions of the Great Comet of 1680, he identified its orbit as being nearly parabolic.

HALLEY AND HIS COMET

Newton's friend, the astronomer Edmond Halley, endeavoured to compute the orbits of 24 comets for which he had found accurate enough historical documents. Applying Newton's method, he presupposed a parabola as an approximation for each orbit. Among the 24 parabolas, 3 were identical in size and superimposed in space. The three relevant cometary passages (1531, 1607, and 1682) were separated by two time intervals of 76 and 75 years. Halley concluded that the parabolas were actually the end of an extremely elongated ellipse. Instead of three curves open to infinity, the orbit is closed and brings the same comet periodically back to Earth. As a consequence, it would return in 1758, he predicted.

Observed on Christmas night, 1758, by Johann Georg Palitzsch, a German amateur astronomer, the comet passed at perihelion in March 1759 and at perigee (closest to Earth) in April 1759. The perihelion date of 1759 had been predicted with an accuracy of one month by Alexis-Claude Clairaut, a French astronomer and physicist. Clairaut's work contributed much to the acceptance of Newton's theory on the Continent. With this, the until-then anonymous comet came to be called Halley's comet.

Since 1759, Comet Halley has reappeared three more times—in 1835, 1910, and 1986. Its trajectory has been computed backward, and all of its 30 previous passages described in historical documents over 22 centuries have been authenticated. Comet Halley's period has irregularly varied between 74.4 years (from 1835 to 1910) and 79.6 years (from 451 to 530 CE). These variations, which have been accurately predicted, result from the changing positions of the giant planets, mainly Jupiter and Saturn, whose variable attractions perturb the trajectory of the comet. The space orientation of the orbit has been practically constant, at least for several centuries. Since its returns are not separated by an integer number of years, however, the comet encounters Earth each time on a different point of its orbit around the Sun; thus, the geometry of each passage is different and its shortest distance to the planet varies considerably. The closest known passage to Earth, 0.033 AU, occurred on April 9, 837 CE.

The perigee distance of most of Comet Halley's historical passages has been between 0.20 and 0.50 AU. The last perigee, on April 11, 1986, took place at 0.42 AU from Earth. By contrast, the comet passed at only 0.14 AU from Earth in 1910. Seen from closer range, it was brighter and had a longer tail than on its return in 1986. This is one reason why the 1986 passage proved so disappointing to most lay observers. Yet, a far more important factor had to do with geometry: in the latitudes of the major Western countries, the comet was hidden by the southern horizon during the few weeks in April 1986 when it was at its brightest. Moreover, the night sky of most Western countries is brightly and constantly illuminated by public and private lights. Even in the absence of moonlight, the nighttime sky is pervaded by a milky glare that easily hides the tail of a comet.

Each century, a score of comets brighter than Comet Halley have been discovered. Yet, they appear without warning and will not be seen again. Many are periodic comets like Comet Halley, but their periods are extremely long (millennia or even scores or hundreds of millennia), and they have not left any identifiable trace in prehistory. For example, the bright Comet Hale-Bopp will reappear in about 2,380 years.

Comet Bennett, taken at Cerro Tololo Interamerican Observatory, Chile, March 16, 1970.
Courtesy of the Department of Astronomy, University of Michigan, Ann Arbor

Bright Comet Bennett 1970 II will return in 17 centuries, whereas the spectacular Comet West 1976 VI will reappear in about 500,000 years. Among the comets that can easily be seen with the unaided eye, Comet Halley is the only one that returns in a single lifetime. More than 200 comets whose periods are between 3 and 200 years are known, however. Unfortunately they are or have become too faint to be readily seen without the aid of telescopes.

MODERN COMETARY RESEARCH

During the 19th century it was shown that the radiant (i.e., spatial direction) of the spectacular meteor showers of 1866, 1872, and 1885 coincided well with three known cometary orbits that happened by chance to cross Earth's orbit at the dates of the observed showers. The apparent relationship between comets and meteor showers was interpreted by assuming that the cometary nucleus was an aggregate of dust or sand grains without any cohesion, through a concept known as the "sandbank" model. Meteor showers were explained by the spontaneous scattering of the dust grains along a comet's orbit, and the cometary nucleus began to be regarded only as the densest part of a meteor stream.

At the end of the 19th and the beginning of the 20th century, spectroscopy revealed that the reflection of sunlight by the dust was not the only source of light in the tail, showing the discontinuous emission that constitutes the signature of gaseous compounds. More specifically, it revealed the existence in the coma of several radicals—molecular fragments such as cyanogen (CN) and the carbon forms C_2 and C_3, which are chemically unstable in the laboratory because they are very reactive in molecular collisions. Spectroscopy also enabled investigators to detect the existence of a plasma component in the cometary tail by the presence of molecular ions, as,

for example, those of carbon monoxide ($CO+$), nitrogen (N_2+), and carbon dioxide (CO_2+). The radicals and ions are built up by the three light elements carbon (C), nitrogen (N), and oxygen (O). Hydrogen (H) was added when the radical CH was discovered belatedly on spectrograms of Comet Halley taken in 1910. The identification of CH was proposed by the American astronomer Nicholas Bobrovnikoff in 1931 and confirmed in 1938 by Marcel Nicolet of Belgium. In 1941 another Belgian astronomer, Pol Swings, and his coworkers identified three new ions: CH+, OH+, and CO2+. The emissions of the light elements hydrogen, carbon, oxygen, and sulfur and of carbon monoxide were finally detected when the far ultraviolet spectrum (which is absorbed by Earth's atmosphere) was explored during the 1970s with the help of rockets and satellites. This included the very large halo (10^7 kilometres [62 million miles]) of atomic hydrogen (the Lyman-alpha emission line) first observed in Comets Tago-Sato-Kosaka 1969 IX and Bennett 1970 II.

Although the sandbank model was still seriously considered until the 1960s and '70s by a small minority (most notably the British astronomer Raymond A. Lyttleton), the presence of large amounts of gaseous fragments of volatile molecules in the coma suggested to Bobrovnikoff the release by the nucleus of a bulk of unobserved "parent" molecules such as H_2O, CO_2, and NH_3 (ammonia). In 1948, Swings proposed that these molecules should be present in the nucleus in the solid state as ices.

In a fundamental paper, the American astronomer Fred L. Whipple set forth in 1950 the so-called "dirty snowball" model, according to which the nucleus is a lumpy piece of icy conglomerate wherein dust is cemented by a large amount of ices—not only water ice but also ices of more volatile molecules. This amount must be substantial enough to sustain the vaporizations for a large number of revolutions. Whipple noted that the nuclei of some comets at least are solid enough to graze the Sun without experiencing total destruction, since they apparently survive unharmed. (Some but not all Sun-grazing nuclei split under solar tidal forces.)

Finally, argued Whipple, the asymmetric vaporization of the nuclear ices sunward produces a jet action opposite to the Sun on the solid cometary nucleus. When the nucleus is rotating, the jet action is not exactly radial. This explained the theretofore mysterious nongravitational force identified as acting on cometary orbits. In particular, the orbital period of 2P/Encke mysteriously decreased by one to three hours per revolution (of 3.3 years), whereas that of 1P/Halley increased by some three days per revolution (of 76 years). For Whipple, a prograde rotation of the nucleus of 2P/Encke and a retrograde rotation of that of 1P/Halley could explain these observations. In each case, a similar amount of some 0.5 to 0.25 percent of the ices had to

be lost per revolution to explain the amount of the nongravitational force. Thus, all comets decay in a matter of a few hundred revolutions. This duration is only at most a few centuries for Encke and a few millennia for Halley. At any rate, it is millions of times shorter than the age of the solar system. However, comets are constantly replenished from the Kuiper Belt and the Oort cloud.

TYPES OF ORBITS

In the absence of planetary perturbations and nongravitational forces, a comet will orbit the Sun on a trajectory that is a conic section with the Sun at one focus. The total energy E of the comet, which is a constant of motion, will determine whether the orbit is an ellipse, a parabola, or a hyperbola. The total energy E is the sum of the kinetic energy of the comet and of its gravitational potential energy in the gravitational field of the Sun. Per unit mass, it is given by $E = \frac{1}{2}v^2 - GMr^{-1}$, where v is the comet's velocity and r its distance to the Sun, with M denoting the mass of the Sun and G the gravitational constant. If E is negative, the comet is bound to the Sun and moves in an ellipse. If E is positive, the comet is unbound and moves in a hyperbola. If E = 0, the comet is unbound and moves in a parabola.

In polar coordinates written in the plane of the orbit, the general equation for a conic section is $r = q(1+e)/(1 + e \cos \theta)$, where r is the distance from the comet to the Sun, q the perihelion distance, e the eccentricity of the orbit, and θ an angle measured from perihelion. When $0 \leq e < 1$, $E < 0$ and the orbit is an ellipse (the case $e = 0$ is a circle, which constitutes a particular ellipse); when $e = 1$, $E = 0$ and the orbit is a parabola; and when $e > 1$, $E > 0$ and the orbit is a hyperbola.

In space, a comet's orbit is completely specified by six quantities called its orbital elements. Among these are three angles that define the spatial orientation of the orbit: i, the inclination of the orbital plane to the plane of the ecliptic; , the longitude of the ascending node measured eastward from the vernal equinox; and ω, the angular distance of perihelion from the ascending node (also called the argument of perihelion). The three most frequently used orbital elements within the plane of the orbit are q, the perihelion distance in astronomical units; e, the eccentricity; and T, the epoch of perihelion passage.

Identifying Comets and Determining Their Orbits

Up to the beginning of the 19th century, comets were discovered exclusively by visual means. Many discoveries are still made visually with moderate-size telescopes by amateur astronomers. Although comets can be present in any region of the sky, they are often discovered near the western horizon after sunset or near the eastern horizon before sunrise, since they are brightest when closest to the Sun. Because of Earth's rotation and direction of motion in its orbit, discoveries before sunrise are more likely, as confirmed by discovery statistics.

At discovery a comet may still be faint enough not to have developed a tail; therefore, it may look like any nebulous object—e.g., an emission nebula, a globular star cluster, or a galaxy. The famous 18th-century French comet hunter Charles Messier (nicknamed "the ferret of comets" by Louis XV for his discovery of 21 comets) compiled his well-known catalog of "nebulous objects" so that such objects would not be mistaken for comets. The final criterion remains the apparent displacement of the comet after a few hours or a few days with respect to the distant stars; by contrast, the nebulous objects of Messier's catalog do not move. After such a displacement has been indisputably observed, any amateur wishing to have the comet named for himself must report his claim to the nearest observatory as soon as possible.

Most comets are and remain extremely faint. Today, a larger and larger proportion of comet discoveries are thus made fortuitously from high-resolution photographs, as, for instance, those taken during sky surveys by professional astronomers engaged in other projects. The faintest recorded comets approach the limit of detection of large telescopes (those that are 8 metres [26 feet] or more in diameter). Several successive observations of these faint moving objects are necessary to ensure identification and simultaneous calculation of a preliminary orbit. In order to determine a preliminary orbit as quickly as possible, the eccentricity $e = 1$ is assumed since some 90 percent of the observed eccentricities are close to one, and a parabolic motion is computed. This is generally sufficient to ensure against "losing" the comet in the sky.

The best conic section representing the path of the comet at a given instant is known as the osculating orbit. It is tangent to the true path of the chosen instant, and the velocity at that point is the same as the true instantaneous velocity of the comet. Nowadays, high-speed computers make it possible to produce a final ephemeris (table of positions) that is not only based on the definitive orbit but also includes the gravitational forces of the Sun and of all significant planets that constantly change the osculating orbit. In spite of this fact, the deviation between the observed and the predicted positions usually grows (imperceptibly) with the square of time. This is the signature of a "neglected" acceleration, which comes from a nongravitational force. Formulas representing the smooth variation of the nongravitational force with heliocentric distance are now included for many orbits. The most successful formula assumes that water ice prevails and controls the vaporization of the nucleus.

PERIODIC COMETS

The *Catalog of Cometary Orbits*, compiled by astronomer Brian Marsden, remains the standard reference for orbital statistics. Its 1989 edition lists 1,292 computed orbits from 239 BCE to 1989 CE; only 91 of them were computed using the rare accurate historical data from before the 17th century. More than 1,200 are therefore derived from cometary passages during the last three centuries. The 1,292 cometary apparitions of Marsden's catalog involve only 810 individual comets; the remainder represents the repeated returns of periodic comets.

Periodic comets are usually divided into short-period comets (those with periods of less than 200 years) and long-period comets (those with periods of more than 200 years). Of the 155 short-period comets, 93 have been observed at two or more perihelion passages. Four of these comets have been definitely lost, and three more are probably lost, presumably because of their decay in the solar heat. Some authors have found it advantageous to change the definition of short-period comets by diminishing their longest-period cutoff to 20 years. This leaves 135 short-period comets (new style) in the *Catalog*; the 20 others having periods between 20 and 200 years are called intermediate-period comets.

These two new classes are separated by a small period gap. The average short-period comet has a seven-year period, a perihelion distance of 1.5 AU, and a small inclination (13°) on the ecliptic. All short-period comets (new style) revolve in the direct (prograde) sense around the Sun, just as the planets do. The intermediate-period comets have on average a larger inclination of the ecliptic, and five of them turn around the Sun in a retrograde direction. The most famous of the latter is 1P/Halley (30 appearances). Eleven of the 20 intermediate-period comets have been observed during a single appearance.

The comets with long-period orbits are distributed at random in all directions of the sky, and roughly half of them turn in the retrograde direction. Of the 655 comets of long period contained in the *Catalog*, 192 have osculating elliptic orbits, and 122 have osculating orbits that are very slightly hyperbolic. Finally, 341 are listed as having parabolic orbits, but this is rather fallacious because either it has not been possible to detect unequivocal deviations from a parabola on the (sometimes very short) arc along which the comets have been observed or, more simply, the final calculations have never been made. The parabola is always assumed first in the preliminary computation as it is easier to deal with. If the osculating orbit is computed backward to when the comet was still far beyond the orbit of Neptune and if the orbit is then referred to the centre of mass of the solar system, the original orbits almost always prove to be elliptic. (The centre of mass of the solar system is different from the centre of the Sun primarily because of the position of massive Jupiter.) Twenty-two original orbits remain (nominally) slightly hyperbolic beyond the orbit of Neptune, but 19 remain not significantly different from a parabola. Even the three that are significantly

different near 50 AU are likely to become elliptic when they are 50,000 or 100,000 AU from the Sun. The reason is that, though the mass of the Oort cloud remains uncertain, it should be added to the mass of the inner solar system to compute the orbits. The smallest possible mass of the Oort cloud is likely to transform the orbits into ellipses. It is thus reasonable to believe that all observed comets were initially in elliptic orbits bound to the solar system. Accordingly, all parabolic and nearly parabolic comets are thought to be comets of very long period.

The future orbit of a long-period comet is obtained when the osculating orbit is computed forward to when the comet will be leaving the planetary system (beyond the orbit of Neptune) and is referred to the centre of mass of the solar system. Because of the planetary perturbations, slightly more than half of the future orbits become strongly elliptic, whereas slightly less than half become strongly hyperbolic. Roughly half of the long-period comets are thus "captured" by the solar system on more strongly bound orbits; the other half are permanently ejected out of the system.

Among the very-long-period comets, there is a particular class that Oort showed as having never passed through the planetary system before (see above), notwithstanding the fact that their original orbits were elliptic, which implies repeated passages. This paradox vanishes when it is understood that their perihelia were outside of the planetary system before their first appearance but that their orbits have been perturbed near aphelia (either by stellar or dark interstellar-cloud passages or by galactic tides) in such a way that their perihelia were lowered into the planetary system. The first passage of a "new" comet is usually brighter than an average passage (a large fraction of the famous bright historical comets were such new comets). This is possibly explained by the presence of more volatile gases and of a larger component of very fine dust. The most volatile gases may have disappeared during subsequent passages, and the finest dust may have agglomerated into larger dust grains that reflect less light for the same production rate. About 90 comets have been identified as new in long-period orbits. If the same proportion exists in the poorly computed parabolic orbits, the total must be close to 170 new comets in Marsden's catalog, but 80 of them have not been identified.

GROUPS OF COMETS AND OTHER UNUSUAL COMETARY OBJECTS

Some comets travel in strikingly similar orbits, only the time of perihelion passages being appreciably different. Members of such a group of comets are thought to be fragments from a larger comet that was tidally disrupted earlier by the Sun or in some cases by the differential jet action of nongravitational forces on a fragile nucleus. Many such breakups have been observed historically. Slight

differences in the resultant velocities—though they occur very gently—are sufficient to cause cometary fragments to separate along orbits close to but distinct from each other, particularly as far as their total energy is concerned. A very slight variation in a^{-1} introduces an orbital period that may vary by several years, and when the cometary fragments return they will go through perihelion at widely separated epochs. The best-known example is the famous group of "Sun-grazing" comets (also called the Kreutz group), which has 12 definite members (plus one probable) with perihelion distances between 0.002 and 0.009 AU (less than half a solar radius). Their periods are scattered from 400 to 2,000 years, and their last passages occurred between 1880 and 1970. The most famous fragment of the group is Comet Ikeya-Seki, C/1965 S1.

Comet 29P/Schwassmann-Wachmann 1, which has a period of 15 years, is in a quasi-circular and somewhat unstable orbit between Jupiter and Saturn, with a perihelion q that equals 5.45 AU and an aphelion of 6.73 AU. It can be observed every year for several months when opposite to the Sun in the sky. Without any visible tail, it has irregular outbursts that make its coma grow in size for a few weeks and become up to 1,000 times as bright as normal.

Another unusual object is the so-called asteroid 2060 Chiron, which has a similar orbit between Saturn and Uranus. Though first classified as an asteroid, its icy nucleus of some 300 kilometres

(186 miles) suggests that it is a giant comet provisionally parked on a quasi-circular but unstable orbit. Indeed, Chiron develops weak, sporadic outbursts, and in 1989 a transient nebulosity surrounding it (a "coma") was reported for the first time. Within a few thousand years, Chiron might be perturbed enough by Saturn to come closer to the Sun and become a spectacular comet.

For faraway objects that contain volatile ices, the distinction between asteroids and comets becomes a matter of semantics because many orbits are unstable; an asteroid that comes closer to the Sun than usual may become a comet by producing a transient atmosphere that gives it a fuzzy appearance and that may develop into a tail. Some objects have been reclassified as a result of such occurrences. For example, asteroid 1990 UL3, which crosses the orbit of Jupiter, was reclassified as Comet 137P/Shoemaker-Levy 2 late in 1990. Conversely, it is suspected that some of the Earth-approaching asteroids (Amors, Apollos, and Atens) could be the extinct nuclei of comets that have now lost most of their volatile ices.

Two bright comets, Morehouse 1908 III and Humason 1962 VIII, exhibited a peculiar tail spectrum in which the ion CO^+ prevailed in a spectacular way, possibly because of an anomalous abundance of a parent molecule (carbon monoxide, carbon dioxide, or possibly formaldehyde [CH_2O]) vaporizing from the nucleus. Finally, Comet Halley is the brightest and therefore the most famous of all short- and intermediate-period comets as the only one that returns in a single lifetime and can be seen with the naked eye.

THE COMETARY NUCLEUS

As previously noted, the traditional picture of a comet with a hazy head and a spectacular tail applies only to a transient phenomenon produced by the decay in the solar heat of a tiny object known as the cometary nucleus. In the largest telescopes, the nucleus is never more than a bright point of light at the centre of the cometary head. At substantial distances from the Sun, the comet seems to be reduced to its starlike nucleus. The nucleus is the essential part of a comet because it is the only permanent feature that survives during the entire lifetime of the comet. In particular, it is the source of the gases and dust that are released to build up the coma and tail when a comet approaches the Sun. The coma and tail are enormous: typically the coma measures a million kilometres (621,371 miles) or more in diameter, and the tail may extend about 100 million kilometres in length. They scatter and continuously dissipate into space but are steadily rebuilt by the decay of the nucleus, whose size is usually in the range of 10 kilometres (6 miles).

The evidence on the nature of the cometary nucleus remained completely circumstantial until March 1986, when the first close-up photographs of the nucleus of Comet Halley were taken during a flyby by the Giotto spacecraft of the

Composite image of the nucleus of Comet Halley produced from 68 original photographs taken by the Halley Multicolour Camera on board the Giotto spacecraft on March 13 and 14, 1986. Courtesy of H.U. Keller; copyright Max-Planck-Institut für Aeronomie, Lindau, Ger., 1986

If there was any surprise, it was not over its irregular shape (variously described as a potato or a peanut), which had been expected for a body with such small gravity (10^{-4}g, where g is the gravity of Earth). Rather, it was over the very black colour of the nucleus, which suggests that the snows or ices are indeed mixed together with a large amount of sootlike materials (i.e., carbon and tar in fine dust form). The very low geometric albedo (2 to 4 percent) of the cometary nucleus puts it among the darkest objects of the solar system. Its size is thus somewhat larger than anticipated: the roughly elongated body measures 15 by 8 kilometres (9 by 5 miles) and has a total volume of some 500 cubic kilometres (120 cubic miles). Its mass is rather uncertain, estimated in the vicinity of 10^{17} grams, and its bulk density is very small, ranging anywhere from 0.1 to 0.8 g/cm³ (0.06 to 0.46 oz/in³). The infrared spectrometer on board the Soviet Vega 2 spacecraft estimated a surface temperature of 300 to 400 K for the inactive "crust" that seems to cover 90 percent of the nucleus. Whether this crust is only a warmer layer of outgassed dust or whether the dust particles are really fused together by vacuum welding under contact is still open to speculation.

European Space Agency. Whipple's basic idea that the cometary nucleus was a monolithic piece of icy conglomerate had been already well supported by indirect deductions in the 1960s and '70s and had become the dominant though not universal view. The final proof of the existence of such a "dirty snowball," however, was provided by the photographs of Comet Halley's nucleus.

The 10 percent of the surface of Halley's nucleus that shows signs of activity seems to correspond to two large and a few smaller circular features resembling volcanic vents. Large sunward jets of dust originate from the vents; they are clearly dragged away by the gases vaporizing from the nucleus. This vaporization has to be a sublimation of the ices that cools them down to no more than 200 K in the open vents. The chemical composition of the vaporizing gases, as expected, is dominated by water vapour (about 80 percent of the total production rate). The next most abundant volatile (close to 10 percent) appears to be carbon monoxide (CO), though it could come from the dissociation of another parent molecule (e.g., carbon dioxide [CO_2] or formaldehyde [CH_2O]). Following CO in abundance is CO_2 (close to 4 percent). Methane (CH_4) and ammonia (NH_3), on the other hand, seem to be close to the 0.5 to 1 percent level, and the percentage of carbon disulfide (CS_2) is even lower; at that level, there also must be unsaturated hydrocarbons and amino compounds responsible for the molecular fragments observed in the coma.

This is not identical to—though definitely reminiscent of—the composition of the volcanic gases on Earth, which also are dominated by water vapour. However, their CO_2:CO, CO_2:CH_4, and SO_2:S_2 ratios are all larger than in Comet Halley, meaning that the volcanic gases are more oxidized. The major difference may stem from the different temperature involved—often near 1,300 K in terrestrial volcanoes, as opposed to 200 K for cometary vaporizations. This may make the terrestrial gases closer to thermodynamic equilibrium. The dust-to-gas mass ratio is uncertain but is possibly in the vicinity of 0.4 to 1.1.

The dust grains are predominantly silicates. Mass spectrometric analysis by the Giotto spacecraft revealed that they contain as much as 20–30 percent carbon, which explains why they are so black. There also are grains composed almost entirely of organic material (molecules made of atoms of hydrogen, carbon, nitrogen, and oxygen).

There is some uncertainty concerning the rotation of Halley's nucleus. Two different rotation rates of 2.2 days and 7.3 days have been deduced by different methods. Both may exist, one of them involving a tumbling motion, or nutation, that results from the irregular shape of the nucleus, which has two quite different moments of inertia along perpendicular axes.

Scientific knowledge of the internal structure of the cometary nucleus was not enhanced by the flyby of Comet Halley, and so it rests on weak circumstantial evidence from the study of other comets. Earlier investigations had established that the outer layers of old comets were processed by solar heat. These layers must have lost most of their volatiles and developed a kind of outgassed crust, which probably measures a few metres in thickness. Inside the crust there is thought to exist an internal structure that is radially the same at any depth. Arguments supporting this view are based on the fact that cometary comas and tails do not become essentially different when comets decay. Since they lose more and more of their outer layers, however, the observed phenomena come from material from increasingly greater depths. These arguments are specifically concerned with the dust-to-gas mass ratio, the atomic and molecular spectra, the splitting rate, and the vaporization pattern during fragmentation.

Before the Giotto flyby of Comet Halley, other cometary nuclei had never been resolved optically. For this reason, their albedos had to be assumed first in order to compute their sizes. Techniques proposed to deduce the albedo yielded only that of the dusty nuclear region made artificially brighter by light scattering in the dust. In 1986 the albedo of Comet Halley's nucleus was found to be very low (2 to 4 percent). If this value is typical for other comets, then 11 of 18 short-period comets studied would be between 6 and 10 kilometres (3 and 6 miles) in diameter; only 7 of them would be somewhat outside these limits. Comet Schwassmann-Wachmann 1 would be a giant with a diameter of 96 kilometres; 10 long-period comets would all have diameters close to 16 kilometres (59 miles; within 10 percent).

Since short-period comets have remained much longer in the solar system than comets having very long periods, the smaller size of the short-period comets might result from the steady fragmentation of the nucleus by splitting. Yet, the albedo may also diminish with aging. At the beginning, if the albedo were close to that of slightly less dirty snow (10 percent), the nuclear diameter of long-period comets would come very close to that of the largest of the short-period comets. The diameters of new comets also have been shown to be rather constant and most likely measure close to 10 kilometres (6 miles). Of course, these are mean "effective" diameters of unseen bodies that are all likely to be very irregular.

The region around the nucleus, up to 10 or 20 times its diameter, contains an amount of dust large enough to be partially and irregularly opaque or at least optically thick. It scatters substantially more solar light than is reflected by the black nucleus. Dust jets develop mainly sunward, activated by the solar heat on the sunlit side of the nucleus. They act as a fountain that displaces somewhat the centre of light from the centre of mass of the nucleus. This region also is likely to contain large clusters of grains that have not yet completely decayed into finer dust; the grains are cemented together by ice.

THE GASEOUS COMA

The coma, which produces the nebulous appearance of the cometary head, is a short-lived, rarefied, and dusty atmosphere escaping from the nucleus. It is seen as a spherical volume having a diameter of 10^5 to 10^6 kilometres (6.2×10^5

to 6.2 × 10^6 miles), centred on the nucleus. The coma gases expand at a velocity of about 0.6 kilometre (0.3 mile) per second. This velocity can be measured from the motion of expanding "halos" triggered by outbursts in the nucleus, from the speed required to produce the Greenstein effect (see below), and from the fluid dynamics required to drag dust particles away at those places where they are observed in the dust tails. This expansion velocity, v, varies somewhat with heliocentric distance r: $v = 0.58r^{-0.5}$ (in kilometres per second, when r is in astronomical units).

The light of the spherical coma comes mainly from molecular fragments that have been produced by the dissociation of unobserved "parent molecules" in a zone on the order of 10^4 kilometres (6.2 × 10^4 miles) around the nucleus. This also is the approximate size of the zone where molecular collisions continue to occur; beyond that zone, the gas becomes too rarefied for such interaction to occur. The zone simply expands radially without molecular collisions into the vacuum of space. The parent molecules (e.g., those of water vapour, carbon dioxide, and hydrogen cyanide [HCN]) are generally not observed because they do not fluoresce in visible light. So far, only a few have been observed at millimetre or centimetre wavelengths by radio telescopes; many more are needed if they are to be regarded as the source of the various radicals and ions that have been detected.

If the mixture of original parent molecules has been frozen out of thermodynamic equilibrium in the nuclear ices, many chemical reactions can still take place in the molecular collision zone. At the usually cold temperature of vaporization, the kinetics of fast ion-molecular reactions would prevail. The reactions might reshuffle the original molecules present in the nucleus into new parent species, which would be the ones subsequently photodissociated into observed fragments by solar light. (This complex situation is still far from being completely understood.) In turn, the observed fragments, after having absorbed and reemitted photons from the solar light several times, would photodissociate or photoionize, which make them disappear from sight at the fuzzy limit of the light-emitting coma (typically 2–5 × 10^5 kilometres [1.2–3.1 × 10^5 miles]).

The organic radicals were seen in cometary heads as visual or ultraviolet emission lines or bands. The exceptions were water vapour, along with hydrogen cyanide and methyl cyanide (CH_3CN); these species, which could be called parent molecules, were observed as pure rotation lines at radio frequencies. The metals—except for sodium (Na), which is observed in many comets—were seen as visual lines in Sun-grazing comets alone. They are assumed to result from the vaporization of dust grains by solar heat. Sodium is a volatile metal that is not unlikely to vaporize easily from dust grains at large distances from the Sun (more than 1 AU). The ions were seen in the visual or ultraviolet emission lines or bands at the onset of the plasma tail or detected by spacecraft. The silicate signature was found in infrared emission bands at the onset of dust tails. The occurrence of the silicate elements, as well as the presence of a rather large amount of organic compounds, was confirmed by the mass spectrometric analysis of dust grains during the Giotto flyby of Comet Halley.

An extremely weak coma appeared in 1984 when Comet Halley still was 6 AU from the Sun. In February 1991, the Belgian astronomers Olivier Hainaut and Alain Smette detected a giant outburst from Comet Halley, which was already at a distance of 14.5 AU from the Sun and had the form of a fanlike structure in the direction of the Sun; this is the best case study to date. Rarely have comas been detected beyond 3 or 4 AU, where they are still quite small; they grow to a maximum near 1.5 AU and seem to contract as they approach closer to the Sun. This effect comes from the more rapid decay in solar light (by photoionization or photodissociation) of the visible radicals that emit the coma light. The discrete emission of light by cometary atoms, radicals, or ions is due to the selective absorption of sunlight, followed by its reemission either at the same wavelength (resonance) or at a different wavelength (fluorescence).

In 1941, astrophysicist Pol Swings explained the peculiar appearance of some of the molecular bands in comets by the irregular spectral distribution of the exciting solar radiation owing to the presence of Fraunhofer lines (dark, or absorption, lines) in this radiation. The temporal variations that occur in the molecular bands as a comet approaches the Sun were explained quantitatively by the variable shift in the apparent wavelengths of the solar Fraunhofer lines due to the variable radial velocity of the comet. This is the so-called Swings effect. Later, the American astronomer Jesse Greenstein explained, by a differential Swings effect, the observed differences in the molecular bands in front of and behind the nucleus: the radial expansion velocity of the coma introduces a different shift forward and backward. This differential Swings effect is often referred to as the Greenstein effect.

Exceptions to the resonance-fluorescence mechanism are known and are exemplified by the case of the emission of the "forbidden" red doublet of atomic oxygen at wavelengths of 6300 and 6364 angstroms. Such an emission cannot be excited by direct absorption of sunlight but is produced directly by the photodissociation of H_2O into H_2 + O (in the ^1D state) and, in an accessorial manner, of CO_2 into CO + O (in the ^1D state). The ^1D state is an excited state of the oxygen atom that decays spontaneously into the ground (lowest energy) state by emitting the forbidden red doublet, provided that it had not been quenched earlier by molecular collisions.

The large atomic hydrogen halo detected up to 10^7 kilometres (6.2×10^7

miles) from the nucleus is simply a large coma visible in ultraviolet (Lyman-alpha line). It is two orders of magnitude larger than the comas that can be seen in visible light only because the hydrogen atoms, being lighter, move radially away 10 times faster and are ionized 10 times more slowly than the other radicals.

COMETARY TAILS

The tails of comets are generally directed away from the Sun. They rarely appear beyond 1.5 or 2 AU but develop rapidly with shorter heliocentric distance. The onset of the tail near the nucleus is first directed toward the Sun and shows jets curving backward like a fountain, as if they were pushed by a force emanating from the Sun. The German astronomer Friedrich Wilhelm Bessel began to study this phenomenon in 1836, and Fyodor A. Bredikhin of Russia developed, in 1903, tail kinematics based on precisely such a repulsive force that varies as the inverse square of the distance to the Sun. Bredikhin introduced a scheme for classifying cometary tails into three types, depending on whether the repulsive force was more than 100 times the gravity of the Sun (Type I) or less than one solar gravity (Types II and III). Subsequent research showed that Type-I tails are plasma tails (containing observed molecular ions as well as electrons not visible from ground-based observatories), and Types II and III are dust tails, the differences between them

being attributable to a minor difference in the size distribution of the dust grains. As a result of these findings, the traditional classification formulated by Bredikhin is no longer considered viable and is seldom used. Most comets (but not all) simultaneously show both types of tail: a bluish plasma tail, straight and narrow with twists and nods, and a yellowish dust tail, wide and curved, which is often featureless.

The plasma tail has its onset in a region extremely close to the nucleus. The ion source lies deep in the collision zone (typically 1,000 kilometres [621 miles]). It is likely that charge-exchange reactions compete with the photoionization of parent molecules, but the mechanism that produces ions is not yet quantitatively understood. In 1951 the German astronomer Ludwig Biermann predicted the existence of the solar wind in order to account for the rapid accelerations observed in plasma tails as well as their aberration (i.e., deviation from the direction directly opposite the Sun). The cometary plasma is blown away by the magnetic field of the solar wind until it reaches its own velocity—nearly 400 kilometres (248 miles) per second. This action explains the origin of the large forces postulated by the Bessel-Bredikhin theory. Spectacular changes observed in the plasma tail, such as its sudden total disconnection, have been explained by discontinuous changes in the solar wind flow (e.g., the passage of magnetic sector boundaries).

In 1957 the Swedish physicist Hannes Alfven predicted the draping of the magnetic lines of the solar wind around the cometary ionosphere. This phenomenon was detected by the International Cometary Explorer spacecraft, launched by the U.S. National Aeronautics and Space Administration (NASA), when it passed through the onset of the plasma tail of Comet 21P/Giacobini-Zinner on Sept. 11, 1985. Two magnetic lobes separated by a current-carrying neutral sheet were observed as expected. A related feature known as the ionopause was detected by the Giotto space probe during its flyby of Comet Halley in 1986. The ionopause is a cavity without a magnetic field that contains only cometary ions and is separated from the solar wind by a sharp discontinuity. Halley's ionopause lies about 4,000 to 5,000 kilometres (2,500 to 3,100 miles) from the nucleus of the comet. An analysis of all the encounter data indicates that a complete understanding of cometary interaction with the solar wind has not yet been achieved. It is well understood, however, that the neutral coma remains practically spherical. The solar wind is so rarefied that there are no direct collisions of its particles with the neutral particles of the coma, and, as these particles are electrically neutral, they do not "feel" the magnetic field.

The source of the dust tail is the dust dragged away by the vaporizing gases that emanate from the active zones of the nucleus, presumably from vents like those observed on Comet Halley's nucleus.

The dust jets are first directed sunward but are progressively pushed back by the radiation pressure of sunlight. The repulsive acceleration of a particle varies as $(sd)^{-1}$ (with linear size s and density d). For a given density, it thus varies as s^{-1}, separating widely the particles of different sizes in different parts of the tail. Studying the dust tail isophotes of varying brightnesses therefore yields the dust grain distribution. This distribution may peak for very fine particles near 0.5 micrometre (0.00002 inch), assuming a density of two, as in the case of Comet Bennett; however, it falls off with s^{-n} (with n ranging from three to five) for larger particles. This mechanism neglects particles much smaller than the mean wavelength of sunlight. Because such particles do not reflect light, they do not feel its radiation pressure. (They are not detected from ground-based observations anyway.)

One of the major results of the Giotto flyby of Halley's nucleus was the detection of abundant particles much smaller than the wavelength of light, indicating that the size distribution does not peak near 0.5 μm (0.00002 inch) but seems rather to grow indefinitely with a slope close to d^{-2} for finer and finer particles down to possibly 0.05 μm (10^{-17} gram). The dust composition analyzers on board the Giotto and Vega spacecraft revealed the presence of at least three broad classes of grains. Class 1 contains the light elements hydrogen, carbon, nitrogen, and oxygen only (in the form of either ices or polymers of organic compounds). The particles of class 2 are analogous to the meteorites known as CI carbonaceous chondrites but are possibly slightly enriched in carbon and sulfur. Class 3 particles are even more enriched in carbon, nitrogen, and sulfur; they could be regarded as carbonaceous silicate cores (like those of class 2) covered by a mantle of organic material (similar to that of class 1) that has been radiation-processed. Most of the encounter data were excellent for elemental analyses but poor for determining molecular composition, because most molecules were destroyed by impact at high encounter velocity. Hence, there still remains much ambiguity regarding the chemical nature of the organic fraction present in the grains.

Meteors are extraterrestrial particles of sand-grain or small-pebble size that become luminous upon entering the upper atmosphere at very high speeds. Meteor streams have well-defined orbits in space. More than a dozen of these orbits have practically the same orbital elements as the orbits of the identical number of short-period comets. Fine cometary dust consists primarily of micrometre- or sub-micrometre-size particles that are much too small to become visible meteors (they are more like cigarette smoke than dust). Moreover, they are scattered in the cometary tail at great distance from the comet orbit. The size distribution of cometary dust grains, however, covers many orders of magnitude; a small fraction of them may reach

0.1 millimetre (0.004 inch) to even a few centimetres. Because of their large size, these dust grains are almost not accelerated by the radiation pressure of sunlight. They remain in the plane of the cometary orbit and in the immediate vicinity of the orbit itself, even though they separate steadily from the nucleus.

They sometimes become visible as an anti-tail—i.e., as a bright spike extending from the coma sunward in a direction opposite to the tail. This phenomenon occurs as a matter of geometry: it takes place for only a few days when Earth crosses the plane of the cometary orbit. At such a time, this plane is viewed through the edge, and all large grains are seen accumulated along a line. The same grains scatter farther and farther away from the nucleus until some are along the entire cometary orbit. When Earth's orbit intersects such an orbit (an event that occurs year after year at the same calendar date), these large grains produce meteor showers.

Extremely fine cometary grains also may penetrate Earth's atmosphere, but they can be slowed down gently without burning up. Some have been collected by NASA's U-2 aircraft at very high altitudes. Grains of this kind are known as Brownlee particles and are believed to be of cometary origin. Their composition is chondritic, though they show somewhat more carbon and sulfur than the CI carbonaceous chondrites, and their structure is fluffy with many pores. Similar grains were found in space

Comet Arend-Roland photographed on April 25, 1957. The prominent anti-tail extending from the coma appears to precede the comet, though it actually trails from behind. Courtesy of Lick Observatory, University of California

during the space probe exploration of Comet Halley.

COMETARY MODELS

As previously noted, the sandbank model of the cometary nucleus fell into disregard by the late 1950s and early 1960s and was supplanted by the dirty snowball (or icy conglomerate) concept. Much circumstantial evidence supported the latter, but confirmation was lacking until 1986, when the Giotto spacecraft returned detailed, close-up photographs of Comet Halley's nucleus. Yet, while these photographs corroborated the general idea of the model, they revealed that "dirty snowball" was in fact a misnomer because snow (even when dirty) is suggestive of something white or at least gray in colour. In actuality, the cometary nucleus proved to be pitch black owing to the large amount of very fine, black sootlike particles intermixed with the volatile ices.

Many variations of the icy conglomerate model have been proposed since the early 1980s, as, for example, the fractal model, rubble-pile model, and icy-glue model. These names, however, suggest only slightly different types of accretion of primordial particles; they all share common features—namely, irregular shape, heterogeneous mixture, and very low density because of cavities and pores. The existence of a crust or dust mantle of a different nature had already been proposed before the 1986 spacecraft encounter with Comet Halley for two reasons. First, cosmic-ray processing of the outer layers had been described by Leonid M. Shul'man of the Soviet Union (1972) and later advocated by Fred Whipple and Bertram Donn of the United States, while the outgassing of the outer layers by solar heat had also been assumed since the proposal of Whipple's model (1950). Second, detailed models of the formation and disruption of such mantles due to solar-radiation processing of the upper layers had been studied by Devamitta Asoka Mendis of the United States (1979) and M. Horanyi of Hungary (1984).

An average heuristic model for the elemental abundances of the cometary nucleus was developed by the American astronomer Armand H. Delsemme in 1982. Delsemme computed the H:C:N:O:S ratios from ultraviolet and visual observations of atomic and molecular species in bright comets detected during the 1970s and deduced the abundances of metals from the chondritic composition of cometary dust. In this model, hydrogen was depleted by a factor of 1,000 with respect to solar or cosmic abundances, and carbon was depleted by a factor of 4 in the gaseous fraction. The results of the 1986 study of Comet Halley confirmed the average chemical model and showed that the carbon missing in the gas was actually present in the dust. Except for hydrogen (and presumably helium), it appears that all elements are roughly in cosmic proportions in comets in spite of their extremely low gravity (10^{-4} times that of Earth). This emphasizes the pristine nature of comets. Unlike most bodies of the solar system, comets obviously have never been severely processed by any heating episode since their formation. If the accretion of comets occurred at very low temperatures, near absolute zero, the water ice in a newly formed comet must be amorphous. Idealized models show that the transition to cubic ice might be the cause of sudden flare-ups between 3 and 6 AU.

ORIGIN AND EVOLUTION OF COMETS

All observed comets make up an essentially transient system that decays and disappears almost completely in less than one million years. Since they all pass through the solar system, planetary perturbations eject a fraction of them into deep space on hyperbolic orbits and capture another fraction on short-period orbits. In turn, those that have been captured decay rapidly in the solar heat. Fortunately, there is a permanent source of new comets that maintains the steady state—namely, the outer margin of the Oort cloud. Comets within the bulk of the Oort cloud are unobservable, not only because they do not develop comas and tails but also because they are too far away.

COMETARY FORMATION AND THE OORT CLOUD

Any modern theory about cometary origins has to consider the origin of the Oort cloud. None of the comets observed today left the Oort cloud more than three or four million years ago. The Oort cloud is, however, gravitationally bound to the solar system, which it follows in its orbit around the Milky Way Galaxy. Therefore, it is likely that the Oort cloud has existed for a long time. The most probable hypothesis is that it was formed at the same time as the giant planets by the very process that accreted them. The Soviet astronomer Viktor S. Safronov developed this accretionary theory of the planetary system mathematically in 1972. According to his model, the planets originated from a disk or a ring of dust around the Sun, and cometary nuclei are nothing

more than primordial planetesimals that accreted first and became the building blocks of the planets. From the accreted mass of the giant planets, Safronov predicted the correct order of magnitude of the mass of the Oort cloud, which was built up by those planetesimals that missed colliding with the planetary embryos and were thrust far away by their perturbations. In effect, the Oort cloud in this theory becomes the necessary consequence and the natural by-product of the accretion of the giant planets.

Later, in the 1970s, the American astronomer A.G.W. Cameron developed a much more massive model of the protostar nebula, in which the comets accreted in a circular ring at some 1,000 AU from the Sun, which is far beyond the present limits of the planetary system. The primeval circular orbits were then transformed into the elongated ellipses present in the Oort cloud by mass loss of the primitive solar nebula. Both the Cameron and Safronov models put the origin of comets together with that of the solar system some 4.6 billion years ago. Plausibility is given to the general idea of accretion from dust disks by the existence of such disks around many young stars—a fact established by infrared observations in the 1980s and confirmed visually in at least one case (β Pictoris). Further support is found in clues derived from meteorites.

Since the early 1980s, new ideas have been explored to determine whether the Oort cloud could be much younger than the solar system or at least periodically replenished. The role of the massive and dense molecular clouds that exist in interstellar space has been reexamined in different ways. Could comets have accreted in these clouds directly from interstellar grains? Mechanisms for later capturing them into the Oort cloud cannot be very effective, but the efficiency is not capital, and some possibilities have been proposed. Since the solar system itself was probably formed from the gravitational collapse of such a molecular cloud, it seems more likely that either comets or the interstellar grains that were going to accrete into comets followed suit during gaseous collapse and were put into the Oort cloud at the same time that the planets were being formed. Elemental isotopic ratios deduced from the Comet Halley flyby have not brought about any conspicuous anomalies that could be attributed to matter coming from outside the solar system. So far, observational clues all favour the idea of cometary matter deriving from the same primeval reservoir as the stuff of the solar system, but it must be recognized that the evidence remains weak.

POSSIBLE PRE-SOLAR-SYSTEM ORIGIN OF COMETS

Telltales based on the chemical constitution of cometary nuclei as well as on the evolution of their orbits suggest that the origin of comets goes back beyond that of the planets and their satellites. Two scenarios are among the likeliest possibilities. In the first, comets had already accreted in all dense molecular clouds of the Milky Way Galaxy by the agglomeration of interstellar grains covered by a frost of organic molecules that cemented them together. Later, such a cloud collapsed to form the solar system. In the second scenario, dense molecular clouds were not able to accrete their frosty interstellar grains into larger bodies. When one of these molecular clouds collapsed to form the future solar system, however, the interstellar grains did likewise and eventually formed a dusty disk around the central star—the proto-Sun. Accretion into objects of 10-kilometre (6.2 mile) diameter is more likely in dusty disks of this type. The outer grains of the disk had not lost their frost, and some of them were ejected into the Oort cloud during the accretion of planetesimals into giant planets after some very moderate processing by heat. It is hoped that one day, space probes will secure data that will make it possible to determine whether frosty interstellar grains have lost their identity or can still be recognized as pristine and unaltered objects in cometary dust.

Comets seem to be the most pristine objects of the solar system, containing intact the material from which they were formed. Included are the hydrogen, carbon, oxygen, nitrogen, and sulfur atoms needed to build the volatile molecules present in the terrestrial biosphere (including the oceans and the atmosphere). Comets also seem to be the link between interstellar molecules and the most primitive meteorites known—the carbonaceous chondrites. The molecules required to initiate prebiotic chemistry (e.g., hydrogen cyanide, methyl cyanide, water, and formaldehyde) are present in interstellar space just as they are in comets; larger prebiotic chemistry molecules (e.g., amino acids, purines, and pyrimidines) occur in some chondrites and possibly in comets. An early cometary bombardment of Earth, predicted in some accretion models of the solar system, may have brought the oceans and the atmosphere, as well as a veneer of the molecules needed for life to develop on Earth. Comets could well be the link between interstellar chemistry and life.

NOTABLE COMETS

Comets have inspired and frightened humanity since the dawn of history. Some of the more notable are discussed here.

COMET AREND-ROLAND

Comet Arend-Roland (C/1956 R1) was a long-period comet remarkable for its anomalous second tail, which projects toward rather than away from the Sun. It was one of the brightest naked-eye comets of the 20th century. It was discovered photographically on the night of Nov. 8–9, 1956, by S. Arend and P. Roland at the Royal Observatory, Uccle, Belg. Its perihelion passage (i.e., its closest approach to the Sun) occurred on April 20, 1957. Because it was discovered months before perihelion, lengthy observations could be carried out. The anomalous tail appeared for a few nights late in April, changing direction from night to night and appearing as a sharp spike aimed at the Sun. This was an effect of perspective, of viewing edgewise a fan of debris from the comet, scattered ahead of it along its orbit.

BIELA'S COMET

Biela's Comet was a short-period comet discovered (1826) by and named for the Austrian astronomer Wilhelm, Baron von Biela (1782–1856). It was identified by Biela as a periodic comet that returned every 6.6 years.

Biela's Comet underwent remarkable transformations; it was observed in 1846 to break in two, and in 1852 the fragments returned as twin comets that were never seen thereafter. In 1872 and 1885, however, when Earth crossed the path of the comet's known orbit, bright meteor showers (known as Andromedids, or Bielids) were observed, lending strength to astronomers' deduction that all meteor showers are composed of fragments of disintegrated comets. The official designation is 3D/Biela, where the letter D stands for "dead."

CHIRON

Chiron was once thought to be the most distant known asteroid. It is now believed to have the composition of a comet nucleus—i.e., a mixture of water ice, frozen gases, and dust.

Chiron was discovered in 1977 by the American astronomer Charles Kowal and classified as an asteroid with the number

2060. It is about 200 km (125 miles) in diameter and travels in an unstable, eccentric orbit between the orbits of Saturn and Uranus with a period of about 50.7 years. In 1989 two other Americans, Karen J. Meech and Michael Belton, detected a fuzzy luminous cloud around Chiron. Such a cloud, termed a coma and being a distinguishing feature of comets, consists of dust and entraining gases expelled from the cometary nucleus when sunlight vaporizes its ices. On the basis of this discovery, Chiron was reclassified as a comet. Subsequently, additional asteroid-size icy bodies in orbits similar to that of Chiron were discovered and given the class name Centaur objects.

ENCKE'S COMET

The faint Encke's Comet has the shortest orbital period (about 3.3 years) of any known; it was also only the second comet (after Halley's) to have its period established. The comet was first observed in 1786 by Pierre Méchain. Johann Franz Encke in 1819 calculated that sightings of apparently different comets in 1786, 1795, 1805, and 1818 were in fact appearances of the same comet, whose short orbital period he was able to deduce. The comet was named in his honour. Encke also found the comet's period to be decreasing by about 2 ½ hours in each revolution and showed that this behaviour could not be explained by gravitational perturbations (slight changes in an orbit) caused by planets. The American astronomer Fred Whipple explained it in 1950 as the effect of jet forces produced by vaporization of the comet's nucleus in combination with the rotation of the nucleus.

COMET HALE-BOPP

Comet Hale-Bopp was a long-period comet that was spectacularly visible to the naked eye, having a bright coma and a thick white dust tail. It was discovered independently in July 1995 by Alan Hale and Thomas Bopp, two American amateur astronomers, at the unusually far distance of 7 AU, about 1 billion km (600 million miles) from the Sun, well beyond Jupiter's orbit. The comet reached perihelion (closest distance to the Sun) at 0.914 AU on April 1, 1997, without ever coming very close to Earth (nearest distance 1.31 AU), because its orbit was almost perpendicular to that of Earth. In addition to its broad dust tail, the comet possessed a narrower bluish plasma tail slanting away from the dust tail. From the comet's rate of gas production, its nucleus was estimated to be at least 30 km (20 miles) in diameter.

HALLEY'S COMET

Halley's Comet was the first comet whose return was predicted and, almost three centuries later, the first to be photographed up close by spacecraft. In 1705 the English astronomer Edmond Halley published a work that included his calculations showing that comets observed in 1531, 1607, and 1682 were really one comet and predicting that comet's return in 1758.

Halley's Comet, 1986. NASA/National Space Science Data Center

Conquest of England (1066) and shown in the Bayeux Tapestry of that time. Its passage in 1301 appears to have inspired the form of the Star of Bethlehem that the Italian painter Giotto used in his "The Adoration of the Magi." Its passages have taken place about 76 years apart on average, but the gravitational influence of the planets on the comet's orbit have caused the orbital period to vary by a year or two from one reappearance to the next. During the comet's return in 1910, Earth probably passed through part of its tail, which was millions of kilometres in length, with no apparent effect.

As predicted, the comet passed Earth in November–December 1985, reached perihelion on Feb. 9, 1986, and came closest to Earth on April 11, 1986. Its passage was observed by two Japanese spacecraft (Sakigake and Suisei), two Soviet spacecraft (Vega 1 and Vega 2), and a European Space Agency spacecraft (Giotto). Close-up images of the comet's nucleus made by Giotto show an oblong object with dimensions of about 15 × 8 km (9 × 5 miles). Dust particles shed during the comet's slow disintegration over the millennia are distributed along its orbit. The passage of Earth through this debris stream every year is responsible for the Orionid and Eta Aquarid meteor showers in October and May, respectively.

The comet was sighted late in 1758, passed perihelion (closest distance to the Sun) in March 1759, and was named in Halley's honour.

Dozens of earlier passages of Halley's Comet were later calculated and checked against historical records of comet sightings. Its earliest recorded appearance, witnessed by Chinese astronomers, was in 240 BCE. Its closest approach to Earth took place in April 837. It was the large, bright comet seen during the Norman

Halley's Comet is next expected to return to the inner solar system in 2061.

COMET HYAKUTAKE

Comet Hyakutake (C/1996 B2) was a long-period comet that, because of its relatively close passage to Earth, was observed as one the brightest comets of the 20th century. It was discovered on Jan. 30, 1996, by the Japanese amateur astronomer Hyakutake Yuji using large binoculars. Visible to the naked eye in late February of that year, it became spectacular in March, developing a long blue plasma tail and a white dust tail that was much shorter but wider. It finally became five or six times as bright as a first-magnitude star when it passed Earth at a mere 0.1 AU (15 million km [9.3 million miles]) on March 24–25. It faded away in early April and reached perihelion (closest distance to the Sun) at 0.23 AU from the Sun on May 1.

COMET IKEYA-SEKI

The long-period Comet Ikeya-Seki is one of a group of Sun-grazing comets having similar orbits, including the Great Comet of 1882. Comet Ikeya-Seki was discovered Sept. 18, 1965, by

Comet Ikeya-Seki, 1966. Roger Lynds/NOAO/AURA/NSF

two Japanese amateur astronomers, Ikeya Kaoru and Seki Tsutomu. Moving in a retrograde orbit, the comet made its closest approach to the Sun on Oct. 21, 1965, at a distance less than a solar radius from the surface. The comet was then bright enough to be seen with the naked eye in daylight. Like the similarly spectacular Great Comet of 1882, it was fragmented by tides induced by its proximity to the Sun; Ikeya-Seki gave astronomers their first chance since 1882 to study a comet in such conditions. It is assumed that the group of Sun-grazing comets to which Ikeya-Seki belongs represents the remnants of a single, larger comet that also was fragmented by solar tides at some time in the past.

COMET MOREHOUSE

Comet Morehouse was a very bright comet in a retrograde, quasi-parabolic orbit, remarkable for variations in the form and structure of its tail. It was named after Daniel Walter Morehouse, a U.S. astronomer, and was observed from September 1908 to May 1909. On several occasions the tail appeared to break into fragments and to be completely separated from the head. Also, the tail became visible at twice Earth's

CENTAUR OBJECTS

The Centaur objects are a population of small bodies, similar to asteroids in size but to comets in composition, that revolve around the Sun in the outer solar system, mainly between the orbits of Jupiter and Neptune. The first known member of the group, Chiron, was discovered in 1977, although its close affinity with icy comet nuclei was not recognized until more than a decade later. Since the discovery of the second known representative, Pholus, in 1992, additional Centaur objects, or Centaurs, have been reported, and astronomers have speculated that hundreds or thousands more may exist.

Centaur objects, which are as large as about 200 km (125 miles) in diameter, are thought to have originated beyond the orbits of Neptune and Pluto, in the Kuiper Belt. Having been perturbed inward by Neptune's gravitational influence, they presently travel in unstable orbits that cross the paths of the giant planets. Because of the likelihood that they will collide with a planet or be flung by a planet's gravity into a new orbit either far from the Sun or toward the inner planets, these objects are thought to spend a short lifetime, in astronomical terms, as Centaurs. This implies that the population of Centaurs is being continually replenished from the Kuiper Belt.

At the large distances of the Centaurs from the Sun, customary distinctions between comets and asteroids can become blurred. By traditional definition, comets contain more frozen water and other volatile compounds than rocky material, and they give off gases when these ices vaporize. At the very low temperatures in the outer solar system, however, only Chiron and two other Centaurs have shown such activity.

distance from the Sun (2 AU), whereas most comets start to produce a visible tail only at about 1.5 AU from the Sun. These characteristics suggest that Morehouse was a "new" comet, coming straight from the Oort cloud.

COMET SCHWASSMANN-WACHMANN 1

In 1927, the short-period Comet Schwassmann-Wachmann 1 was discovered photographically by the German astronomers Friedrich Carl Arnold Schwassmann and Arthur Arno Wachmann. It has the most nearly circular orbit of any comet known (eccentricity 0.131) and remains always between the orbits of Jupiter and Saturn, having an orbital period of 16.4 years. It is also remarkable for outbursts in its brightness, which sometimes increases by several magnitudes in a matter of hours. These outbursts are determined to be the result of the transient development of a coma (faint atmosphere) of gas and dust, but, because this event occurs at random along the comet's orbit, it cannot be explained by variations in solar heating of the comet's nucleus. Rather, it is thought to be caused by heat-evolving chemical reactions occurring inside the nucleus or from the buildup and occasional release of internal gas as solar radiation gradually evaporates volatile materials below the crust of the nucleus.

APPENDIX A: MOONS OF JUPITER

NAME	TRADITIONAL NUMERICAL DESIGNATION	MEAN DISTANCE FROM CENTRE OF JUPITER (ORBITAL RADIUS; KM)	ORBITAL PERIOD (SIDEREAL PERIOD; EARTH DAYS)*	INCLINATION OF ORBIT TO PLANET'S EQUATOR (DEGREES)
Metis	XVI	128,000	0.295	0.021
Adrastea	XV	129,000	0.298	0.027
Amalthea	V	181,400	0.498	0.389
Thebe	XIV	221,900	0.675	1.070
Io	I	421,800	1.769	0.036
Europa	II	671,100	3.551	0.467
Ganymede	III	1,070,400	7.155	0.172
Callisto	IV	1,882,700	16.69	0.307
Themisto	XVIII	7,284,000	130.02	43.08
Leda	XIII	11,165,000	240.92	27.46
Himalia	VI	11,461,000	250.56	27.5
Lysithea	X	11,717,000	259.2	28.3
Elara	VII	11,741,000	259.64	26.63
S/2000 J 11		12,555,000	287	28.27
Carpo	XLVI	17,058,000	456.3	51.4
S/2003 J 12		17,833,000	489.72 R	145.8
Euporie	XXXIV	19,304,000	550.74 R	145.8
S/2003 J 3		20,224,000	583.88 R	143.7
S/2003 J 18		20,426,000	596.58 R	146.5
Orthosie	XXXV	20,720,000	622.56 R	145.9
Euanthe	XXXIII	20,797,000	620.49 R	148.9
Harpalyke	XXII	20,858,000	623.32 R	148.6
Praxidike	XXVII	20,908,000	625.39 R	149.0
Thyone	XXIX	20,939,000	627.21 R	148.5

NAME	TRADITIONAL NUMERICAL DESIGNATION	MEAN DISTANCE FROM CENTRE OF JUPITER (ORBITAL RADIUS; KM)	ORBITAL PERIOD (SIDEREAL PERIOD; EARTH DAYS)*	INCLINATION OF ORBIT TO PLANET'S EQUATOR (DEGREES)
S/2003 J 16		20,956,000	616.33 R	148.6
Mneme	XL	21,035,000	620.04 R	148.6
Iocaste	XXIV	21,060,000	631.6 R	149.4
Helike	XLV	21,069,000	626.32 R	154.8
Hermippe	XXX	21,131,000	633.9 R	150.7
Thelxinoe	XLII	21,164,000	628.09 R	151.4
Ananke	XII	21,276,000	629.77 R	148.9
S/2003 J 15		22,630,000	689.77 R	140.8
Eurydome	XXXII	22,865,000	717.33 R	150.3
S/2003 J 17		22,983,000	714.51 R	163.7
Pasithee	XXXVIII	23,004,000	719.44 R	165.1
S/2003 J 10		23,044,000	716.25 R	164.1
Chaldene	XXI	23,100,000	723.72 R	165.2
Isonoe	XXVI	23,155,000	726.23 R	165.2
Erinome	XXV	23,196,000	728.46 R	164.9
Kale	XXXVII	23,217,000	729.47 R	165.0
Aitne	XXXI	23,229,000	730.18 R	165.1
Taygete	XX	23,280,000	732.41 R	165.2
Kallichore	XLIV	23,288,000	728.73 R	165.5
Eukelade	XLVII	23,328,000	730.47 R	165.5
Arche	XLIII	23,355,000	731.95 R	165.0
S/2003 J 9		23,388,000	733.3 R	164.5
Carme	XI	23,404,000	734.17 R	164.9
Kalyke	XXIII	23,483,000	742.06 R	165.2
Sponde	XXXVI	23,487,000	748.34 R	151.0
Megaclite	XIX	23,493,000	752.86 R	152.8

NAME	TRADITIONAL NUMERICAL DESIGNATION	MEAN DISTANCE FROM CENTRE OF JUPITER (ORBITAL RADIUS; KM)	ORBITAL PERIOD (SIDEREAL PERIOD; EARTH DAYS)*	INCLINATION OF ORBIT TO PLANET'S EQUATOR (DEGREES)
S/2003 J 5		23,498,000	738.74 R	165.0
S/2003 J 19		23,535,000	740.43 R	162.9
S/2003 J 23		23,566,000	732.45 R	149.2
Hegemone	XXXIX	23,577,000	739.88 R	155.2
Pasiphae	VIII	23,624,000	743.63 R	151.4
Cyllene	XLVIII	23,809,000	752 R	149.3
S/2003 J 4		23,933,000	755.26 R	144.9
Sinope	IX	23,939,000	758.9 R	158.1
Aoede	XLI	23,980,000	761.5 R	158.3
Autonoe	XXVIII	24,046,000	760.95 R	152.9
Callirrhoe	XVII	24,103,000	758.77 R	147.1
Kore	XLIX	24,543,000	779.17 R	145.0
S/2003 J 2		28,455,000	981.55 R	151.8

NAME	ECCENTRICITY OF ORBIT	ROTATION PERIOD (EARTH DAYS)**	RADIUS OR RADIAL DIMENSIONS (KM)	MASS (10^{17} KG)***	MEAN DENSITY (G/CM³)
Metis	0.0012	sync.	21.5	(1)	
Adrastea	0.0032	sync.	8.2	(0.07)	
Amalthea	0.0032	sync.	83.5	20.8	0.86
Thebe	0.0176	sync.	49.3	(15)	
Io	0.0041	sync.	1,821.6	893,200	3.53
Europa	0.0094	sync.	1,560.8	480,000	3.01
Ganymede	0.0013	sync.	2,631.2	1,482,000	1.94
Callisto	0.0074	sync.	2,410.3	1,076,000	1.83

NAME	ECCENTRIC- ITY OF ORBIT	ROTATION PERIOD (EARTH DAYS)**	RADIUS OR RADIAL DIMENSIONS (KM)	MASS (10^{17} KG)***	MEAN DENSITY (G/CM^3)
Themisto	0.2428		4.0	(0.007)	
Leda	0.1636		10.0	(0.11)	
Himalia	0.1623	0.4	85.0	42	1.3–2.4
Lysithea	0.1124		18.0	(0.63)	
Elara	0.2174	0.5	43.0	(8.7)	
S/2000 J 11	0.248		2.0	(0.0005)	
Carpo	0.4316		1.5	(0.0005)	
S/2003 J 12	0.492		0.5	(0.00002)	
Euporie	0.1432		1.0	(0.0002)	
S/2003 J 3	0.1969		1.0	(0.0002)	
S/2003 J 18	0.0601		1.0	(0.0002)	
Orthosie	0.2808		1.0	(0.0002)	
Euanthe	0.2321		1.5	(0.0005)	
Harpalyke	0.2269		2.2	(0.001)	
Praxidike	0.2311		3.4	(0.0043)	
Thyone	0.2286		2.0	(0.0009)	
S/2003 J 16	0.2266		1.0	(0.0002)	
Mneme	0.2301		1.0	(0.0002)	
Iocaste	0.2158		2.6	(0.0019)	
Helike	0.1506		2.0	(0.0009)	
Hermippe	0.2096		2.0	(0.0009)	
Thelxinoe	0.2194		1.0	(0.0002)	
Ananke	0.2435		14.0	(0.3)	
S/2003 J 15	0.1944		1.0	(0.0002)	
Eurydome	0.2759		1.5	(0.0005)	
S/2003 J 17	0.2381		1.0	(0.0002)	
Pasithee	0.2675		1.0	(0.0002)	
S/2003 J 10	0.4294		1.0	(0.0002)	

NAME	ECCENTRIC- ITY OF ORBIT	ROTATION PERIOD (EARTH DAYS)**	RADIUS OR RADIAL DIMENSIONS (KM)	MASS (10^{17} KG)***	MEAN DENSITY (G/CM^3)
Chaldene	0.2521		1.9	(0.0008)	
Isonoe	0.2471		1.9	(0.0008)	
Erinome	0.2664		1.6	(0.0005)	
Kale	0.2599		1.0	(0.0002)	
Aitne	0.2643		1.5	(0.0005)	
Taygete	0.2525		2.5	(0.0016)	
Kallichore	0.2503		1.0	(0.0002)	
Eukelade	0.2634		2.0	(0.0009)	
Arche	0.2496		1.5	(0.0005)	
S/2003 J 9	0.2627		0.5	(0.00002)	
Carme	0.2533		23.0	(1.3)	
Kalyke	0.2471		2.6	(0.0019)	
Sponde	0.3121		1.0	(0.0002)	
Megaclite	0.4198		2.7	(0.0021)	
S/2003 J 5	0.2476		2.0	(0.0009)	
S/2003 J 19	0.2559		1.0	(0.0002)	
S/2003 J 23	0.2738		1.0	(0.0002)	
Hegemone	0.3396		1.0	(0.0005)	
Pasiphae	0.409		30.0	(3)	
Cyllene	0.4115		1.0	(0.0002)	
S/2003 J 4	0.362		1.0	(0.0002)	
Sinope	0.2495		19.0	(0.7)	
Aoede	0.4311		2.0	(0.0009)	
Autonoe	0.3168		2.0	(0.0009)	
Callirrhoe	0.2829		4.3	(0.0087)	
Kore	0.3245		1.0	(0.0002)	
S/2003 J 2	0.4074		1.0	(0.0009)	

*R following the quantity indicates a retrograde orbit.

**Sync. = synchronous rotation; the rotation and orbital periods are the same.

***Quantities given in parentheses are poorly known.

APPENDIX B: MOONS OF SATURN

NAME	TRADI-TIONAL NUMERICAL DESIGNA-TION	MEAN DISTANCE FROM CENTRE OF SATURN (ORBITAL RADIUS; KM)	ORBITAL PERIOD (SIDEREAL PERIOD; EARTH DAYS) {1}	INCLINATION OF ORBIT TO PLANET'S EQUATOR (DEGREES)	ECCEN-TRICITY OF ORBIT
Pan	XVIII	133,580	0.575	0.001	0
Daphnis	XXXV	136,500	0.594	0	0
Atlas	XV	137,670	0.602	0.003	0.0012
Prometheus	XVI	139,380	0.603	0.008	0.0022
Pandora	XVII	141,720	0.629	0.05	0.0042
Epimetheus {4}	XI	151,410	0.694	0.351	0.0098
Janus {4}	X	151,460	0.695	0.163	0.0068
Aegaeon	LIII	167,500	0.808	0	0
Mimas	I	185,540	0.942	1.53	0.0196
Methone	XXXII	194,440	1.01	0.007	0.0001
Anthe	XLIX	197,700	1.01	0.1	0.001
Pallene	XXXIII	212,280	1.1154	0.181	0.004
Enceladus	II	238,040	1.37	0.02	0.0047
Tethys	III	294,670	1.888	1.09	0.0001
Telesto {5}	XIII	294,710	1.888	1.18	0.0002
Calypso {5}	XIV	294,710	1.888	1.499	0.0005
Polydeuces {6}	XXXIV	377,200	2.737	0.177	0.0192
Dione	IV	377,420	2.737	0.02	0.0022
Helene {6}	XII	377,420	2.737	0.213	0.0071
Rhea	V	527,070	4.518	0.35	0.001
Titan	VI	1,221,870	15.95	0.33	0.0288
Hyperion	VII	1,500,880	21.28	0.43	0.0274
Iapetus	VIII	3,560,840	79.33	15{7}	0.0283
Kiviuq	XXIV	11,110,000	449.22	45.708	0.3289

NAME	TRADI-TIONAL NUMERICAL DESIGNA-TION	MEAN DISTANCE FROM CENTRE OF SATURN (ORBITAL RADIUS; KM)	ORBITAL PERIOD (SIDEREAL PERIOD; EARTH DAYS) {1}	INCLINATION OF ORBIT TO PLANET'S EQUATOR (DEGREES)	ECCEN-TRICITY OF ORBIT
Ijiraq	XXII	11,124,000	451.42	46.448	0.3164
Phoebe	IX	12,947,780	550.31 R	175.3	0.1635
Paaliaq	XX	15,200,000	686.95	45.084	0.363
Skathi	XXVII	15,540,000	728.2 R	152.63	0.2698
Albiorix	XXVI	16,182,000	783.45	34.208	0.477
S/2007 S2		16,725,000	808.08 R	174.043	0.1793
Bebhionn	XXXVII	17,119,000	834.84	35.012	0.4691
Erriapus	XXVIII	17,343,000	871.19	34.692	0.4724
Siarnaq	XXIX	17,531,000	895.53	46.002	0.296
Skoll	XLVII	17,665,000	878.29 R	161.188	0.4641
Tarvos	XXI	17,983,000	926.23	33.827	0.5305
Tarqeq	LII	18,009,000	887.48	46.089	0.1603
Griep	LI	18,206,000	921.19 R	179.837	0.3259
S/2004 S13		18,404,000	933.48 R	168.789	0.2586
Hyrokkin	XLIV	18,437,000	931.86 R	151.45	0.3336
Mundilfari	XXV	18,628,000	952.77 R	167.473	0.2099
S/2006 S1		18,790,000	963.37 R	156.309	0.1172
S/2007 S3		18,795,000	977.8 R	174.528	0.1851
Jarnsaxa	L	18,811,000	964.74 R	163.317	0.2164
Narvi	XXXI	19,007,000	1003.86 R	145.824	0.4308
Bergelmir	XXXVIII	19,336,000	1005.74 R	158.574	0.1428
S/2004 S17		19,447,000	1014.7 R	168.237	0.1793
Suttungr	XXIII	19,459,000	1016.67 R	175.815	0.114
Hati	XLIII	19,846,000	1038.61 R	165.83	0.3713
S/2004 S12		19,878,000	1046.19 R	165.282	0.326
Bestla	XXXIX	20,192,000	1088.72 R	145.162	0.5176

NAME	TRADITIONAL NUMERICAL DESIGNATION	MEAN DISTANCE FROM CENTRE OF SATURN (ORBITAL RADIUS; KM)	ORBITAL PERIOD (SIDEREAL PERIOD; EARTH DAYS) {1}	INCLINATION OF ORBIT TO PLANET'S EQUATOR (DEGREES)	ECCENTRICITY OF ORBIT
Thrymr	XXX	20,314,000	1094.11 R	175.802	0.4664
Farbauti	XL	20,377,000	1085.55 R	155.393	0.2396
Aegir	XXXVI	20,751,000	1117.52 R	166.7	0.252
S/2004 S7		20,999,000	1140.24 R	166.185	0.5299
Kari	XLV	22,089,000	1230.97 R	156.271	0.477
S/2006 S3		22,096,000	1227.21 R	158.288	0.3979
Fenrir	XLI	22,454,000	1260.35 R	164.955	0.1363
Surtur	XLVIII	22,704,000	1297.36 R	177.545	0.4507
Ymir	XIX	23,040,000	1315.14 R	173.125	0.3349
Loge	XLVI	23,058,000	1311.36 R	167.872	0.1856
Fornjot	XLII	25,146,000	1494.2 R	170.434	0.2066

NAME	ROTATION PERIOD (EARTH DAYS) {2}	RADIUS OR RADIAL DIMENSIONS (KM)	MASS (10^17 KG){3}	MEAN DENSITY (G/CM³)
Pan		10	0.049	0.36
Daphnis		3.5	(0.002)	
Atlas		19 × 17 × 14	0.066	0.44
Prometheus		70 × 50 × 34	1.59	0.48
Pandora		55 × 44 × 31	1.37	0.5
Epimetheus	sync.	69 × 55 × 55	5.3	0.69
Janus	sync.	99 × 96 × 76	19	0.63
Aegaeon		0.3	(0.000001)	
Mimas	sync.	198	373	1.15
Methone		1.5	(0.0002)	
Anthe		1	(0.00005)	

NAME	ROTATION PERIOD (EARTH DAYS) {2}	RADIUS OR RADIAL DIMENSIONS (KM)	MASS (10^{17} KG){3}	MEAN DENSITY (G/CM³)
Pallene		2	(0.0004)	
Enceladus	sync.	252	1,076	1.61
Tethys	sync.	533	6,130	0.97
Telesto		15 × 13 × 8	(0.07)	
Calypso		15 × 8 × 8	(0.04)	
Polydeuces		6.5	(0.015)	
Dione	sync.	562	10,970	1.48
Helene		16	(0.25)	
Rhea	sync.	764	22,900	1.23
Titan	sync.	2,576	1,342,000	1.88
Hyperion	chaotic	185 × 140 × 113	55	0.54
Iapetus	sync.	735	17,900	1.08
Kiviuq		8	(0.033)	
Ijiraq		6	(0.012)	
Phoebe	0.4	107	83	1.63
Paaliaq		11	(0.082)	
Skathi		4	(0.003)	
Albiorix		16	(0.21)	
S/2007 S2		3	(0.001)	
Bebhionn		3	(0.001)	
Erriapus		5	(0.008)	
Siarnaq		20	(0.39)	
Skoll		3	(0.001)	
Tarvos		7.5	(0.027)	
Tarqeq		3.5	(0.002)	
Griep		3	(0.001)	
S/2004 S13		3	(0.001)	
Hyrokkin		4	(0.003)	
Mundilfari		3.5	(0.002)	

NAME	ROTATION PERIOD (EARTH DAYS) {2}	RADIUS OR RADIAL DIMENSIONS (KM)	MASS (10^{17} KG){3}	MEAN DENSITY (G/CM³)
S/2006 S1		3	(0.001)	
S/2007 S3		2.5	(0.0009)	
Jarnsaxa		3	(0.001)	
Narvi		3.5	(0.003)	
Bergelmir		3	(0.001)	
S/2004 S17		2	(0.0004)	
Suttungr		3.5	(0.002)	
Hati		3	(0.001)	
S/2004 S12		2.5	(0.0009)	
Bestla		3.5	(0.002)	
Thrymr		3.5	(0.002)	
Farbauti		2.5	(0.0009)	
Aegir		3	(0.001)	
S/2004 S7		3	(0.001)	
Kari		3.5	(0.002)	
S/2006 S3		3	(0.001)	
Fenrir		2	(0.0004)	
Surtur		3	(0.001)	
Ymir		9	(0.049)	
Loge		3	(0.001)	
Fornjot		3	(0.001)	

{1} R following the quantity indicates a retrograde orbit.

{2} Sync. = synchronous rotation; the rotation and orbital periods are the same.

{3} Quantities given in parentheses are poorly known.

{4} Co-orbital moons.

{5} "Trojan" moons: Telesto precedes Tethys in its orbit by 60°; Calypso follows Tethys by 60°.

{6} "Trojan" moons: Helene precedes Dione in its orbit by 60°; Polydeuces follows Dione by 60° on average, but with wide variations.

{7} Average value. The inclination oscillates about this value by 7.5° (plus or minus) over a 3,000-year period.

Appendix C: Moons of Uranus

NAME	MEAN DISTANCE FROM CENTRE OF URANUS (ORBITAL RADIUS; KM)	ORBITAL PERIOD (SIDEREAL PERIOD; EARTH DAYS)*	INCLINATION OF ORBIT TO PLANET'S EQUATOR** (DEGREES)	ECCENTRICITY OF ORBIT
Cordelia	49,800	0.335	0.085	0.0003
Ophelia	53,800	0.376	0.104	0.0099
Bianca	59,200	0.435	0.193	0.0009
Cressida	61,800	0.464	0.006	0.0004
Desdemona	62,700	0.474	0.113	0.0001
Juliet	64,400	0.493	0.065	0.0007
Portia	66,100	0.513	0.059	0.0001
Rosalind	69,900	0.558	0.279	0.0001
Cupid	74,392	0.613	0.099	0.0013
Belinda	75,300	0.624	0.031	0.0001
Perdita	76,417	0.638	0.47	0.0116
Puck	86,000	0.762	0.319	0.0001
Mab	97,736	0.923	0.134	0.0025
Miranda	129,900	1.413	4.338	0.0013
Ariel	190,900	2.52	0.041	0.0012
Umbriel	266,000	4.144	0.128	0.0039
Titania	436,300	8.706	0.079	0.0011
Oberon	583,500	13.46	0.068	0.0014
Francisco	4,276,000	266.56 R	(145.22)	0.1459
Caliban	7,231,000	579.73 R	(140.881)	0.1587
Stephano	8,004,000	677.36 R	(144.113)	0.2292
Trinculo	8,504,000	749.24 R	(167.053)	0.22
Sycorax	12,179,000	1288.3 R	(159.404)	0.5224
Margaret	14,345,000	1687.01	(56.63)	0.6608
Prospero	16,256,000	1978.29 R	(151.966)	0.4448
Setebos	17,418,000	2225.21 R	(158.202)	0.5914
Ferdinand	20,901,000	2887.21 R	(169.84)	0.3682

NAME	ROTATION PERIOD (EARTH DAYS)***	RADIUS OR RADIAL DIMENSIONS (KM)	MASS (10^{20} KG)	MEAN DENSITY (G/CM^3)
Cordelia		20		
Ophelia		21		
Bianca		26		
Cressida		40		
Desdemona		32		
Juliet		47		
Portia		68		
Rosalind		36		
Cupid		5		
Belinda		40		
Perdita		10		
Puck		81		
Mab		5		
Miranda	sync.	240 × 234.2 × 232.9	0.66	1.2
Ariel	sync.	581.1 × 577.9 × 577.7	13.5	1.67
Umbriel	sync.	584.7	11.7	1.4
Titania	sync.	788.9	35.2	1.71
Oberon	sync.	761.4	30.1	1.63
Francisco		11		
Caliban		36		
Stephano		16		
Trinculo		9		
Sycorax		75		
Margaret		10		
Prospero		25		
Setebos		24		
Ferdinand		10		

*R following the quantity indicates a retrograde orbit.

**Inclination values in parentheses are relative to the ecliptic.

***Sync. = synchronous rotation; the rotation and orbital periods are the same.

APPENDIX D: MOONS OF NEPTUNE

NAME	MEAN DISTANCE FROM CENTRE OF NEPTUNE (ORBITAL RADIUS; KM)	ORBITAL PERIOD (SIDEREAL PERIOD; EARTH DAYS)*	INCLINATION OF ORBIT TO PLANET'S EQUATOR (DEGREES)	ECCENTRICITY OF ORBIT
Naiad	48,227	0.2944 R	4.75	0.0004
Thalassa	50,075	0.3115 R	0.21	0.0002
Despina	52,526	0.3347 R	0.22	0.0002
Galatea	61,953	0.4287 R	0.05	0
Larissa	73,548	0.5548 R	0.25	0.0014
Proteus	117,647	1.1223 R	0.52	0.0005
Triton	354,800	5.8768 R	157.3	0
Nereid	5,513,400	360.1468 R	32.6	0.7512
Halimede	15,728,000	1,879.71 R	134.1	0.5711
Sao	22,422,000	2,914.07 R	48.5	0.2931
Laomedeia	23,571,000	3,167.85 R	35	0.4237
Psamathe	46,695,000	9,115.91 R	146.6	0.4499
Neso	48,387,000	9,373.99 R	132	0.4945

NAME	ROTATION PERIOD (EARTH DAYS)**	RADIUS OR RADIAL DIMEN- SIONS (KM)	MASS $(10^{20}$ KG$)$***	MEAN DENSITY (G/CM³)
Naiad	likely sync.	48 × 30 × 26	(0.002)	
Thalassa	likely sync.	54 × 50 × 26	(0.004)	
Despina	likely sync.	90 × 74 × 64	(0.02)	
Galatea	likely sync.	102 × 92 × 72	(0.04)	
Larissa	likely sync.	108 × 102 × 84	(0.05)	
Proteus	likely sync.	220 × 208 × 202	(0.5)	
Triton	sync.	1,353.40	214	2.061
Nereid	not sync.	170	(0.3)	

NAME	ROTATION PERIOD (EARTH DAYS)**	RADIUS OR RADIAL DIMEN- SIONS (KM)	MASS (10^{20} KG)***	MEAN DENSITY (G/CM^3)
Halimede		31	(0.001)	
Sao		22	(0.001)	
Laomedeia		21	(0.001)	
Psamathe		20	(0.0002)	
Neso		30	(0.001)	

*R following the quantity indicates a retrograde orbit.

**Sync. = synchronous rotation; the rotation and orbital periods are the same.

***Mass values in parentheses are poorly known.

APPENDIX E: NOTABLE KUIPER BELT OBJECTS

ERIS

The dwarf planet Eris is the largest KBO. It was discovered in 2005 in images taken two years earlier at Palomar Observatory in California, U.S. Before it received its official name, Eris was known by the provisional designation 2003 UB313; it was nicknamed "Xena" by its discoverers and also briefly termed the "10th planet."

Eris's diameter of roughly 2,500 km (1,550 miles) makes Eris slightly larger than Pluto. Eris revolves once about every 560 Earth years in a highly tilted, elliptical orbit. From its spectrum its surface appears to be coated with white methane ice. Eris has at least one moon, Dysnomia, about one-eighth its size, with an orbital period about two weeks long.

HAUMEA

Haumea is an unusual KBO. It was discovered in 2003 by a team of American astronomers at Cerro Tololo Inter-American Observatory. Originally called 2003 EL61, Haumea is named for the Hawaiian goddess of birth and fertility. Haumea is an elongated object, unusual for a dwarf planet; its dimensions are 980 × 750 × 500 km (610 × 470 × 310 miles). It has a fast rotation period of 3.9 hours, which may be the reason for Haumea's elongation. Eight other Kuiper Belt objects have orbits similar to Haumea's; these objects and Haumea's fast rotation may have been caused by a collision of Haumea with some object in the distant past. Unlike most objects in the Kuiper Belt, Haumea is not an equal mixture of ice and rock but has a thin icy crust covering a rocky interior. (The name Haumea alludes to this structure since the goddess Haumea is also associated with stone.) In 2005 two moons of Haumea were discovered and were subsequently named after daughters of Haumea. The larger moon, Hi'iaka, is named after the goddess of the island of Hawaii and of the hula; the smaller moon, Namaka, is named after a water spirit. In September 2008 the IAU designated Haumea as the fifth dwarf planet and the fourth plutoid.

MAKEMAKE

Originally called 2005 FY9, Makemake is named after the creator god of the Polynesian inhabitants of Easter Island; the name alludes to its discovery by astronomers at Palomar Observatory on March 31, 2005, a few days after Easter. Since Makemake has a diameter of 1,500 km (900 miles), it is large enough for gravity to have made its shape round, and thus in 2008 it was designated as a dwarf planet as well as a plutoid. Makemake orbits the Sun every 306 years and is reddish in colour.

SEDNA

Sedna is a small body in the Kuiper Belt that may be the first discovered object from the Oort cloud. It was discovered in 2003 by a team of American astronomers at Palomar Observatory on Mount Palomar, Calif. At that time, it was the most distant object in the solar system that had ever been observed, at a distance of 13 billion km (8.1 billion miles) from the Sun. Its discoverers named the new object Sedna, after the Inuit goddess said to live in a cave at the bottom of the

Arctic Ocean. Sedna is between 1,200 and 1,600 km (700 and 1,000 miles) in diameter, and it was found to have a highly elliptical orbit, which took it from 76 AU to 981 AU and back in a period of 12,159 years.

Observations of Sedna quickly raised a number of puzzling questions. Astronomers had thought that all objects in the outer solar system would be icy and therefore white or gray in appearance, but Sedna was almost as red as Mars. Its extremely elliptical orbit resembled the orbits of objects thought to exist in the Oort cloud. Sedna, however, was observed at a distance 10 times closer than the predicted inner edge of the Oort cloud. The proposal that Sedna had been kicked toward the inner solar system by the gravitation of a passing star is an idea that could account for its orbit.

GLOSSARY

ablation The loss of mass from the surface of a meteoroid by vaporization or as molten droplets.

albedo The ratio between the amount of light actually reflected and that which would be reflected by a uniformly scattering disk of the same size, both observed at opposition.

aqueous Related to, containing, or dissolvable in water.

asteroid Any of a host of rocky small bodies, about 1,000 km (600 miles) or less in diameter, that orbit the Sun.

aubrites Easily crumbled stony meteorites made mostly of the magnesium silicate enstatite.

basalt A hard, dense, dark volcanic rock composed chiefly of plagioclase, pyroxene, and olivine, which often has a glassy appearance.

Bode's law An empirical rule giving the approximate distances of planets from the Sun.

chondrites The most abundant type of stony meteorite.

chondrules Small spherical bodies found in chondrites, which are believed to have once been free-floating molten droplets in the solar nebula.

comet Any of a class of small celestial objects orbiting the Sun that develop diffuse gaseous envelopes and often long luminous tails when near the Sun.

Coriolis force An effect that causes material moving on a rotating planet to appear to be deflected to either the right or the left.

eccentric Deviating from a circular path; having an elongated, elliptical orbit.

flux tube A tube-shaped area of space that contains a strong magnetic field.

fragmentation When an object breaks into pieces, usually as the result of a collision or an explosion.

heliocentric Related to the Sun, the center of all solar system activity.

homogeneous Of a similar nature, or having the same composition throughout.

hyperbola A plane curve formed by the intersection of a plane with both halves of a right circular cone at an angle parallel to the axis of the cone.

incandescent Emitting visible light as the result of being heated.

isotropic Identical in all directions.

magnetosphere Region in the atmosphere where magnetic phenomena and the high atmospheric conductivity caused by ionization are important in determining the behaviour of charged particles.

meteorid A relatively small stony or metallic natural object from space that sometimes enters Earth's atmosphere and heats to incandescence.

meteoritics The branch of astronomy dealing with meteorites.

millibar A unit of pressure equal to one thousandth (10^{-3}) of a bar, which is equal to one million (10^6) dynes per square centimeter.

occulation The interruption of light as an object passes in front of a viewed object, as during an eclipse.

perihelion The point of a celestial body's orbit that is nearest the sun.

prograde Having an orbit that is the same as most other celestial bodies; in the solar system, the prograde orbit is counterclockwise.

radiant Point in the sky from which a meteor shower appears to originate.

radiometry A technique used to derive the diameter of an asteroid by balancing the infrared radiation (heat) emitted by the asteroid with the solar radiation it absorbs.

radionuclides Radioactive isotopes that decay at characteristic rates.

regolith A layer of pulverized rock, produced by bombardment with meteorites, that is thought to cover asteroids.

retrograde Moving in the opposite direction than is normal; in the solar system, the retrograde orbit is clockwise.

synchronous Moving at the same rate, at the same time.

triangulation Measuring the distance to an object by observations from two separate points.

ureilites Grainy, dark grey or brown stony meteorites with carbon-rich veins.

FOR FURTHER READING

Balogh, André. *The Heliosphere Through the Solar Activity Cycle.* New York, NY: Springer, 2007.

Barucci, M.A., et al., ed. *The Solar System Beyond Neptune.* Tucson, AZ: University of Arizona Press, 2008.

Crovisier, Jacques, and Thérèse Encrenaz. *Comet Science: The Study of Remnants from the Birth of the Solar System.* New York, NY: Cambridge University Press, 2000.

Davies, John. *Beyond Pluto.* New York, NY: Cambridge University Press, 2001.

Elkins-Tanton, Linda. *Uranus, Neptune, Pluto, and the Outer Solar System.* New York, NY: Chelsea House, 2006.

Jenniskens, Peter. *Meteor Showers and Their Parent Comets.* New York, NY: Cambridge University Press, 2008.

Levy, David H. *Impact Jupiter: The Crash of Comet Shoemaker-Levy 9.* Jackson, TN: Basic Books, 2003.

Littman, Mark. *Planets Beyond: Discovering the Outer Solar System.* Mineola, NY: Dover Publications, 2004.

Lorenz, Ralph, and Jacqueline Milton. *Titan Unveiled: Saturn's Mysterious Moon Explored.* Princeton, NJ: Princeton University Press, 2008.

Matloff, Gregory L. *Deep Space Probes: To the Outer Solar System and Beyond.* New York, NY: Springer, 2005.

Norton, O. Richard, and Lawrence A. Chitwood. *Field Guide to Meteors and Meteorites.* New York, NY: Springer, 2008.

Schmude, Richard W., Jr. *Uranus, Neptune, and Pluto and How to Observe Them.* New York, NY: Springer, 2008.

Seargent, David. *The Greatest Comets in History: Broom Stars and Celestial Scimitars.* New York, NY: Springer, 2008.

Stern, Alan, and Jacqueline Mitton. *Pluto and Charon: Ice Worlds on the Ragged Edge of the Solar System.* New York, NY: John Wiley & Sons, 2005.

Trigo-Rodriguez, J.M. *Advances in Meteoroid and Meteor Science.* New York, NY: Springer, 2008.

Tyson, Neil deGrasse. *The Pluto Files: The Rise and Fall of America's Favorite Planet.* New York, NY: W.W. Norton & Co., 2009.

Weintraub, David A. *Is Pluto a Planet? A Historical Journey Through the Solar System.* Princeton, NJ: Princeton University Press, 2008.

Wilkinson, John. *Probing the New Solar System.* Collingwood, Australia: CSIRO Publishing, 2009.

INDEX